# The product management handbook

# The product management handbook

Your practical guide to improving and sustaining results

Richard S. Handscombe

## McGRAW-HILL BOOK COMPANY

**London** · New York · St Louis · San Francisco · Auckland · Bogotá
Guatemala · Hamburg · Lisbon · Madrid · Mexico · Montreal
New Delhi · Panama · Paris · San Juan · São Paulo · Singapore
Sydney · Tokyo · Toronto

Published by
McGRAW-HILL Book Company (UK) Limited
MAIDENHEAD · BERKSHIRE · ENGLAND

**British Library Cataloguing in Publication Data**
Handscombe, Richard S.
  The product management handbook.
  1 New products. Management
  I. Title
  658.5′75
  ISBN 0–07–707082–8


**Library of Congress Cataloging-in-Publication Data**
Handscombe, Richard S.
  The product management handbook: your practical guide to improving and sustaining results /
Richard S. Handscombe.
      p.     cm.
  Includes index.
  ISBN 0–07–707082–8
  1. Product management — Handbooks, manuals, etc. I. Title. HF5415.15.H354 1989
  658.5 — dc19                                             88-27556

1234 CUP 9089

Typeset by Kudos Graphics, Slinfold, Horsham, West Sussex
Printed and bound in Great Britain at the University Press, Cambridge

*To product champions
with courage to seek
product, personal
and corporate effectiveness*

# Contents

# Preface

Product management is at the heart of organizational competitiveness in both the private and public sector, and will remain so in the turbulent competitive environment of the 1990s. It is now used world-wide, as much in industrial product and service companies as in consumer product companies where it began. Further expansion is inevitable in the 1990s as more and more organizations try to achieve or stay in the first division.

The practical and productive application of the concepts of product management offers organizations a wide range of benefits. The most important of these include:

- A focus on making important products and services competitive in national and international markets
- An integrated corporate drive towards product profit performance and productivity
- A timely reappraisal of marketing and product development plans in good time for the single European market from 1992
- The development of a new generation of business-aware general managers, heads of department and rounded mid-career change agents understanding and able to lead multifunctional competitive activity

*The Product Management Handbook* was inspired by the recognition that although these benefits are potentially available to all organizations, many achieve only suboptimal results. Discussion with numerous product managers and senior management teams — introducing or accountable for product management systems — indicated a need for practical guidelines and support in improving the performance and productivity of the 'art'. During the 1980s, a broad spectrum of types of product manager and variations in product management structures, systems and styles has emerged. *The Product Management Handbook* presents a framework for a generic profit-effective approach, based on observation and experience in a wide range of national and international situations. Concepts and methods of application are presented in a practical hands-on approach to aid understanding and application by corporate sponsors of product management, by product managers themselves and by the broad range of functional management affected by product management decisions, structures, systems and procedures. There is a concentration on generic concepts, processes and skills, with reference to theory where essential to understanding and to the relationship with classical functional management concepts.

*The Product Management Handbook* provides a broadly based source of ideas, operating guidelines and a framework of reference to the practising executive director and manager faced with the task of improving current levels of both corporate and personal performance. The book will also be of significant help to the business school student and graduate required to analyse effective international management practice and interested in preparing for an early career in product management. To the human resource and training manager the book provides a relevant text and framework of reference for in-company development programmes for product managers.

The approach to product management presented is relevant to a broad range of small and large organizations: national and international companies, multinationals, entrepreneurial high-technology start-ups, charities, university campuses and government agencies.

Effective product management is about improving product group performance, productivity and leadership, and involves and affects all functional departments and activities. It employs a general management rather than solely a marketing management approach, embracing the management and championing of a product or service from seedcorn concept through development (Chapter 3), marketing (Chapter 4), sales (Chapter 6), manufacture (Chapter 7) and financial management (Chapter 8).

Fundamental product management concepts are explored in Chapters 1 and 2. Chapters 9 and 10 concentrate on how best to introduce and sustain effective management practices. The practical product management audit, featured in Chapter 10, will provide food for thought.

Numerous checklists, questionnaires and process charts are included in the text to aid translation from words to tomorrow's real-time management practice. Purposely, reference to case situations is anonymous to enable the reader to consider ideas against his own experience and needs, without the diversion of attempting to match with named corporate culture and practice. This approach is deliberate as companies inevitably move up and down the international league tables for performance, image and visibility for reasons often unrelated to underlying management concepts and practices.

*The Product Management Handbook* is planned as an ongoing management timepiece without the dangers of early obsolescence of content. It is hoped that the reader will appreciate this approach.

In the main, the contents of the book are based on personal observations and practice as a manager, consultant and trainer, rather than on an in-depth review and reassembling of previous publications and papers. In this context, an appreciative acknowledgement must be made to the many companies, colleagues and clients who have provided a rich range of opportunities and insights over some 30 years. Space and confidentiality do not allow a total listing. However, special thanks are due to Khawar Ansari, Norman Hunter, Vinoo Iyer, Philip Norman, Pieter Papendrecht and the late Klaus Westphal who challenged and contributed to specific aspects of the final text.

Lastly, deep gratitude is due to my wife and partner, Ria Handscombe, who gave continuous support and guidance to the project and who, together with Janet, mastered the complexities of the original manuscript. Without their perseverance the publishing deadline would not have been achieved.

# 1. The contribution of product management

**Senior managers' and product managers' key task**
To strengthen personal and organizational awareness of the nature and benefits of product management

### Definition

Product management is defined as the *dedicated* management of a specific product or service to *increase its profit contribution* from current and potential markets, in both the long and short term, *above that which would otherwise be achieved* by means of traditional approaches to the management of territorial sales activity, marketing and product development. Effective product management is a practical, purposeful and positive approach to improving company results through the efforts of a competent and committed team coordinating and progressing the development, manufacture, marketing, sales and sales support of a strategically important group of products.

### The implications

The phrase 'dedicated management' implies the appointment and acceptance of, and corporate support for, product *champions* committed to the coordination of the multifunctional effort involved in progressing competitive products and/or services through the processes of development, manufacture, marketing, sales and customer support. Such dedication is becoming essential to the achievement of creative breakthroughs in product competitiveness. These breakthroughs are needed to create, offer and support products and services which will become integrated with the strategic and operational plans of both corporate and personal customers.

Product management, as defined above, is being adopted by an increasing number of organizations to anticipate and cope with rapid changes in market conditions, in particular the steady intensification of national and international competition.

### Potential benefits

In practice the concepts, processes and practices of product management offer chief executives, general managers, international vice presidents and marketing directors a profit- and customer-orientated management culture which is professional, practical and integrative. It is an approach which will help corporate managers achieve practical solutions to such common problems as:

- How to establish strategic management disciplines at all levels in the company
- How to accelerate and secure improvements in the development and launch of new products and services to the marketplace
- How to achieve parallel and consistent drives for premium prices and margins, and for improvement in total productivity to reduce the total cost base — the dual drive that achieves above average levels of profitability in both the short and long term
- How to achieve coordination among marketing, sales and product development departments to secure successful growth in sales, market share, profitability and a reputation for strategically important groups of products or services which offer customers value for money
- How to direct and drive the multidisciplined, multifunctional and innovative design and development process essential to the creation of profit-effective new products and creative product improvements
- How to achieve useful conflict but harmony between corporate headquarters and overseas subsidiary and affiliate companies, accomplishing coordination of corporate product and territorial marketing and product support activity
- How to prevent precious high-quality technical and marketing resources from drifting into corporate projects with low opportunity levels
- How to anticipate and prepare, at a sub-corporate level, for significant changes in markets, such as the opening up of European and South East Asian markets
- How to achieve and sustain both the commitment of the best Western companies to retaining international leadership, and the determination of companies in Japan and the Far East follower countries like Korea, to capture that lead
- How to develop the next generation of business-aware general managers and heads of department and, in particular, harness the combined talents of the young generation of MBA-type marketers and the older generation of technocrats
- How to develop a critical mass of rounded mid-career middle management change agents

In today's dynamic world, these questions must constantly be confronted. They require structured and detailed strategic analysis, changes in culture and improved day-to-day operational management and problem-solving capability.

Product management, properly introduced and sustained, can be of major benefit in designing and implementing profit-effective management practices and processes that provide practical answers to the above questions.

### Extent of application

Product management began as a management style used by leading consumer product companies. Early promise and success led to its adoption by many successful companies of all kinds. Success in the private sector led to the adoption

**Table 1.1**   Scope of application of product management

| Private sector | Public sector | Personal sector |
| --- | --- | --- |
| Multinational companies | Government agencies | Charities |
| International companies | Health services | Voluntary organizations |
| National companies | Universities | |
| Multiproduct companies | Railways | Sports clubs |
| Single product companies | Nationalized industrial companies | Social clubs |
| Venture capital companies etc. | Police service etc. | Religious orders |

of product management concepts, practices and processes in public sector organizations and by enthusiastic individual directors and managers in voluntary organizations. The scope of current applications is shown in Table 1.1.

Surveys of emergent company stuctures and human resourcing programmes indicate that:

- Product management is likely to be a dominant form of organization structure in the 1990s
- Companies in all industries are actively expanding their product management organizations
- Companies in the engineering and financial service industries, with the entwined issues of market management and technology management, are often taking a broader perspective of the scope and benefits of product management than many consumer product companies
- The level of product manager positions, and the experience and knowledge required, vary considerably from organization to organization
- The exact needs, objectives, organization structure and planning and control systems associated with product management vary from organization to organization and from division to division
- The companies most likely to make a success of the concept are those with a common, realistic and tough vision of the nature of product management: with individual product managers established and accepted as challenging change agents, coordinators and, above all, *product champions*

*The Product Management Handbook* provides a vivid explanation of that vision and practical guidelines for turning the vision into reality.

### The basic concepts

The following basic concepts provide a vision of the fundamental rationale behind professional product management, and a firm base for its introduction into specific organizations.

1. Operating profits and cash flow are derived from competitive and competitively managed products and services
2. The products and services offered by companies vary in importance with

respect to tomorrow's marketing needs and demands and competitive conditions
3. Sustaining a focus on strategically important products and services and achieving timely changes in priorities requires a management process that directs, coordinates, supports and controls corporate development across functions, across locations, across countries and across international boundaries
4. The management process required needs to be integrative and to stimulate, secure and cement a multidisciplined approach to the management of markets and technology, as illustrated in Fig. 1.1
5. The integrative process is required to ensure that:

   (a) Product development and market priorities are consistent with the

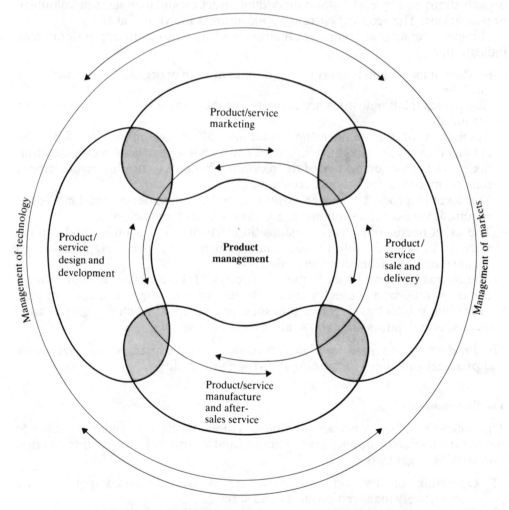

**Figure 1.1** Product management: an integrative concept

corporate strategy for the business and are accepted by all the directors and managers involved

(b) The product/service design and development process takes account of:

- What is required by customers
- What can be designed
- What can be manufactured

(c) The product/service marketing takes account of and integrates:

- what the company wants to achieve in the marketplace
- what individual territorial sales teams, subsidiaries or affiliate companies want to achieve
- what specific major companies and customer groups are attempting to achieve strategically

(d) Product/service selling takes account of:

- the strategic importance of specific products/services
- the need to sell to achieve profit, cash flow and reputation, not only volume

(e) Product manufacture or service preparation takes account of and integrates:

- the demands of present customers for provision and servicing of orders placed
- the negotiating demands of present customers in respect of important future orders
- the company's strategic priorities
- the need to prepare for and manufacture new prototypes and new products for timely product launches

6. Above all, an integrated process is required to ensure that the potential of products is not diminished as the result of:

(a) interfunctional combat and jealousies
(b) short-term operational crises in specific departments or overseas territories
(c) short-term cost cropping
(d) problems of international communication between headquarters, subsidiaries and affiliates

7. In smaller less complex organizations the integrating product management role can be provided by the chief executive or managing director

8. As companies grow in scale, complexity and extent of internationalization, the same integrating and innovation can only be achieved by dedicated *product champions* or product managers

9. Product managers need corporate sponsorship, commitment and support, for success.

10. The level and scope of the role of product managers and their teams needs to be matched to the strategic and operational needs of the organization.

Experience has demonstrated that the successful application of product management requires effective sponsorship, commitment, detailed analysis and understanding of what product management can offer an organization.

*The Product Management Handbook* provides the basis for a thorough analysis, and the design and implementation of effective day-to-day product management processes and procedures. The analysis needs to start with an understanding of the reasons for the growth in interest in product management.

### Reasons for growth in application

Typical reasons for appointing product managers as part of a formal product management structure and process can be treated under two headings: market pressures and internal pressures. The pressures described below apply equally to formal approaches in large companies and to semi-formal approaches to product management, particularly in the business unit or smaller company.

Market pressures include:

- The increased level, complexity and interaction of domestic, European Community and world-wide competition leading to uncertainty and instability of today's business environment
- The need to manage competition professionally, giving more attention than previously to tracking the ways in which competitors are responding, and are likely to respond, to the speed of technological change, user needs, design concepts and manufacturing process intensification and integration
- The need to balance the conflicts between possibilities for shorter product lives resulting from new technology, new user needs, affluence and lifestyles, and the longer product life requirements of purchasers and end users that emanate from constraints on capital investment as well as the search for low life-time costs
- The ever-broadening family of products and more and more complex or comprehensive product packages that can create confusion in the eyes and minds of buyers, and require skilful product differentiation and market segmentation for commercial success
- The attempts to globalize products in market segments where a commonality of needs and applications can be perceived in industrial and consumer markets
- The amazingly consistent focus on the customer as number one achieved by Japanese companies, even for global products
- Permanent shifts in the location of scientific, technological and marketing power as companies in the Far East demonstrate their strength compared with Western companies
- Advantages of possibilities of transnational innovation as language and communication barriers come down through improvements in education and information technology
- The trend towards world-wide technical support for mass market products and services
- The need for a more proactive and coordinated international outlook in response to stronger customer protection legislation in an increasing number of countries, particularly within the EEC and USA

- An increasing scrutiny of the buying process by customers and particularly by multinationals in response to significant differences in the products, pricing and service levels offered to different subsidiaries; differences in value for money often arise through lack of internal coordination, nationalism and open interfunctional rivalry
- The speed of change of technology and the enhancement of the ability to apply technology to product development, process development and distribution systems

Internal pressures include:

- The need for detailed integrated planning among all functions, divisions, branches and subsidiaries if special market events, such as the Big Bang in the financial services industry, are to be exploited successfully
- The desire to benefit from a coordination of market research and analysis where there are common ground and overlaps in strategic decision-making between the marketing and research and development departments, and between corporate headquarters and international subsidiaries
- The need to establish and maintain a corporate approach to monitoring and reacting to issues such as total product quality and product liability
- The vital need to introduce and sustain active change programmes focused on the dual achievement of improvements in product margins and productivity as illustrated in Fig 1.2
- The need to accelerate the achievement of a culture of innovation, inspiration and a desire for excellence
- The need to establish strategically focused and controlled internal competition between product development and marketing teams and consistently to seek out and achieve earlier and continuing market benefits from current products

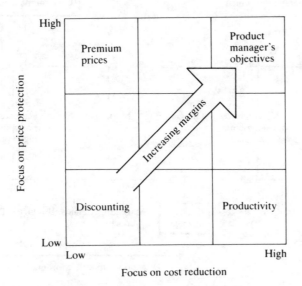

**Figure 1.2** Product management objectives

and product applications; such benefits are often overdue or overtaken by events due to tension and stresses in the organization. After a period of cuts in research and development budgets to improve short-term profits and cash flow, such inertia can be a corporate killer disease

– The need to improve the productivity of multidisciplined groups of knowledge workers to secure the integration of information technology with products and service systems and concentrate resources on strengthening those product groups important to the future, whether by internal product development, process development, factoring, licensing or joint ventures

It is most important that product managers are appointed to *champion* the development, launch, marketing, sales, and customer support of tomorrow's products; to achieve in the process multifunctional, multilocation and, where appropriate, multinational enthusiasm and commitment to the selected products and their customers. In short, product management has become an essential factor in the formula for international competitive success.

### The product manager's team

Fig. 1.3 illustrates the position of a typical team of product managers within an organization structure. The position provides company-wide direction of, support for, and coordination of a group of specific products and/or services. It implies a role which offers considerable challenge, involving responsibility, if not total accountability, for making things happen. The product manager is expected to

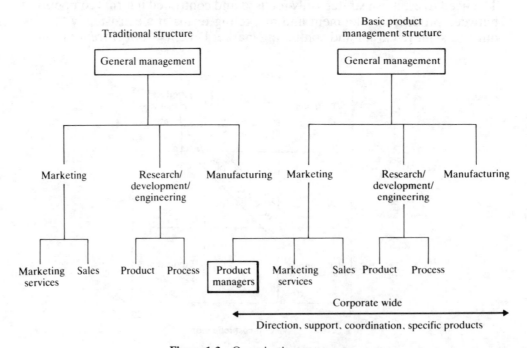

**Figure 1.3** Organization structures

achieve results operating from a limited power base. He often works alone, or controls no more than six product managers or even assistant product managers. How, then, can he function? The answer lies in his role as a leader, with the determination, perseverance, personality and interpersonal skills needed to motivate other people, mostly not direct subordinates but employed by other functions, divisions or territories.

The team typically 'assembled' by an effective product group manager is illustrated in Fig. 1.4.

The three tier team comprises:

*Level 1* The product group manager himself and subordinate product managers or assistant product managers.

The product group manager may be accountable for the management of an existing group of products or the launch and management of an entirely new group of products

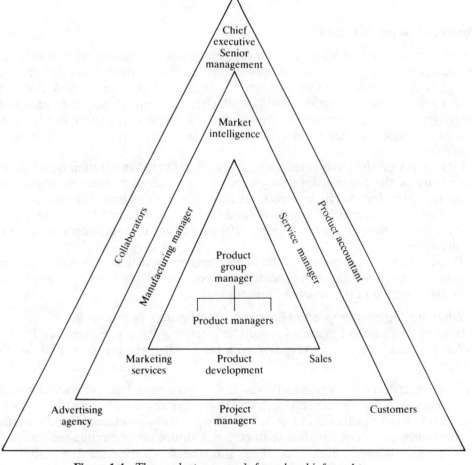

**Figure 1.4** The product manager's formal and informal team

*Level 2*   The immediate associate members of the team; managers on whom the product manager relies for day-to-day information and action
*Level 3*   Associates, internal and external to the company on whom the product manager relies for medium-term information and action.

Their direct and indirect involvement and input are vital to longer-term strategic decisions and short-term market competitiveness of products

In practice, the exact mix and balance of the team will be influenced by the role defined for each product manager.

In a strongly decentralized national company with numerous single product subsidiaries or business units, the subsidiary general manager or business unit managers are *de facto* product managers. Much of this is relevant to their needs.

In each situation, the organization structure and the specific role of product managers needs careful consideration and communication to ensure understanding and commitment. Organizational relationships are expanded on as the book progresses, but see especially chapters 3, 4, 6, and 7. Each relationship is vital to successful product management.

**The role of the product manager**

The role of the product manager, in terms of purpose, key tasks, relationships and accountability, requires sensitive planning, communication and support, and recognition that an effective product manager will cut across and challenge traditional functional positions and boundaries. It is a tough job and needs to be properly constructed, introduced and sustained. However, experience indicates that all too often in practice much confusion surrounds the role of the product manager.

First, many product managers themselves are confused about their own role and the nature of the relationships they need to establish with other managers and specialists in order to achieve a committed product management team.

Second, many managers associated and interacting with product managers are confused as to the real role of the latter, often resenting their influence or attempts to influence.

Third, senior management may be unable to overcome the confusion of product managers and those interacting with them because of inadequate preplanning. Adequate preplanning consists of identifying:

– What are the most important corporate competitive problems
– In what way product managers could help resolve these problems, and
– What would be the most effective role for product managers to play in such areas

In practice, the role of individual product managers, brand managers and product group managers does, and needs to, vary from company to company. A number of typical options is illustrated in Fig. 1.5. Each option can be effective under certain circumstances and, equally, less than effective under other circumstances.

An understanding of the choice of roles available is important to a number of decisions related to the introduction of product management, concerning, first,

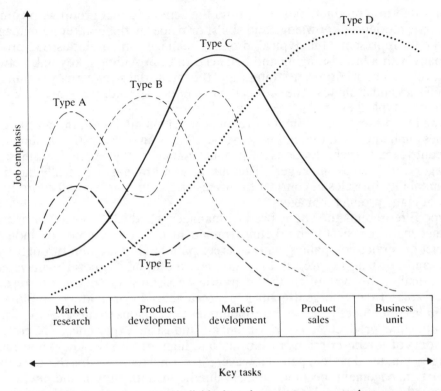

**Figure 1.5**  Variations in the role of individual product managers or product group managers

the form and style of product management most suited to a specific organization at a specific point in time and the recruitment and development of product managers; and second, whether product manager appointments are to be profit-generating or personal development posts or, at best, a combination of both.

Type A in Fig. 1.5 represents a typical consumer product manager, primarily involved in market development, market segmentation, promotional activity, pricing analysis, able to base his decisions on accurate and frequent market share and reaction data from regular shelf-count surveys or consumer interview surveys.

Type B represents the product manager given the task of masterminding the introduction of new high-technology products from concept design to handover to the sales force after product trials with key customers. Often this type of product manager is only partially involved in determining market strategy. In many companies type B represents the product manager appointed from a technical function as a mid-career move, perhaps aged 40–45 years. The strength of this type of appointment is that the product manager has a deep knowledge of emergent customer needs and technologies, and is known and respected within the company. The potential weakness is that the product manager is inexperienced in marketing. In such situations decisions on marketing strategy are shared

or allocated to a product manager within the same product group with complementary experience, knowledge and skills, or made by the marketing manager.

Type C represents the typical product manager in an industrial product
company with a broad-ranging and balanced role, providing a key link between
the development of corporate strategy and the territorial sales activity within sales
subsidiaries and affiliates. The product manager in a speciality chemical company
would be a typical example.

Type D represents the ultimate level of product management; the profit-centre
business-unit approach that has become popular as an organizational philosophy
in recent years. In such situations the product manager may be titled 'business unit
manager', or 'business manager'. The business unit manager typically has direct
accountability for sales in contrast to the restricted supportive and coordinating
roles of many product managers.

Type E represents the young product manager, aged 23–26 years, or assistant
product manager, or the marketing trainee in either consumer or industrial
product or service companies, whose career path might take him through Types
A, C and D as he progresses to senior marketing and general management.
Traditionally, this was often the 'marketing assistant' or 'marketing research
officer' role of the emergent management trainee. Unfortunately, employment
conditions sometimes result in the appointment of persons to this type of position
under the title 'product manager' without any industrial experience. The cosmetic
upgrading of job descriptions to substantiate higher salaries to help and recruit
young graduates does happen. However, it is one reason why the concept of
product management becomes undervalued, misunderstood and ineffectual,
particularly in industrial product companies. The selection and training of
product managers is discussed in depth in Chapter 9.

The above roles are outlined to assist managers to:

– Consider a range of options before deciding on the most fruitful role for their
  specific organizational situation
– Communicate and achieve understanding of the intended role for product
  managers
– Explain the difference in their company between the range of product
  management roles that might exist
– Understand the benefits and risks of common overlapping between the
  different types of product management job
– Establish an appropriate recruitment and training programme for product
  managers

### Defining the key tasks

The purpose of the product manager's role is to champion the product for which
he is responsible by planning and influencing the achievement of enhanced
profits, market share, cash flow and product reputation. But what are the key
tasks, and what are typical accountabilities? The range of key tasks performed
by product managers is illustrated in Fig. 1.6 in the form of a checklist for the
reader's personal use. The checklist is designed to aid the review of current and

potential roles for a variety of product management positions. Detailed job descriptions are discussed later in the book

1. *Product group manager*
   Accountable for the overall strategic and operational management of a homogeneous group of products, from product vision to replacement in the marketplace by a new generation of products, on an ongoing basis. This is a central theme throughout the book.
2. *Product line manager*
   Normally accountable for the management of a specific product or subgroup within a total product range
3. *Product manager*
   A title synonymous in practice with (1) and (2) dependent on the structure and job classification of a specific company
4. *New product manager*
   Accountable for the development and launch of new products and in some cases their subsequent marketing. This is discussed in detail in Chapter 3
5. *Product market manager or marketing engineer*
   Accountable for product management within a specific territorial market or world-wide market segment. Normally only accountable for the marketing aspects of the product management role. This is discussed in detail in Chapter 5
6. *Product marketing manager*
   A corporate appointment, accountable only for the marketing aspects of the product management role
7. *Product business manager*
   Essentially a product group manager with direct accountability for sales and possibly product development and product manufacture
8. *Product business engineer*
   Accountable for developing new business for a range of high-technology engineering products
9. *Brand manager*
   Accountable for the marketing of a specific line of branded products

Properly structured, the product management role can, in its variety of forms, have significant impact on the source and level of sales, margins and profit, and the establishment of a market and customer orientation throughout the organization. The latter constitutes a vital support to corporate managers determined to establish a commitment to the customer and marketing concept (see Chapter 4) throughout the organization. Examples of specific product manager job descriptions are provided in Chapters 3, 6 and 9.

### Styles of product management

The purpose, benefits, role and team of the product manager have now been discussed. Clarity and realism in each of these areas is critical to the successful launch, maintenance and perhaps relaunch of product management in a company. However, there are three more critical factors:

## JOB TITLES

1. *Current title:* .............................................................................................

2. *Possible future title:* .................................................................................

The following tasks are typical of those assigned to Product Managers.
What are the priorities of the particular job under review.

| Typical Task | Relative importance (H, M, L) | Relative difficulty (H, M, L) |
|---|---|---|
| 1. *International marketing strategy* | | |
| 1.1 Coordination of market research intelligence and assessment | | |
| 1.2 Identification of market sector/product opportunities | | |
| 1.3 Market selection and definition | | |
| 1.4 Development of product/market strategy | | |
| 1.5 Specification of emerging product needs/opportunities | | |
| 1.6 Selling of marketing strategy/guidelines to subsidiaries, sales force, etc. | | |
| 1.7 Maintenance of up-to-date analysis of competitors' strengths/weaknesses, strategies | | |
| 1.8 Coordination of promotional activities | | |
| 1.9 Coordination of pricing policy | | |
| 1.10 Coordination of discount policy | | |
| 1.11 Coordination of customer service package (e.g. finance, training, servicing, etc.) | | |
| 1.12 Management of agents and distributors | | |
| 1.13 Management of joint ventures, license agreements, etc. | | |
| 1.14 Competitor liaison/agreement | | |
| 1.15 Other: please specify | | |
| 1.16 | | |
| 2. *Product strategy* 2.1 Development of product specifications | | |
| 2.2 Development of product development programme | | |
| 2.3 Liaison with product development engineering/design | | |

| Typical Task | | Relative importance (H, M, L) | Relative difficulty (H, M, L) |
|---|---|---|---|
| 2.4 | Commercial/technical evaluation of new product proposals | | |
| 2.5 | Tracking of competitors' product initiatives | | |
| 2.6 | Planning and management of product launches | | |
| 2.7 | Development and management of product business plan | | |
| 2.8 | Other: please specify | | |
| 2.9 | | | |
| 3. *Accountability* 3.1 | Sales volume | | |
| 3.2 | Profit | | |
| 3.3 | Margins profit/sales | | |
| 3.4 | Return on investment | | |
| 3.5 | Cash flow | | |
| 3.6 | Corrective actions | | |
| 3.7 | Product management audits (Chapter 10) | | |

**Figure 1.6**  Review of current and future product management roles

1. The style of product management and product manager's role which the company plans to introduce. A product management audit is outlined in Chapter 10 to help in reaching this corporate decision
2. The capability and motivation of the product managers appointed. This is discussed in depth in Chapter 9
3. The time the product manager has to do the real job: the role of a product champion. This is discussed in depth in Chapter 10

All three factors and the ultimate contribution of product managers are influenced by the corporate culture and management style of the company. The characteristics of product management styles are illustrated in Table 1.2; they provide guidelines for good practice.

Effective product group managers are selected, trained and motivated towards the leadership style. The tasks included in the management and administrative styles are incorporated within a time-effective strategic management process (Chapter 2), and delegated, where time-effective, to full-time and part-time associate members of the product management team.

In many instances, the majority of basic administrative tasks are best managed by the traditional functional organization structure, as are some of the management-type activities. In this way the product manager can concentrate on

**Table 1.2**  Characteristics of three product manager styles

| Management function | Product manager style | | |
| --- | --- | --- | --- |
| | *Administrative* | *Management* | *Leadership* |
| Planning | Budgets | Operational plans | Product/market strategy within the framework of corporate strategy |
| Organizing | Emphasis on activity charts and job descriptions | Emphasis on relationships and accountability | Integration and coordination of the multidisciplined multifunctional 'team' impacting product success |
| Leading | Internal memos and letters | Verbal requests/ communication of priorities for change | Verbal communication of strategic direction to total product team |
| Monitoring | Basic computer printouts | Extraction of principal information | Trend analysis — graphs and matrices |
| Controlling | Detailed analysis | Exception principle | Key ratios and milestones |
| Developing | Asking to be booked on courses | Coaching subordinates and arranging seminars | Coaching and counselling 'total' product team and arranging audit workshops |
| Coordinating | Clearing-house for memos, etc. | Regular meetings and visits | Leading strategy sessions and progressing follow-up |
| Satisfying the customer | Processes customer complaints regarding yesterday's/today's needs | Careful analysis of sales reports and market research of today's/ tomorrow's needs | Meets active cutomers to understand tomorrow's needs |

the important directing and coordinating of roles. Personal experience demonstrates that the potential added value inherent in product management is achieved where corporate managers define and support a leadership role, and the product managers plan and act accordingly. To ensure success, the product management process and training of product managers need to support the concept. The product management process is discussed in Chapter 2 and the training of product managers and the characteristics of effective product managers in Chapter 9.

### Communicating the concepts and culture

One of the most common reasons for poor acceptance, support and achievement of product management as a concept is a lack of understanding of the organization's interpretation of the concept and implied culture.

In view of the interdisciplinary nature of effective product management activity, the chief executive has the main role in establishing communication with the many departments, subsidiaries and affiliates involved in the total product management process. The message communicated needs to emphasize:

- The purpose and importance of product management to the company
- The basic product management concept, process and practices as interpreted by the company
- The level at which product managers will be appointed within the company
- The mission, role, accountability and extent of authority of product managers
- The role of functional management in responding to and supporting the concept of multifunctional and multidisciplinary processing and promotion of plans
- The downside risks if products fail to be competitive and profitable

The message needs to be clearly communicated, using appropriate means. Typical approaches involve primary (face-to-face) communication and secondary supportive communication. Examples of primary (face-to-face) communication are:

- Discussion and agreement at an executive board meeting
- Presentations at corporate conferences
- The opening speech at a world-wide product management strategy session involving representatives of all key functions and territories
- Supportive presentations by the marketing executive, research and development executive, the national sales executive, international executive, and manufacturing executives at their own functional departmental meetings and to multidisciplinary project or management meetings that they might lead

Examples of secondary supportive communication are:

- The inclusion of an appropriate descriptive communication in the briefing notes for the annual planning and budgeting cycle
- The write-up of product management purpose, concept, philosophy, practices and processes as a section in the corporate policy and procedure manual
- The incorporation of product management modules in the executive training and development programme
- A write-up of the concept and successes in the house journal or company magazine

Such expression and reinforcement of company culture can do much to foster meaningful product management and give product managers the support and motivation to succeed.

The product management audit process described in Chapter 10 will be found to be of benefit in determining the corporate message to communicate and the urgency for corrective competitive actions. Chapter 5 discusses the role of senior management in the communication process in more detail.

**Chapter 1 – Key point summary**

*Achieving the maximum contribution from product managers*

1. Decide on 'real' needs
2. Select the role option most likely to be effective
3. Define the role with clarity
4. Communicate the role
5. Support the informal team concept
6. Give product managers room to move as champions
7. Focus product managers on customer plans and needs

# 2. The operation of the product management process

**Senior managers' and product managers' key task**

To develop, introduce and manage a professional approach to the planning and control of all plans and activities impacting the commercial success of a product or service

### The customer focus of product management

Product managers work in a competitive arena, both in the marketplace in achieving a secure and profitable customer base, and internally in securing the necessary financial investment and organizational commitment and support to ensure product group success. The role is both strategic and operational and has parallels with that of a managing director of a division but without full authority and the field marshall's baton.

The managing director is appointed to improve and sustain company or divisional results. Success is achieved by establishing clear, innovative and realistic strategy direction, the matching of operational resources, capability and actions to strategic needs, and a consistent drive for total productivity, the latter measured in terms of ratios such as unit shareholder value to assets, profit to sales, working capital to sales, and added value per unit of salaries and wages.

The product manager is appointed to direct and coordinate the management of a specific product group as near as possible as a business, by providing a direct link between delivering value for money to the customer and an enhanced value of the product group to the company and shareholders when assessed as a strategic business unit or opportunity.

Through the variety of roles discussed in Chapter 1, the product manager strives for results by giving strategic direction to the marketing, development and manufacture of strategically important products, a sustained customer service effort, productivity in all activities associated with the product group, and the coordination of functional and territorial plans, investments and actions.

The links between corporate strategy and results and product group strategy and results are illustrated in Fig. 2.1.

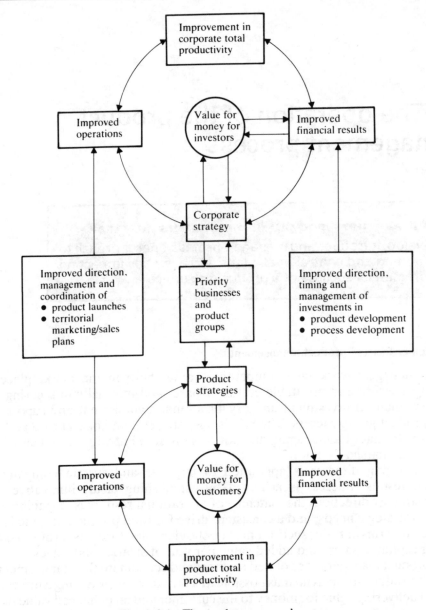

**Figure 2.1**  The product manager's arena

The basic planning and control processes are developed in this chapter and are explained in more detail in the chapters shown below:

Product development process and plans — Chapter 3
Market development process and plans — Chapter 4
Sales development process and plans — Chapter 6
Manufacturing development process and plans — Chapter 7

Financial planning and control — Chapter 8
Product manager selection, development and support — Chapter 9
The product management audit — Chapter 10

### The product planning process

A product planning process is outlined in Fig. 2.2. The process links the several
dimensions of product planning to the corporate-level strategic planning process.
Implementation of the planning process cuts across organization levels and
boundaries to achieve informed strategic decisions related to

- Business areas and priority product groups.
- Industry and territorial priorities.
- Investments in product development, process development, and technology
  development against the background of emergent customer needs, investments
  by competitors and emergent technological possibilities.
- Independent and collaborative investments in market, product and technological developments.
- Own manufacture, local content, international sourcing, and international
  collaborative links.

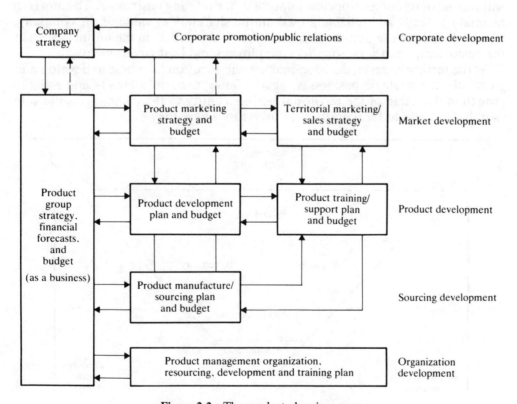

**Figure 2.2**   The product planning process

- Corporate directions to international subsidiaries and territories.
- The need for adjustments to organization structure and culture, and the need to invest in the development of capabilities important to strategic success.
- The capabilities required to develop, communicate and implement strategies successfully. This will include a consideration of the future need for and role of product managers, who will eventually be appointed to direct and manage the core growth portfolio of products towards optimum profit; develop and launch the next generation of products; and direct and manage the divestment of obsolete products with the minimum disruption to customers and at the least cost.

The process is essentially challenging and integrative, and aimed at establishing a disciplined and informed focus on the most attractive market opportunities appropriate to the company.

### Levels of strategic planning

Strategic analysis, decision-making and planning take place at a number of levels, as illustrated in Fig. 2.3. At corporate and divisional level, the end result of strategic thinking will be decisions on priority businesses by industry, commercial activity and territory, the allocation of resources to priority businesses, and the withdrawal of resources from less important or declining businesses. The aim is to maintain a steady and reliable growth in the shareholder value of the company, while satisfying the legitimate needs of other stakeholders in the business such as the customers, financiers, suppliers, employees and host governments.

At the territorial level, decision-making will focus on how best to develop and grow selected strategic businesses, again aiming towards a steady and reliable growth in the value of the territorial business entity to the company as the sole shareholder, and to local partners or investors where they exist.

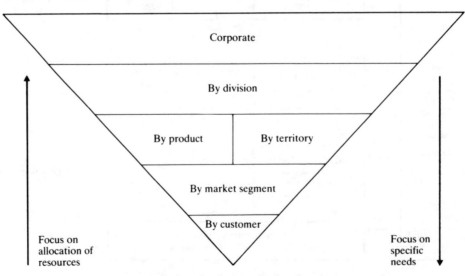

**Figure 2.3** Levels of strategic planning

At the market segment level, the focus is on the professional marketing and sale of the product range to achieve a steady growth in sales, profit contribution, cash flow, and return on assets employed.

At the specific customer level, the focus is on planning to secure maximum sales penetration at premium margins by helping the customer achieve medium-term strategic objectives and resolve short-term operational problems.

Strategic planning at the product group level is essentially integrative, aimed at the establishment of a natural link between

– Corporate strategy and territorial strategies.
– Marketing strategy and functional strategies.
– Functional strategies for product marketing, development, manufacture, distribution and service.

There are two basic aims: first, to achieve a common and cohesive sense of purpose and mission; second, to establish a dedicated and committed drive towards improved levels of profit, return on investment, cash flow, and the value of the product group as a business — above those that would be achieved without the stimulus and coordination of product managers.

By nature product management and product managers constitute a challenge to the organization. Challenge can cause stress. However, such stress can be harnessed and diffused by a participative and co-operative approach to the development and review of product group strategy.

### The nature of product strategies

Product strategy statements need to

– Define the business that the product group represents, whether or not treated financially as a formal business unit
– Provide a sense of direction, focus and practical framework for individual product decisions, the development of marketing strategies and plans for specific products or closely related product clusters, the development of product development plans, and the development of manufacturing strategy and plans
– Identify priorities for market and product development in order to allocate available financial resources to the most strategically important products to enable available financial resources to be allocated selectively to the most important products, market segments and territories
– Be comprehensive but concise, and easily communicated
– Be in a language that can be understood and gain the interest and commitment of a wide range of managers in corporate departments and territories
– Stimulate and accelerate the development of corporate or functional capabilities to support the implementation of agreed strategic initiatives in the marketplace and within the company

The framework for a statement of product group strategy is provided in Table 2.1. The development of such statements of strategy is best achieved through a participative process. Inputs are desirable from the territories and functions

**Table 2.1**   Typical framework for product group strategy

1. *Product group*

2. *Focus of strategy 1989–1992*
   A.  Business mission
   B.  Priority strategic direction and offensive or defensive initiatives

3. *Product priorities*
   3.1   Definition of types of product/service to be included in future product range
   3.2   Priorities for marketing and improving existing products
   3.3   Priorities for developing and launching new products/services
   3.4   Priorities, if any, for phasing out existing low-profit products/services

4. *Market priorities for market development by product or product subgroup*
   4.1   By user and/or buyer group
   4.2   By industrial sector
   4.3   By territory
   4.4   By specialist market research

5. *Sourcing priorities*
   5.1   Own manufacture
   5.2   International sourcing
   5.3   Local content facilities
   5.4   Factored products
   5.5   Licensing in
   5.6   Franchise operations

6. *Acquisition plans*
   If any, to accelerate product or market development programmes

7. *Key capabilities that must be developed*
   To give the product group a fair chance of implementing the strategic decisions defined in Sections 1–6
   Capabilities requiring investment in people, training and development may include product design and development, manufacturing, project management, marketing, sales, sales promotion and advertising

8. *Financial and related objectives for 1989–1992*
   8.1   £ turnover
   8.2   Profit
   8.3   Profit/turnover %
   8.4   £ value added per £ salary/wages/direct employee benefits
   8.5   Return on net assets
   8.6   Cash flow
   8.7   Investment requirements £ and timing

9. *Phase 1 — Implementation plan*
   A.   Resolution of critical issues
   B.   Implementation of urgent strategic initiatives and change

10.   Back up analyses as addendum for reference and update prior to next strategy review

dependent on and in a position to influence the business success of the product group. This cannot be achieved as a desk-bound paper exercise; it needs to involve informed people.

## Typical objectives of product strategy reviews

There are seven typical objectives for the establishment and design of a product strategy review led by a product group or business unit manager.

1. To carry out an objective, open-minded reappraisal of the future opportunities, objectives and risks for the product group.
2. To update, refine and fine-tune an existing statement of strategy in the light of
   recent implementation, successes and failures, trends in the business
   environment, and the deeper knowledge of the factors impacting competitiveness gained since the last strategy review.
3. To evaluate and test tentative strategic decisions in an objective, relatively
   unbiased manner.
4. To involve those persons with most knowledge, experience and foresight in
   relation to the business environment and markets in which the product group
   does business.
5. To establish commitment to the product group by involving as participants the
   direct product team (the group product manager and subordinate product
   managers); and associate members referred to in Chapter 1 (product
   development manager, selected territorial managers, marketing services or
   sales promotion and advertising manager, manufacturing manager, customer
   service manager, product group accountant).
6. To establish priorities for seeking corporate funds for product improvement
   and/or new product development programmes, and for the opening up of new
   markets.
7. To establish a focus for the development of detailed marketing strategies and
   plans for individual products or product subgroups and selected market
   segments and territories. This will be discussed in detail in Chapter 4.

Product strategy reviews organized with these objectives in mind are likely to
establish an innovative entrepreneurial climate and accelerate the building of a
cohesive product team.

The needs are no different to the needs of corporate strategy sessions at
divisional or company level. The only difference is the more dedicated analysis
and evaluation of opportunities and risks for a specific product group as against
the total range of product groups and businesses. For smaller companies with only
a few products, the product strategy review and corporate strategy review would
be one and the same.

### Organizing a participative strategy review

Product strategy reviews may be organized in a number of ways:

1. As a two- or three-day session for a product group team based on members'
   own knowledge, perceptions, ideas and experience.
2. As (1) but with inputs from functions and territories in the form of pre-
   published strategies and plans.
3. As (2) but with replies to a strategic questionnaire.
4. As a participative session involving territorial and functional representatives,
   together with members of the product group team, on a global, national, or
   territorial basis.

In practice the latter approach has much to offer. A typical process chart is
outlined in Fig. 2.4. How can this be implemented in practice?

Company X is a European-based multinational group. The group has expanded internationally through a succession of investments and acquisitions in North and South America, the EEC, EFTA, and Australasia as a stepping-off point to the Far East. A corporate strategy review identified one specific product group as offering the most exciting opportunity for global expansion through the established network of international subsidiaries. Peter was appointed product manager accountable for the world-wide direction and coordination of the product group, which comprised five product lines with a total of 50 individual products. The product manager was also the business unit manager for the product group in his own country in Europe.

Prior to Peter's appointment as product manager, the larger subsidiaries were autonomous in terms of product strategy, product development, manufacturing capacity and international marketing and product support. Inevitably, product management was seen initially as a threat to local authority and even national sovereignty.

Peter, who had previously taken part in a national strategy review, recognized the benefits of establishing an open dialogue with managers involved with the product range world-wide. There were two options: to travel to each of the territories and attempt to sell the need for a coordinated attack on world markets on a step-by-step basis; or to invite all territories to participate in a world-wide

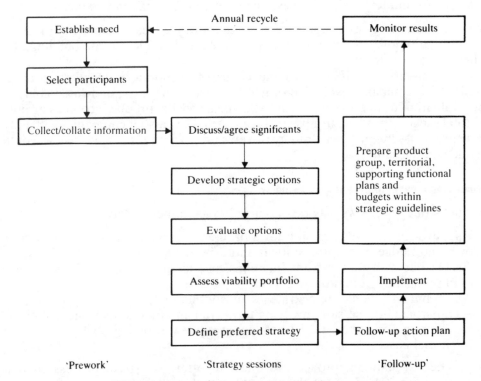

**Figure 2.4** A product group strategy review process

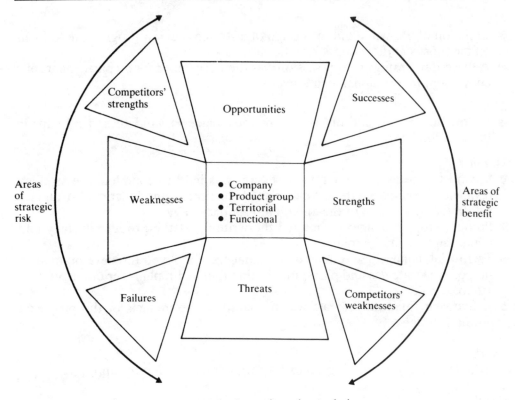

**Figure 2.5**   Strategic wedge analysis

strategy review to decide together what objectives should be set; what should be done; the areas where central direction and allocation of product development resources would be of benefit; where market development direction and support would be of benefit; which products should be launched in the newer territories and which country should provide the product support; where new products should be designed, and where products should be manufactured or sourced.

A product group strategy session was therefore organized with the agreement of corporate management and progressed as follows:

*Month 1*
Participants were agreed, invited and sent a pre-work survey questionnaire based on the strategic wedge analysis outlined in Fig. 2.5.

The participants included:

● The group product manager and territorial product managers from the larger territories
● Market managers from each territory
● Product design and development managers from three centres of technology
● The financial manager servicing the product group
● The manufacturing manager from the three main production facilities

*Month 2*
- Collation of pre-work and the design of a strategy review programme to focus on the most significant opportunities and risks
- A three-day strategy review session was then organized for all participants at a convenient international location

*Month 3*
- Follow-up analysis and investigations took place to validate and fill gaps in information base

*Month 4*
- Second three-day strategy review session was held to complete the strategy review and commence the development of territorial and functional strategies within the framework of the emergent group strategy
- Product group manager completed the write-up of the product strategy and initial implementation plan
- Territorial managers and functional managers completed the development of supportive strategies and plans, integrating them with plans for other product groups
- A five-year financial forecast was prepared of the impacts of the proposed product strategy

*Month 5*
- Product strategy was presented to corporate management for approval

*Month 6*
- One-year budget and action plans to implement the first year of the strategy

*Ongoing*
- Implementation and results were monitored and coordinated by the product group managers
- Ongoing analysis of the competitive environment was begun to confirm anticipations and identify any unexpected events
- Fine-tuning of the strategy as an ongoing process

- Use the statement as a firm statement of direction and priorities, but with flexibility to analyse and respond where appropriate to unexpected competitive shocks.

**The wedge analysis**

The fundamental framework for the competitive strategic analyses required as the input to strategic decisions was illustrated in Fig. 2.5. The framework and basic questions are common to strategic analyses at the level of the total company, division, business unit, product group or individual product, as illustrated in Table 2.2.

In relation to the product group strategy review, the analysis is concerned with identifying significant events, trends and possible happenings that could impact

**Table 2.2**   Use of wedge analysis

| | |
|---|---|
| *The total company division and subsidiary* | In deciding on the most viable future strategy for the company as a total entity, including key decisions on organic growth, acquisition and divestment |
| *The business unit or product group* | In deciding on the most viable competitive strategy for specific priority product groups and territories within the umbrella or framework of the strategy for the total company |
| *The functional department* | In deciding on the most productive strategy for the support of the business and competitive strategies described above |
| *The individual manager including a product manager* | In deciding on the most realistic personal strategy for the current job and possible career paths |

the future direction, strategic options, freedom to operate and success of the product group. The analysis focuses on both positive and negative factors.

*The positives: areas of strategic benefit*
*Opportunities*   The significant customer-related opportunities in today's and tomorrow's marketplace for current and potential products and product technology.
*Strengths*   The most significant current strengths of the product group in terms of the value for money and attractiveness of existing products and services, market shares, product profitabilities, repeat-customer bases and strengths related to product group capabilities in design, marketing, manufacture, sales servicing, and so on: essentially, the strengths that provide a firm base for the future competitiveness of the product group.
*Successes*   The successes that indicate a significant current capability to innovate successfully. An indication of the ability to identify and exploit opportunities and strengths.
*Competitors' weaknesses*   The significant weaknesses of competitors that offer future opportunities to the product group and indicate areas in which competitors might be slow or unable to react to competitive moves by the product group.

*The negatives: areas of strategic risk*
*Weaknesses*   The significant current weaknesses of the product group that, if not corrected, will constrain the ability of the product group to innovate and implement competitive initiatives.
*Failures*   Significant indicators that the product group has recently been unsuccessful in overcoming weaknesses and in implementing new initiatives, and an analysis of the basic causes of failure.
*Threats*   Significant anticipated external trends or occurrences that threaten the competitive success of the product group. The analysis will examine social, political, technological, economic, environmental, competitive and customer trends and possible future shocks.
*Competitors' strengths*   The significant strengths of key competitors that will

create difficulties for the product group in implementing new initiatives and responding to external threats.

The quality of the strategy and realism of the implementation plan developed by a product group will be directly related to the quality — in terms of focus, concentration on the significant, depth of insight, vision and lateral thinking, multidisciplined perspective, rather than volume — of the wedge analysis.

### Opportunity search

A broad-based search and evaluation of opportunities is at the heart of successful strategy reviews — those that result in visionary but realistic competitive strategies which meet and stimulate customer needs better than those of competitors and create new standards that transcend competitors' initiatives. Five bottlenecks typically exist:

1. Time
2. Lack of vision and poor perception of needs
3. Insularity of individual functions
4. Mental myopia
5. Fixed ideas and negative screening

Improvements can be achieved by:

- Designing an opportunity search questionnaire and circulating this to know-ledgeable persons, including those who will take part in the strategy review
- Collating the replies as silent brainstorming
- Evaluating the ideas as a group on the basis of timing, scale, potential profitability, investment required and potential return on investment, level of competition, cost of entry, current product group strengths and capabilities, and ease of exploitation
- Giving consideration to base data in a creative manner that removes functional mind blockages and achieves valuable world-beating ideas

Table 2.3 provides a practical starting point for the process within a product group.

Final opportunities may be identified directly from the survey questionnaire or result from subsequent evaluation and creative questioning along such lines as:

What opportunities could be grouped together?
How can we reshape the opportunity?
Where are the opportunities for synergy?
What if the technology could be accelerated?
What could be the next development beyond the idea?
What developments could replace the idea with better ideas?
In what other ways could the opportunity be interpreted or developed?
How could the opportunity be simplified?

### Basic product market decisions

The range of product market options to be considered by product managers is extensive, as illustrated by the decision matrix shown in Fig. 2.6.

**Table 2.3**  Framework for identification of product opportunities. What are the most significant opportunities for profitable growth over the next five years for each subgroup of products within the total product range?

|  | Product subgroup A | Product subgroup B | Product subgroup C |
|---|---|---|---|
| 1. *Market opportunities* | | | |
|    1.1  Geographic territories | | | |
|    1.2  Industrial sectors | | | |
|    1.3  Specific user groups | | | |
|    1.4  Specialist segments | | | |
| 2. *Application opportunities* | | | |
|    2.1  Current | | | |
|    2.2  New | | | |
|    2.3  Substitute technology | | | |
| 3. *Product opportunities* | | | |
|    3.1  Current products | | | |
|    3.2  Improved products | | | |
|    3.3  New products | | | |
|    3.4  Product packages | | | |
| 4. *Service opportunities* | | | |
|    4.1  Current services | | | |
|    4.2  Improved services | | | |
|    4.3  New services | | | |
|    4.4  Product/service packages | | | |
| 5. *Collaboration opportunities* | | | |
|    5.1  Licensing in and out | | | |
|    5.2  Franchising | | | |
|    5.3  Joint venture | | | |
|    5.4  Acquisition | | | |
| 6. *Technological opportunities* | | | |
|    6.1  Enhanced products | | | |
|    6.2  Step changes | | | |
|    6.3  Cost reductions | | | |
|    6.4  Changes in customer technology | | | |
| 7. *Social opportunities* | | | |
|    7.1  Domestic | | | |
|    7.2  Global | | | |
| 8. *Political opportunities* | | | |
|    8.1  Domestic | | | |
|    8.2  Global | | | |
| 9. *Economic opportunities* | | | |
|    9.1  Domestic | | | |
|    9.2  Global | | | |
| 10. *Major customer opportunities* | | | |
|    10.1  Strategic needs | | | |
|    10.2  Changes in technology | | | |
|    10.3  Expanding markets | | | |

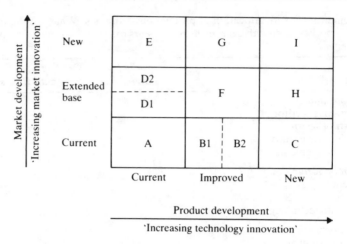

**Figure 2.6**   Product–market decision matrix

*Box A   Current position*
Box A represents the starting point for a newly appointed product manager who inherits an active product range or new product development programme. The products will be those curently marketed or which are about to be launched. The design of products will have been based on previously proven product design and product manufacturing technology. The current market dimension will be defined by the current territories in which the products are sold, the industries and customers to which the products are sold, and the application markets represented by the selected customer groups. The starting point will represent an earlier manager's decision on product and market priorities and the extent of previous commercial creativity in terms of market segmentation and product differentiation. The short-term priority of the product manager is to establish an understanding of the commercial viability of the existing product/market and product/customer mix; and the urgency for exploring profit-effective expansions of the product range or market.

A number of progressive options are illustrated by the other boxes in the matrix. They are presented as a series of questions to enable the product manager to explore the matrix in a progressive and productive manner.

*Box B   Improved products*
B1   How could the current product or service be made more attractive to potential and existing repeat customers, by repacking and minor incremental product and service improvements, utilizing existing technology?
B2   How could the current product, or incrementally improved product, be improved by a major redesign, introduction of new technology or a reformulation?

How could the current service be improved by extending the scope of the service, improving the response time, quality of customer–staff interface and so on?

*Box C    New products*
What new products, attractive to existing customers, could be added profitably to the product range as in-fill products, extension to the range, choice options or replacement products, or complementary entirely new products to enhance the product package?

*Box D    Extended market base*
D1   What profitable expansion of the customer base is possible by an expansion of the sales force, change in method of sale, exploitation of similar product applications in new industries for the product or service?
D2   What expansion of the customer base is possible by seeking out and exploiting new applications of the product within current or new territories/industries?

*Box E    Expansion of customer base*
What profitable expansion of the customer base is possible by developing totally new markets; territories, industries with entirely new applications for the product?

*Box F    Improved products and extended customer base*
What combination of the options represented by boxes B and D could provide profitable options worthy of analysis?

*Box G    Improved products attractive to entirely new customer base*
What entirely new markets would be opened up by improved products?

*Box H    New products and extended customer base*
What new related market opportunities could be opened up by adding a complementary new product to the product range?

*Box I    Diversification*
What new products can be identified that would serve entirely new markets, industries, customer group and territories?


The majority of product managers will operate within the options represented by boxes A–H. Cumulatively, these boxes represent the progressive stages of corporate organic growth.

   Box I represents the territory of the new product manager, business development manager, strategic or planning manager appointed to explore entirely new business opportunities that might be exploited by internal investment or by external acquisition. This box may also represent any unused new business ideas generated from product development brainstorming sessions or product group strategy reviews. Not relevant to the product group, they would normally be communicated to the new product, business development or strategic planning manager for further evaluation.

   The range of options outlined is complex. Each requires detailed analysis and consideration before short-listing and selection of final options for development. In practice, product market decisions will be made at a number of levels, as illustrated in Table 2.4. In theory, the analysis can be commenced at any of the five

**Table 2.4** Levels of product market decision-making

| Level | Process | Illustrative decisions |
|---|---|---|
| 1. *Corporate* | Corporate strategy | Choice of business areas, territories and business groups |
| 2. *Product group* | 2.1 Product group strategy | Decision on priority product innovations and broad market concentration |
| | 2.2 Market strategy | Decision on detailed product differentiation and market segmentation |
| 3. *New product manager* | New business search | Choice of new product/market areas for corporate investigation |
| 4. *Territorial sales manager* | Territorial strategy | Decision on priority customer groups and product matches |
| 5. *Industrial salesmen* | Customer strategy | Decision on product priorities |

levels. However, greatest medium- and long-term impact will be achieved if analysis is commenced at the corporate and product group strategy levels. Lower-level planning can then be done within strategic guidelines communicated by corporate management down the organization structure and laterally across the organization by product managers.

### Market share

The concept of market share (that is, percentage of market volume achieved by a specific product or product group compared to the 'total' market) is an internationally recognized measurement of market penetration and one of the important triad of product measurements illustrated in Fig. 2.7 (the others being the level of reliable profit generated and the product value for money as seen in the eyes of the customer).

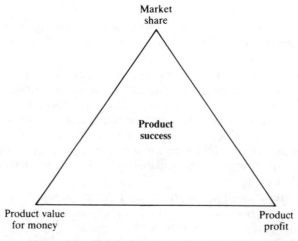

**Figure 2.7.** Triad of product competitive success

In practice, the measurement and communication of market share statistics fulfils four important purposes for the product manager.

1. As a measure of the market penetration of a specific product or product group, at a specific point in time, or the emergent trend.
2. As a means of tracking and illustrating the relative competitive positions of a number of current products, compared to each other and compared to the products marketed by competitors in the same markets.
3. As a means of illustrating the relative competitive success of a specific product group or products in a range of markets, e.g. different geographic markets, distribution channel markets or application markets.
4. As one of the starting points for identifying and analysing options for market segmentation, competitive niches and need for product innovations.

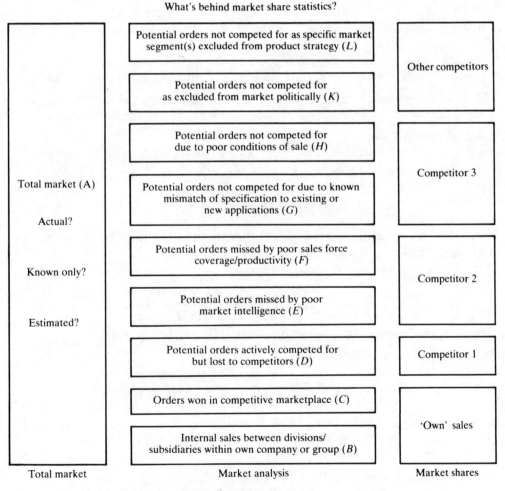

**Figure 2.8**   What's behind market share statistics?

Although simple in concept, application can have a number of difficulties.

1. The reliability of the statistics.
2. The ease with which market share statistics can be modified 'politically'.
3. The need to read behind the statistics.
4. The presentation of market share statistics.

*Reliability of statistics*
As illustrated in Fig. 2.8, a major source of error may be the inability to define the total market size.

For some products a well-defined market exists, with all competitors known and accurate regular measurements of own and competitors' sales reported: for example, for consumer products with regular and reliable shelf-count market returns; or transportation products such as aeroplanes, buses and trains where manufactured volumes and major sales are published internationally.

However, for other consumer or industrial products, the statistics available may be at best:

● the known published and/or observed market based on regular market intelligence;
● the estimated market based on regular or occasional market surveys; or
● based on inadequate sales reports of achieved and missed opportunities.

In these cases some information may be difficult or impossible to obtain, e.g. internal sales within transnational groups or sales to the defence industries.

*'Political' modifications*
Three forms of modification of market share statistics are regularly observed.

(a) Statistics based on active market only:

$$\text{Active market share} = \left( \frac{C \times 100}{C \times D} \right) \%$$

(where $C$ and $D$ are identified in Figure 2.8) without indicating that a large part of the product market has not been exploited.

(b) Statistics based on segment market share:

$$\text{Segment market share} = \left( \frac{C \times 100}{A - L} \right) \%$$

without also indicating the percentage of the total market to which this equates.

(c) Traditional market share:

$$\text{Traditional market share} = \left( \frac{C \times 100}{A - L - K - G} \right) \%$$

where, for example, 13 per cent total market share might also be expressed as a 33 per cent success rate for the contracts the company wanted to achieve.

*The need to read behind the figures*
More information is required before deciding whether a given market share is attractive or successful. In principal a high market share is desirable, but not if it

can only be achieved by loss leader marginal cost pricing. A 25 per cent market share may be a major success in a fragmented market with 25 competitors, but a difficult position if it represents third place in a market dominated by two competitors with, say, 42 and 33 per cent market share, respectively.

*Presentation of market share statistics*
The presentation of market share statistics illustrates very vividly the differences of impact between a number of presentations of the same data. Each diagram in Fig. 2.9 could be included in a report prepared by or for a product manager.

In presenting information on market share and other statistics, the product manager has the opportunity to supply details which can be quickly read, understood and remembered. To this purpose, the product manager should establish:

– For what market segments should information be collected, collated and communicated?
– Who should receive product statistics?
– For what purpose do they need them?
– What format of presentation would be most effective?
– Are alternative presentations required?

### Market segmentation

What will be the most effective way of breaking down the total future market into customer groups in order to achieve:

– A focus on sub-markets with greatest growth and profit potential
– An accurate assessment of customer needs, market conditions and competitive factors
– Cost-effective development of products which are distinctive and offer value for money to sizeable groups of potential customers
– Profit-effective and focused product promotions
– Accurate monitoring of results in comparison to competitors

The question is fundamental to the success of the product management process, and needs to take place at two levels of detail. First, the development of the product group strategy will define market priorities in more detail than within the corporate strategy. Second, the priority markets will be refined and given greater definition and clarity as the initial step in the preparation of marketing strategies for each individual market segment.

A number of problems need to be recognized and avoided:

1. No market is homogeneous, but it would not be possible in most markets to offer a different product to each customer
2. Standard products may be too bland and achieve low customer satisfaction with all customers
3. Market segments chosen may be too broad, resulting in middle-of-the-road products, which do not satisfy the needs of a heterogeneous customer base

| Market (tonnes) | Market size 1989 | Anticipated growth to 1991 (%) | Own sales 1989 | Planned growth to 1991 (%) | Forecast market share 1991 (%) |
|---|---|---|---|---|---|
| EEC | 5 500 | 10.0 | 1 100 | 20.0 | 21.8 |
| USA | 3 300 | 15.0 | 550 | 30.0 | 18.8 |
| Far East | 1 100 | 20.0 | 100 | 10.0 | 8.3 |
| Rest of World | 1 100 | −10.0 | 60 | 10.0 | 6.7 |
| Total | 11 000 | 10.5 | 1 810 | 22.2 | 18.2 |

(a) Table

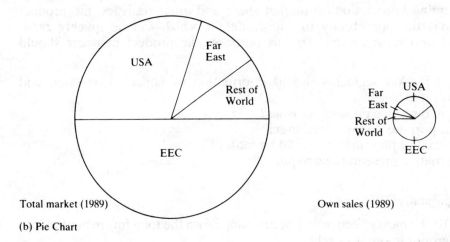

Total market (1989)                                     Own sales (1989)

(b) Pie Chart

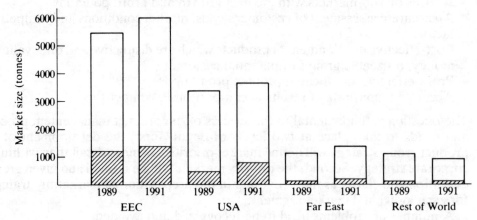

(c) Histogram

**Figure 2.9**  Presentation of market share statistics

4. Market segments chosen may be very narrow specialist niches — products may be defined very specifically for the selective customer base, but have little potential for spin-off sales and other applications and, at worst, will miss out on the real growth in the total market which is in an adjacent segment of the market
5. Segmentation may start by breaking down the current market rather than first visualizing what is the probable market in the short to medium term
6. Segmentation based on analysis of company needs only, without a parallel analysis of current and anticipated competitors' approaches to market segmentations
7. An attempt to focus on too many small segments resulting in confused priorities
8. A lack of lateral thinking to explore novel options. The complexity of the choice is illustrated in Table 2.5
9. Should market segmentation start by defining the product and then looking for the best market segments? Or should the start be the identification of market segments followed by the design of competitive products specific to chosen market segments? In practice, the start may be from either end with final decisions taken at the end of an interactive process (see Fig. 2.10)

The selection of profit-effective market segments needs to be objective, as outlined in Table 2.6.

**Table 2.5** Illustration of range of segmentation options

| Segmentation | Whisky | Soft shampoos | Railway equipment | Hotels |
|---|---|---|---|---|
| Geographic | ✓ | ✓ | ✓ | ✓ |
| Market size | ✓ | ✓ | ✓ | ✓ |
| Aesthetic demands | – | – | ✓ | ✓ |
| Quality requirements | ✓ | ✓ | ✓ | ✓ |
| Company buyers | ✓ | ✓ | ✓ | ✓ |
| Individual buyers | ✓ | ✓ | – | ✓ |
| Social class | ✓ | ✓ | ✓ | ✓ |
| Taste preference | ✓ | – | – | – |
| Sex | – | ✓ | – | ✓ |
| Religion | ✓ | – | – | ✓ |
| Human use | ✓ | ✓ | ✓ | ✓ |
| Animal use | – | ✓ | ✓ | ✓ |
| Family life cycle | ✓ | ✓ | – | ✓ |
| Race/language | ✓ | ✓ | ✓ | ✓ |
| Buying process | ✓ | ✓ | ✓ | ✓ |
| Price sensitivity | ✓ | ✓ | ✓ | ✓ |
| Technological awareness | – | – | ✓ | ✓ |
| Buying power | ✓ | – | ✓ | ✓ |

**Table 2.6**  Process of market segmentation

1. Identify current and creative options
2. Rank attractiveness by assessment against a range of factors, e.g. market size, potential growth, number and strength of competitors, payment and cash-flow behaviour, structure of customer base, price sensitivity, etc.
3. Identify attractive methods of segmentation
4. Assess the risk of each option, including the risk of marring the image of the product and company, for instance as a result of moving from a premium price market to a cut-throat market, or from a socially responsible market to a market which accepts polluting products
5. Select strategic market segments on a balance of attractiveness and risk
6. Build into product group strategy
7. Focus marketing mix strategies on selected market segments (see Chapter 4)

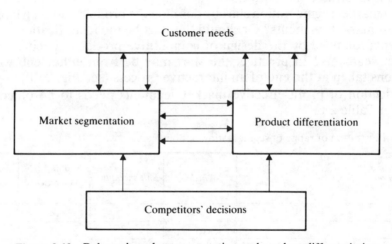

**Figure 2.10**  Balanced market segmentation and product differentiation

The tendency in the emergent markets of the 1990s is that in more and more instances the customer will expect to be treated as king, or competitive companies will persuade the individual consumer or customer that he will be treated as king. Product managers will need to ensure effective segmentation and the offer of value-for-money products and services.

For instance, a product manager in a hotel group was responsible for airport hotels. Traditionally room occupancy had averaged 85 per cent. The product manager set a challenge that room occupancy per day could be increased to 125 per cent. An obvious solution was to let out rooms for interviews and seminar syndicate rooms. But at best this would only achieve a 5 per cent increase, constrained largely by when rooms were vacated and when they would be required by new clients. A number of experiments were run in a pilot hotel, with segmentation by frequent users, family stays, and tour operators. The breakthrough was to segment on the basis of persons with a daily allowance, and persons on a company account or credit card. A discount was offered to persons willing to book in after dinner and book out before breakfast, freeing rooms from 0800 to 2000 hours for letting for stopovers, interviews and small meetings.

Toothpaste used to be segmented by those with own teeth and those with dentures. A browse through the supermarket shelves will now identify toothpaste designed for sensitive teeth, the normal user, the smoker, for healthy gums, unhealthy gums, adults, children, hard-water areas, soft-water areas, and the family dog.

Soft shampoos have been segmented to expand sales by recognizing that the use goes beyond babies to animals, balding males and soft furnishings.

Railway equipment manufacturers segment by a combination of railways that have government finance and those in need of international soft loans, countries that accept open exports and those that require local content, type of power network (electrical, diesel, steam and magnetic levitation), types of operation (city trams, underground, suburban, rural, intercity, trans-continental), type of user (passenger, cattle, freight and mixed), and gauge (broad, standard and narrow).

A university engineering department segments by source of students, industrial research, grants and continuous professional education.

Houses segment by family life cycle, and by income levels and lifestyles, from the first time buyer to the purchaser of a retirement home.

Product managers of consumer products such as confectionery, snack bars and soft drinks increasingly segment by lifestyle considerations.

In essence, effective segmentation decisions are those focused on identifying means of establishing long-term profitable relationships with satisfied customers who purchase products fit for the purpose and giving value for money.

In practice, a combination of approaches to market segmentation and product differentiation can provide a range of strategic options for consideration, as illustrated in Fig. 2.11.

The topic product differentiation is considered in Chapter 3.

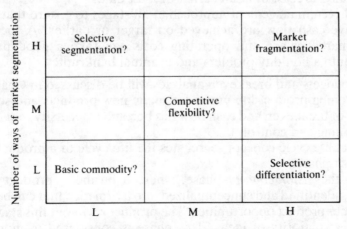

Figure 2.11  Product–market strategic options

### Financial management and the product life cycle

The dimensions of the product manager's financial management task in relation to the product life cycle are illustrated in Fig. 2.12. The financial mission of the product manager is to achieve levels of profit, return on investment, cash flow and breakeven above the company average and comparable with the best corporate performance indices for the industry.

The mission will only be achieved if products are managed professionally from the visionary concept stage until the product is eventually taken off the market in the decline phase.

Professional management requires:

1. A product development programme focused on clear product objectives, planned and controlled against clearly defined milestones in terms of work achieved, time-scales and expenditure against a fully quantified product development budget (this is discussed in detail in Chapters 3 and 8).
2. Specific tough design reviews planned into the programme. The purpose of each design review is to audit in an objective and commercial manner progress and potential problems, and to recommend whether to continue the programme or to abort and minimize potential losses on the project.
3. Specific objectives, detailed strategies, plans and budgets agreed, managed and controlled for the launch of the product, with achievements and potential overruns carefully monitored and controlled.
4. Specific objectives, detailed marketing strategies, plans and budgets developed for the important growth phase of the product life — whether of six months' or six years' duration — the implementation of which is directed with motivation, inspiration, discipline and control. The latter is a difficult but vital mix of success criteria.
5. Specific market reviews planned into the programme, both during the launch phase and the eventual maturity phase, checking whether the downturn occurs when initially forecast or at an earlier or later date.
6. A profit-driven management approach at all stages to ensure that breakeven and positive cash flow are achieved on target or earlier. A focus only on volume, market share and operating costs can take a good product and company into a liquidity problem and eventual bankruptcy.

Formats for budgets and breakeven analyses will be discussed in Chapter 8.

With shortening product life cycles for many new products and services, the management of breakeven and cash flow has become a necessity, not a luxury, in financial planning and control.

The product life cycle concept segregates the life cycle of a product or service into six distinct phases.

Phase 1 is the *vision/concept* phase, where a business, product or market opportunity is identified and conceptualized into a firm idea that can be evaluated along with other product opportunities. The product review at this stage may well reject the great majority of ideas. This phase is considered in more detail in Chapter 3.

Phase 2 is the *design/development* phase, where selected product ideas are

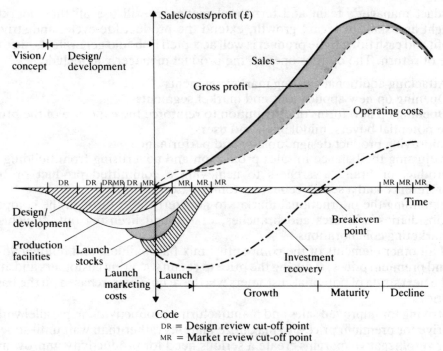

**Figure 2.12**  Product life cycle–product management financial perspectives

progressed through detailed market research, aesthetic and engineering design, design-make and development procedures, initial product testing and authorization to launch onto the marketplace. This takes place over a period of three months in the case of a simple product or service to 10 or more years for an advanced pharmaceutical product.

Phase 3 is the *launch* of the product onto the marketplace following the detailed planning and preparation of phase 2. It is based on a marketing strategy designed to make the potential market aware of the product, eager to have and use it, and to pay the asking price. The launch may be helped by an existing leading brand image for the product group or previous customer preference for the company's products. In other cases the launch may be focused on a few selected customers to prove the product and then speedily to build up sales on successful publishable case situations; or a selected niche market, before expanding into a variety of applications. In all cases the objective is that potential and current customers start to recognize an interesting and useful new buy. Marketing strategy is considered in depth in Chapter 4.

Phase 4 is the *growth phase* – the make or break adult phase of the product or service, when it proves that it is distinctive and gives customer satisfaction. If it offers better value than competing products, it will attract a premium price and an improved probability of achieving planned financial results. Early customers become more enthusiastic and committed, and new customers are added as a result of personal reference or marketing and sales efforts. During this phase the product manager's team and territorial managers will use all their marketing insight and skills to secure growth, extend the product life cycle, and strive for profit and cash flow. If the product is well accepted it should generate its maximum rate of return. The options open to the product manager will include:

- Attacking additional existing market segments
- Opening up new applications and market segments
- Opening up new forms of distribution to reinforce the exposure of the product to potential buyers, middlemen and users
- Improving product design, quality and performance
- Adjusting the balance in sales promotion and advertising from building up a product or brand awareness to achieving a committed product or brand preference and a secure repeat customer base
- Extending the international market to new territories through the company's subsidiaries, affiliates and branches, or through licensing out, franchise or marketing collaborations
- If all other elements of the competitive mix fail, building and holding volume and premium prices; reducing the price to retain wavering customers and attract the next strata of potential customers who have not yet purchased on the basis of price
- Striving for improved sales and manufacturing productivity, in parallel with the drive for premium prices, to maximize margins rather than wait until squeezed or zero/negative margins create a serious need for productivity improvement

Phase 5 is the *maturity* phase, when sales are slowing down. Among the questions the product manager will ask are whether customers have discovered new product options; whether the product has reached an optimum market share; whether all potential buyers know of the product; whether the salesmen are doing a professional job; whether the slowdown is only a plateau before the total market grows and new applications take off; and whether customers are fully aware of the strategic and operational benefits of recent improvements in the product package. The product manager needs to evaluate in depth the likely cause of the plateau and initiate a combination of market investigations and product/market initiatives to test the water and stimulate a new or renewed growth phase.

The classical options available to the product manager are:

1. Launch the product in additional international markets
2. Resegment the market and reposition the product by adjusting product image, sales promotion, advertising and price
3. Search for new applications in new industries for the product
4. Build the product into systems
5. Strive to improve the focus and penetration of the sales force in selected territories where market share is suboptimal
6. Modify the technology of the product, add refinements, new features, extend interservice periods, or improve performance
7. Audit the advertising messages and budget in comparison with those of the competition
8. Acquire competitors within monopoly regulations
9. Persuade current customers to use more and tell others of the benefit

THE OPERATION OF THE PRODUCT MANAGEMENT PROCESS

10. Reposition the product in relation to family and customer life styles
11. License or franchise the product or service into new smaller markets
12. Improve the quality and quality image
13. Restyle packaging of product
14. New pack sizes
15. New colour scheme
16. Co-market with a bigger upmarket volume product to secure synergetic growth (this is a popular creative and productive exercise on many product management training courses)
17. If nothing appears to have a lasting impact, to accelerate the preparation to launch the next new product and hold in readiness
18. New materials
19. New agents and distributors
20. Additional product training
21. A five-star customer campaign, as illustrated in Chapter 6

In the growth and maturity phases all aspects of the competitive mix and marketing mix (Chapter 4) need to be considered individually and in a variety of combinations (see Fig. 2.13). The dual aim is to secure continued profitable growth for the product and continued product reputation until timely replacement by a follow-on product or service.

Phase 6 is the *decline and obsolescence* phase. Customers have decided that the product has been replaced by a more attractive competitive product. Despite

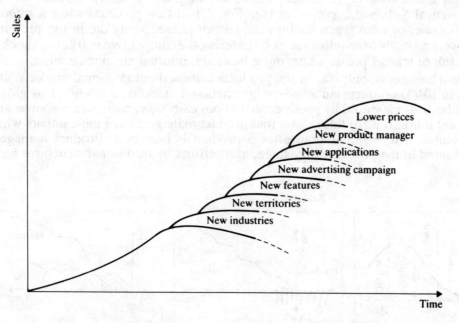

**Figure 2.13**   Impact of product development–market development initatives in premature maturity phase

every effort to sustain sales, the product drifts into a steady decline and extended old age or nosedives towards quick obsolescence. The product manager needs to ensure that the weakening product does not demand increasing time, effort and resources to resolve crisis after crisis. He will aim to time the introduction of the next series product to maximize the medium- and long-term product range and market profitability, territory by territory.

In the early period of decline the product manager may decide to:

1. Reduce the price or introduce larger discount schemes into the pricing guidelines
2. Stop investment in market development and/or product development, and treat the product as a cash cow; or end of life commodity product
3. Worsen delivery and customer service peformance to reduce stock levels and reduce reserved production capacity in order to protect declining gross margins

Care is required. Action in these areas may result in loss of customer confidence in the company. Loss of confidence accelerates the reduction in sales for current products, reduces the receptiveness of customers to a replacement product, and affects customers' belief in other products within the product group. The skilled product manager will attempt to time the introduction of replacement products to achieve optimum lift-off from current customer confidence and commitment.

### Life cycle theory and practice

The theory behind the product life cycle provides the product manager with a useful framework of reference. However, in practice many variants of the theoretical S-shaped curve occur (see Fig. 2.14). Few products show a smooth sales cycle, or even reach far into the launch phase. Many die in the pre-birth phase, and many from initial shock on entering the competitive market — shock as a result of market pressures or, more basically, internal mismanagement.

As a best guess, only one in 100 products launched onto national markets, and one in 10 000 products launched on international markets, is a winner by global standards — measured by profit contribution, cash flow, customer response and market share. It is for this reason that product managers have most impact when appointed before rather than after a product is launched. Product managers appointed in the post-maturity stage, after efforts by traditional structures have

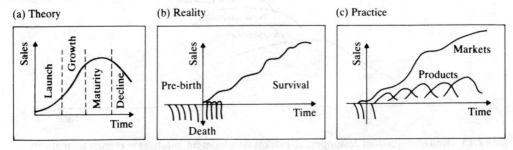

**Figure 2.14** Theory and reality of the product life cycle

failed, face a particularly difficult task. The product is dying, and the new product manager represents even higher overheads.

Product management is about innovation, the aims being to:

- Buck the trend of the product and market life cycles
- Achieve a series of growth/plateau subcycles
- Avoid the need to treat products as cash cows prior to early retirement
- Modify products and market development activity to achieve step-by-step changes in the fortunes of the products
- Stimulate the market

In practice, the product cycle is not an independent phenomenon. Product cycles need to be seen as a series of cycles within the longer-term cumulative market cycle for the given type of product or applications, particularly in those industries where product life cycles become shorter and shorter in time-span.

The product life cycle concept applies most closely where there is stability in the market environment, that is, no fast uncontrollable changes. In periods of instability and uncertainty, there is a need to balance the conflicting possibilities of shorter product life cycles resulting from new technologies and new user needs; and longer product life requirements as a result of constraints on capital and expenditure limits. Effective application of the product life cycle concept requires a thorough understanding of the product group business. The product team needs a reliable process for tracking and anticipating changes in the business environment if product decisions are to be commercially viable and competitive.

### Portfolio analysis

Six examples of portfolio matrices are illustrated; Fig. 2.15. The benefits of such matrices are that they are visual, they look simple, they can be used to illustrate spot situations (i.e. products (1) and (3)) or trends (i.e. product (2)). However, they suffer from four fundamental problems and deceptions:

1. Portfolio analyses do not set strategy, but they do provide a useful framework for visualizing and evaluating the impact of tentative or recent strategic decisions.
2. The visual presentation can be changed dramatically by changing the base of the matrix. For instance, matrix (a) could represent the position of the products in the total market in a specific territory or in a specialist market niche.
3. Positioning products is a matter of judgement, whether it be spot judgements or detailed evaluation. For instance, the dimensions of market attractiveness and product strengths in matrix (b) are complex. Market attractiveness needs to be assessed on the basis of growth, competition, life cycle, profit structure, cost of entry, return on investments achievable, and so on. Product strengths need to be on the basis of a broad range of factors in comparison with competitive products, as will be discussed in Chapter 3. The same is true of matrix (c).
4. The choice of scales can distort the message behind a matrix, such as matrix (d). However, matrix (d) is less likely to be misleading where the scales are related

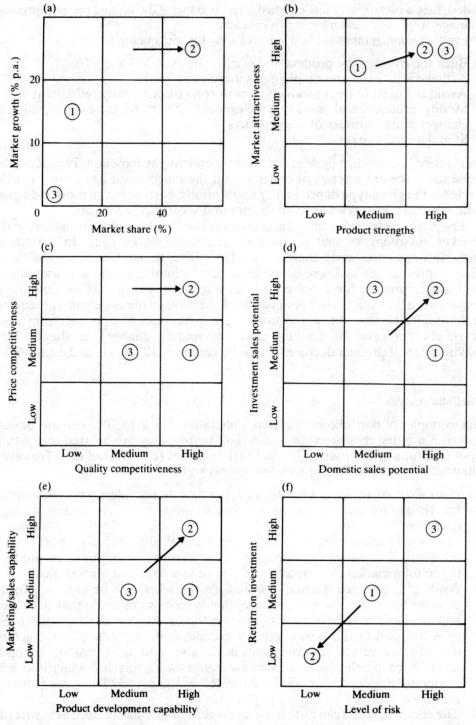

**Figure 2.15** Product group portfolio analyses

to the sales of today's best products, e.g. the boundary between high and medium is set at 80 per cent of the sales of today's best product.

Matrix (e) needs to be judged in comparison with principal competitors and with other product groups in the company.

Matrix (f) describes an important philosophy. In this case the axes can be quantified in terms of return on investment (ROI), e.g. low could be taken to mean 0–10 per cent; medium, 10–20 per cent; and high, 20 per cent or more. The level of risk can be quantified in cash terms, as a percentage of anticipated profit, or as a percentage of ROI. Still, what is appropriate for one company will be inappropriate for another. However, a product opportunity assessed as a medium rate of return and high risk in a country with high interest rates may be regarded by a competitor with a low interest rate as a product with high potential returns and relatively low risk.

Used during strategy sessions to indicate positions and directions that tentative strategic decisions imply, the matrices described can be of benefit, provided the dimensions are defined by the team and used in a consistent manner.

### Product action plans

Product managers are involved in the preparation, communication, monitoring, follow-up and control of a wide range of action plans. These are used to implement specific strategic decisions and to resolve specific operational problems. Areas for specific action plans include market sector development, market research, product development, product launches, promotional campaigns, sales product training, annual planning process, establishment of distributors and agents, and improvement of the operation of product management.

Action plans in each area need to satisfy five effectiveness criteria:

1.  They must focus on specific measureable objectives that can be communicated and monitored. An example might be:

    To develop and launch new product X by 1 January 1990.
    To review and improve distribution network by 1 January 1989.
    To carry out a comprehensive market analysis of competitors between 1 January and 1 April 1989 as a vital input to the 1989 product group strategy review planned for May 1989.
2.  They must identify specific actions required to achieve the objectives.
3.  They must be clear in allocating accountability for the action.
4.  They must indicate clearly the time-scale for the action, highlighting the required start date, completion date and hence planned elapsed time.
5.  They must sequence and assign priority on the basis of a realistic assessment of the impact or benefit of each action and the likely case of implementation. Fig. 2.16 illustrates an impact/ease matrix that aids the assessment and sequencing of actions or tasks. In the example given, high benefit action 3 is held back until actions 4 and 5 have removed bottlenecks to action 3. Tackling action 3 first might alienate people at an early stage and jeopardize the total plan.

A typical action plan format is shown in Fig. 2.17.

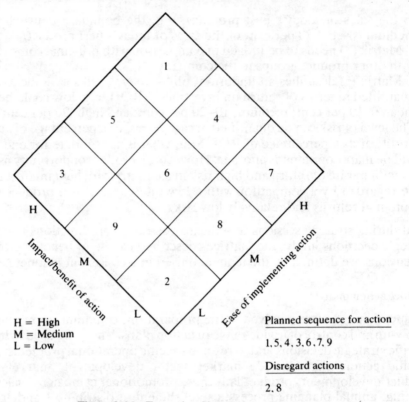

H = High
M = Medium
L = Low

Planned sequence for action

1, 5, 4, 3, 6, 7, 9

Disregard actions

2, 8

**Figure 2.16** Example of impact/ease matrix

---

*PRODUCT GROUP ACTION PLAN No.*       *Prepared by:*                *Date:*

*OBJECTIVES:*   1.
                2.
                3.

| Action required | Priority | By whom | Timescale | | | | | | | | |
|---|---|---|---|---|---|---|---|---|---|---|---|
|  |  |  |  |  |  |  |  |  |  |  |  |

**Figure 2.17** Typical action plan format

Action plans will arise from strategy reviews, operational reviews, territorial visits, customer visits, management meetings, project reviews or personal initiatives.

Product managers need to establish the personal and team discipline required to prepare, issue, communicate and follow up plans in a timely and diligent manner.

### Product risk management

Risk is inherent in all strategic decisions, budgets and action plans. Risks result from a wide variety of possible events such as gaps in information, unreliable information, conflicts between departments or partners, technological break-throughs, new emergent competitors and takeovers of customers, competitors and suppliers.

The assessment and management of risk is therefore an important task of the product manager, who is in a good position to take an overview of likely events and trends in the marketplace and within the business.

The process outlined in Fig. 2.18 needs to be applied at each stage in the process of developing and marketing a product, so as to improve the probability of competitive success.

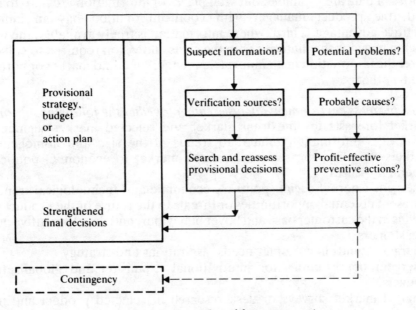

**Figure 2.18** Basic product risk management

### Information needs and sources

The overall planning framework for the product manager was illustrated in Figs 2.2 and 2.6. At the heart of the process is the product management information base. The information base comprises three aspects.

1. *External business environment analysis*
   - a broad assessment of external trends, events and emergent possibilities
2. *External competitive survey*
   - a detailed analysis and forecast of current and likely competitive activity and strategic moves
3. *Internal capability audit*
   - a hard look at the capability of the product group to survive against the background of 1 and 2 above

The extent of the potential information base is considerable and, if collected, would drown any product manager by extent, detail and complexity. Each product manager needs to be selective and determine the information that is essential to an ability to plan, monitor and control; that which is desirable, that which is pure luxury and that which is superfluous. The emphasis should be on identifying what is essential; establishing cost-effective and reliable sources of both base and confirmatory information; and collecting desirable information where it can be obtained and updated on a profit-effective basis.

Typical core information needs are summarized below. Before using the checklist, a number of points must be made. First, in many markets large quantities of data are available, but vital pieces of information are hard to obtain. Second, the product manager with good information has an immediate competitive advantage. Third, where information is freely available, the winning product manager is the manager with the skills and vision required to collate and interpret the information in an innovative manner, and find market opportunities missed by others.

*External business environment analyses gather together the following information:*
1. Market forecasts for the total market and selected market segments and territories. Information related to trends in the size and homogeneity of markets, stability, the sensitivity of the market to economic, political and general pressures.
2. Emergent external social, political, economic and technological trends that represent potential opportunities or threats to the future of the product group.
3. Trends in the customer base and buyer behaviour, and the competitive position of customers.
4. Emergent trends in customer needs, aspirations and strategy.
5. Emergent opportunities for international expansion and globalization of products.
6. Detailed market surveys or desk research of selected product and market opportunities.
7. The potential for collaboration with other companies.
8. Possible acquisitions to accelerate the development of in-fill, add-on or new products, or remove competitors within constraints of monopoly regulations.

*External competitive surveys consider:*
1. Which organizations are current competitors, and which might become competitors over the next five years?

2. What are the most significant current strengths and weaknesses of the competitors in terms of: product range; products; product development and design; quality standards; market share; customer base; location of production; profitability; cash flow; distribution channels; promotion; pricing; political lobbies and connections; access to government finance; organization structure; cost structure; financial resources to sustain a price war; and quality of creative thinking?
3. What are the recent successes and failures of the most significant competitors as an indication of ability or inability to anticipate and respond to changes in market conditions?
4. What major contracts have been obtained recently and are being competed for currently?
5. What significant national and international collaborations exist for sharing research and development risks, joint product development, marketing, sourcing of products, and so on?
6. What significant investments have been recently announced or are being considered?
7. What is the estimated promotion and advertising budget?
8. What is the estimated product development budget?
9. What is the emergent technological strategy of principal competitors?
10. Estimates of cost structures, margins and competitive productivity levels.
11. Analysis of patents and technological/product citations in international technological literature.
12. The extent of competitors' attempts and successes in globalizing products.
13. Emergent strategies, particularly approaches to market segmentation, and sourcing of products.
14. Advertising agents, budgets and focus of activity.
15. The movement of key personnel between competitors.

Basically, the product manager aims to put himself in the competitors' shoes and consider what strategies would be considered viable from the other side of the fence.

Sources of competitive information will include the sales force, commissioned research, day-to-day market intelligence, listening in the marketplace to suppliers, customers and competitors, visiting exhibitions, seminars and conferences, technical meetings and buying in competitive products and services.

In the 1980s the focus of competitive analysis has been on competitors' marketing initiatives and cost structures. Indications are that the monitoring of competitive collaborations and technological competitiveness will become at least as important in the 1990s.

The collection, collation and interpretation of competitive information tends to develop in the form of a flexible picture puzzle (see Fig. 2.19). Information flows from a variety of sources, some more informative and specific than others, some more reliable than others. The product manager needs to assess the quality of information used in making key decisions. Gaps and doubtful information need to be filled and validated before decisions are finalized and implemented.

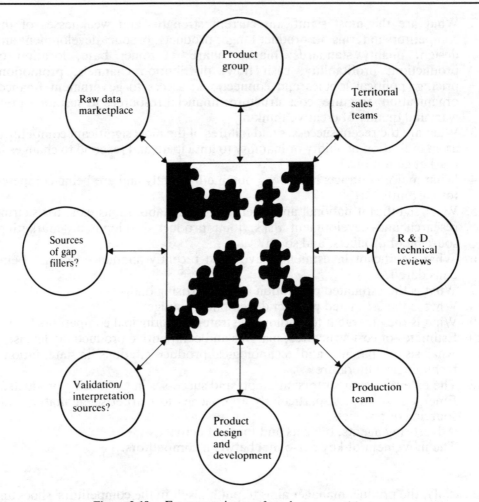

**Figure 2.19.** Emergent picture of product competitiveness

*Internal capability audits consist of the following:*
1. A review of corporate strategic decisions affecting the ability of the product group to secure support and resources.
2. An evaluation of the strengths, successes, weaknesses and failures of the product group at the level of product group, territory and support function.
3. A review of trends in product results, volumes, margins, profit, cash flow, market share, productivity, cost structure, return on investment.
4. Sales forecasts, actuals versus plan, best- and worst-case forecasts against plan, update on potential medium and longer-term major orders.
5. A review of profitability and growth prospects of each product, territory and market segment.
6. A review of product opportunities emergent from the company's research and development activity.

7. A review of product development programmes.
8. A review of product sourcing and manufacturing plans.
9. A review of manufacturing plans for increasing capacity, relocating capacity and for reducing the cost base.
10. Comparison of the financial results of the product group with other product groups within the company.
11. A review of persons allocated full-time or part-time to marketing, sales and product development activity for the product group.
12. A review of corporate promotion and public relations programmes that could benefit the product group.

**Achieving commitment and support**

For personal success, product managers are very dependent on gaining the support and commitment of their direct small product group team and also on a wide range of managers working in other departments and locations.

Therefore, product managers need to ask themselves at an early stage:

– Who do I depend on for success?
– Who currently supports product management and who questions or opposes the concept?
– Who has vital information?
– Who needs to be involved in the preparation of strategies and plans?
– Who needs to be involved in and committed to the implementation of plans?
– How can the essential involvement and commitment be achieved?

A key relationship is that between product managers and territorial managers, the latter being very senior managers in major territories and perhaps equal in rank to the group product manager in smaller territories. The achievement of an effective working relationship requires that product managers are clear about their limits of authority and the value of participation in decision-making.

The spectrum of decision-making in relation to the product–territorial manager dyad is illustrated in Fig. 2.20. Similar patterns need to be thought through in relation to marketing services, product development, manufacturing and customer service.

**Evaluation of product managers**

The objective planning, assessment and evaluation of the performance of product managers is an important feature of the product management process. There is wide variation in the personnel techniques and processes used by companies; some of these techniques are illustrated in Table 2.7. Since more and more companies are moving towards the quantitative approach, the latter is described in detail.

Company A attempted to evaluate product managers entirely on an output basis: the performance of the product group in terms of gross profit before tax and market share. In practice this was not successful. In years of buoyant market conditions the performance assessment was inevitably excellent, although the

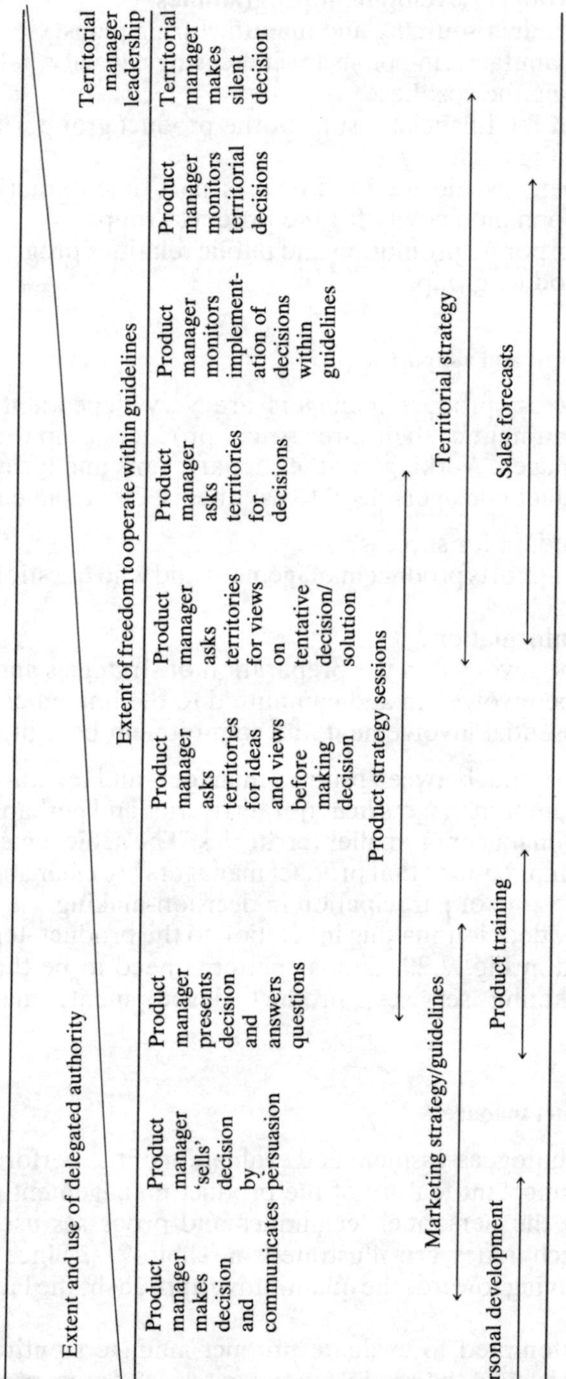

Product manager leadership — Extent and use of delegated authority

Extent of freedom to operate within guidelines — Territorial manager leadership

| Product manager makes and keeps decision to self | Product manager makes decision and communicates | Product manager 'sells' decision by persuasion | Product manager presents decision and answers questions | Product manager asks territories for ideas and views before making decision | Product manager asks territories for views on tentative decision/ solution | Product manager asks territories for decisions | Product manager monitors implement- ation of decisions within guidelines | Product manager monitors territorial decisions | Territorial manager makes silent decision |

Personal development

Product training

Product strategy sessions

Marketing strategy/guidelines

Territorial strategy

Sales forecasts

**Figure 2.20**   The spectrum of product manager – territorial manager decision authority

**Table 2.7**  Trend in product manager's appraisal practices

| Laissez faire | Qualitative evaluation | Quantitative evaluation |
|---|---|---|
| ● No formal system | ● Input related | ● Output/input related |
| ● *Ad hoc* short memory decisions | ● Personal criteria only | ● Personal and shared criteria |
| ● Favouritism | ● Subjective assessment scales | ● Challenging objectives |
| ● Bias | | ● Quantified assessment scales |
| ● Inequity | ● Soft interpretation of results | ● Tough interpretation of results |
| | ● Boss evaluation discussed with subordinate | ● Self evaluation discussed with boss |
| ● Tends to develop 'administration' style of product manager | ● Tends to develop 'management'-style product manager | ● Tends to develop 'leadership'-style product manager |

Observed trend $\longrightarrow$

product manager may have done little to impact the improvement in result directly. In a bad year of deteriorating market conditions and product group results, product managers blamed territorial managers and vice versa, and each claimed that there were too many influences beyond their direct control.

Company B recognized the problems of company A, and introduced an objective input- versus output-related approach. As a fairer and more realistic basis for evaluating the effectiveness of each product manager, the following criteria were introduced:

1. Is the product manager on top of changes in market conditions and requirements and demonstrating that he or she is capable of accurately interpreting the changing needs of the product group business?
2. Does the product manager develop imaginative plans for the product group that are accepted by both corporate management and territorial management?
3. Does the product manager include firm programmes for securing realistic improvements in product profitability and productivity?
4. Does the product manager follow up and, if necessary, modify approved plans to ensure that product objectives are achieved?
5. Is the product manager regarded by other managers as the most knowledgeable about the requirements of the product group, and do they look to him or her for ideas regarding actions to meet customer needs?

Performance against each criterion was assessed on a scale of 0 to 5, 0 denoting unsatisfactory performance and 5 denoting excellent performance.

The approach established a greater awareness of the nature of the influence of product managers on the remainder of the organization but typically product managers, as others, tended to be assessed as at 2.5–3.5, suggesting little differentiation between the poor and good performer.

Company C introduced a realistic balance between output and input criteria, and recognized that some product manager objectives were shared. The aim was

| Part A | Product manager : John Bolt<br>Annual objectives : 1990<br>Discussed/agreed with : ANW<br>Date : 1.12.1989 | | Part B | Product manager performance evaluation<br>Period : 1990<br>Prepared/agreed by : JB/ANW<br>Date : 12.12.1990 | | |
|---|---|---|---|---|---|---|
| Objectives | | Achievement equivalent to % of bonus | | Notes on product manager's personal contribution to achievement of objectives | Agreed % achievement | Weighted bonus performance |
| | | (1) | | | (2) | (1)×(2) |
| 1. *Economic results 1990* | | 50 | | | | |
| 1.1 | 20% improvement in gross profit | | 1.1 | 22% improvement forecast for year end | 100 | |
| 1.2 | 15% improvement in volumes | | 1.2 | Volumes running 14% up | 80 | |
| 1.3 | Market share increased from 33% to 38% | | 1.3 | Market share currently 36% | 75 | |
| 1.4 | Negative cash flow reversed | | 1.4 | Cash flow balanced, forecast +1991 | 85 | 42.5 |
| 2. *Strategic initiatives* | | 25 | | | | |
| 2.1 | Launch of product 'X' on 1.7.1990 | | 2.1 | Product successfully launched and sales 20% up on forecast | 100 | |
| 2.2 | Completion of development programme for product 'Y' to test market phase by end 1990 | | 2.2 | Programme running 3 months late and costs 10% above plan | 0 | 12.5 |
| 3. *Special investigations/analyses* | | 15 | | | | |
| 3.1 | Investigation of impact of 1992 EEC single market on longer-term product group strategy | | 3.1 | Initial analysis complete and circulated for discussion. Review session fixed for 12.1.91. A number of important issues need deeper analysis by then | 70 | 10.5 |
| 4. *Personal development* | | 10 | | | | |
| 4.1 | Attend advanced product management training programme during 1990 and develop follow-up programme for team | | 4.1 | Didn't find time. Booked twice but had to cancel. Now rebooked for February 1991 | 0 | 0 |
| | | | | Recommended % of maximum available bonus award ............65.5% | | |

Note: Final bonus assessment to be made 1.2.1991 when final December results are available

**Figure 2.21** Framework for annual objectives and performance evaluation

to achieve an alignment between business group strategy, financial results and personal development. The company had established a company-wide approach to appraisals.

The approach entailed the following procedures:

1. Product managers carried out a self-appraisal every six months for the first two years in the job and then annually.
2. The product manager evaluated personal performance against the objectives agreed at the last 'personal development and planning review' — the company's name for the appraisal process.
3. The product manager recorded conclusions along the lines of Fig. 2.21, and presented the document verbally to the appropriate group product manager and marketing director. The senior managers listened to the presentation, then highlighted and discussed areas of disagreement. The result was positive and motivational.
4. At alternate sessions, the future development needs and career path of the product manager, again on a self-analysis basis, were discussed. The product manager completed and presented for discussion an analysis based on the following framework of questions:

   (a) What are your demonstrated successes and strengths?
   (b) How can these strengths be utilized over the next 6–24 months?
   (c) What development experience would assist you to develop further the agreed strengths?
   (d) What weaknesses need to be recognized, and corrective action taken, if you are to make the best of your potential capabilities in your current assignment and future career?

The attitude of the company was that everyone had recognizable strengths, which should be further developed as number one priority, and that many weaknesses were a nuisance factor that could be lived with provided consistent ongoing results were achieved.

The style of product manager sought is illustrated by position (3, 3) in each of the three matrices of Fig. 2.22.

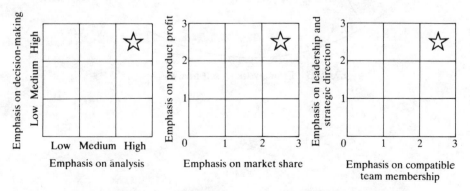

**Figure 2.22**  Preferred emphasis of product manager behaviour

*Self-analysis*
Each of the ten chapters of this book focuses on a particular aspect of the total product management process and task. In total they provide a framework that will assist product managers not only to gather ideas, but also to evaluate their recent performance as product managers. The book is designed to help product managers to complete a personal performance analysis (see Fig. 2.23) and initiate appropriate and timely actions.

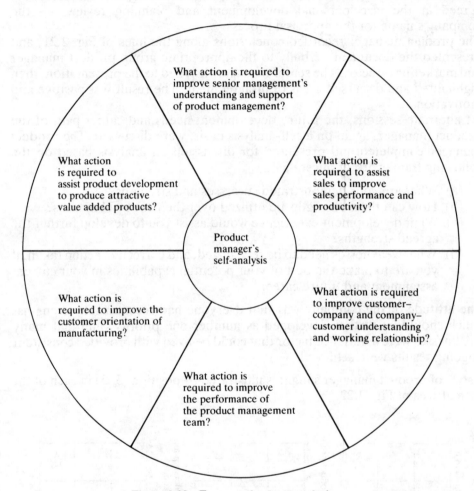

**Figure 2.23**   Framework of self-analysis

**Chapter 2 – Key point summary**

*The operation of the product management process*

1. Focus on the enhanced value of product group as a business
2. Link product planning to corporate strategy
3. Integrate and harmonize product group, territorial and functional planning and control
4. Organize participative product group planning sessions
5. Achieve market focus through objective segmentation
6. Establish strategic financial management of the product life cycle
7. Use action plans to communicate and achieve commitment
8. Ensure that risk analyses are open-minded
9. Establish an informative and reliable intelligence network
10. Evaluate product managers on an objective basis

# 3. Managing product development

**Product managers' key task**

To direct, monitor and control a market-driven programme for the development of improved and new products or services, and to ensure that products or services, fit for purpose and capable of achieving customer satisfaction beyond expectations, are available for introduction and launch into the marketplace on time, in the required quantity and within a competitive cost structure

### The product development task

A professionally managed product development programme is essential to the success of a product group. An effective programme will be characterized by the following important and compatible activities.

1. The establishment of a direct and positive link between product development priorities and plans and the overall strategy for the product group (see Fig. 3.1)
2. Close integration of market, product development and process development plans and activity
3. An ongoing programme of incremental profit-generating improvements to existing products or services to secure enhanced customer satisfaction, sustained and increased demand, and hence extended product lives
4. A progressive programme for the development and phased introduction of timely new products and services, more competitive and profit-effective than the previous generation or series of products. The products will include:

    (a) Add-on products to the current range
    (b) In-fill products within the current range
    (c) Replacement products to follow on from current products in existing markets and for existing application
    (d) Replacement products that will enable the product group to expand sales into related market segments or new international territories, and to meet the demands of related product applications that require an improved product

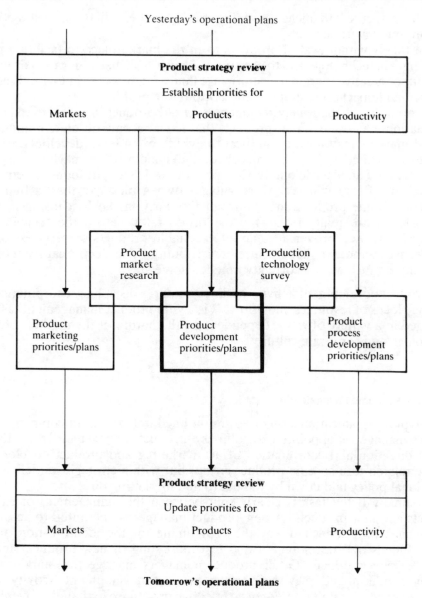

Yesterday's operational plans

**Product strategy review**

Establish priorities for

Markets          Products          Productivity

Product
market
research

Production
technology
survey

Product
marketing
priorities/plans

Product
development
priorities/plans

Product
process
development
priorities/plans

**Product strategy review**

Update priorities for

Markets          Products          Productivity

**Tomorrow's operational plans**

**Figure 3.1**    Focus for product development plans

(e) Entirely new products for new markets and new applications. In this case
the products may be managed by an existing product group, a new product
group or a specially established business unit.

5. The timely withdrawal of product improvement effort from products past their
prime, to be taken out of the market within a relatively short period of time, or

to be refocused in niche specialist markets where they can succeed with minimum investment

6. The timely withdrawal of products from the marketplace to facilitate timely changes in technology and to prevent cash cows from becoming cash drains as a result of creative marginal cost pricing, that sustains sales, but with disastrous eventual impact on cash flows and bottom line profile

7. In certain cases the timely relaunch of an old product in a new market. Two situations can occur. First, products that have become obsolete in industrialized markets may have a significant new life in an underdeveloped or early industrializing market. For instance, the hand sewing machine has been replaced by an electric one in Europe and the USA, but found an emergent need in African villages. More villages own a pick axe than a bulldozer. Second, some products are launched too early in the first instance before customers are really ready for the product, or before the technology is sufficiently well proven to guarantee reliable products or services, or cost effective methods of manufacture or distribution. The electric car is a recurring example which will be correctly timed at some stage.

The product development activity outlined requires discipline, coordination and strategic focus of resources and effort. It is a vital product management task, but managed in a variety of ways, dependent on the nature of the market, product, technology and corporate culture.

### Product development organization

Three typical organization structures are outlined in Fig. 3.2. In company A the product manager is appointed to fulfil the product management role, that of overall direction and coordination of all marketing and product development activity related to a specific product group, but within strategic guidelines and operational policy laid down by the board and marketing director.

In company B the task is clearly split between the management of existing products and new products. A new product manager is appointed to accelerate and manage in a dedicated way the programme for the identification of new product needs, the development and test marketing of new products and the launch of new products. Other product managers manage the marketing for existing products and play no part in product development activity. Such situations need the establishment of an effective procedure for handing over newly launched products from one manager to another without a competitive hiccup.

Company C has decided that products are managed strategically at the chief executive level. There is a clear functional separation between the marketing and technical aspects of product development. The marketing function is only concerned with sales, brand marketing and sales support. The technical function is concerned with the consideration of product development, within strategic guidelines laid down by the chief executive, and the direction and coordination of prototype productions. The manufacturing function is accountable for ensuring that prototypes are turned into production runs, and that products are available to

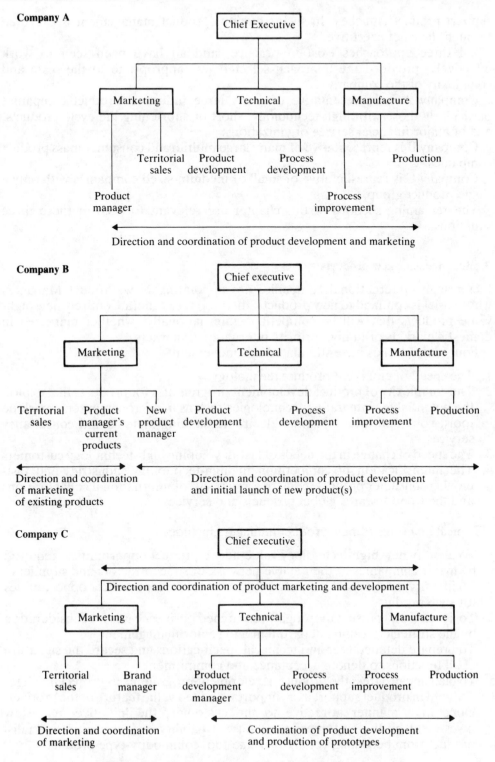

**Figure 3.2**   Variations in product development structure

support product launches. In such situations product management is executed through the chief executive.

All three approaches exist in practice, and all have been seen to work effectively, provided the approach selected was appropriate to the scale and complexity of the company.

Company A is representative of many large industrial product companies particularly those with high-technology, short or shortening life cycle products, and of major financial service organizations.

Company B is representative of many large multibrand consumer mass product companies.

Company C is representative of small or medium-sized companies with only a single product group.

The remaining sections of this chapter are relevant to each of these three situations.


**Product manager new products**

Increasingly, international companies are appointing New Product Managers whose brief is confined to new products; their job is to generate entirely new high-value products that will be competitive internationally, whether marketed in domestic markets or in high-priority international markets.

Four major trends have stimulated this movement:

1. The speed of emergent product technology
2. The complexity of product development programmes for products that exploit the potential for integrating technologies such as in microcomputers, machine tools, communication systems, electronic banking systems and consultancy services
3. The speed of change in the needs of fast-developing high-technology customers
4. The intensification of competition in high-technology industries and fast-moving consumer product industries as a result of international collaborations and the trend towards global products and services

Typical key tasks of new product managers include:

1. To identify new high-technology value-added product opportunities, required by major companies or their stable network of subcontractors and suppliers
2. To identify, specify and quantify existing and emergent market opportunities for such products
3. To develop and present thoroughly researched business cases for consideration by the strategic planning department and senior management
4. To prepare detailed user and technical specifications and secure the signature of all functions to denote acceptance and commitment
5. To plan and progress the product development programme as project manager
6. To build in product support as an important added value feature of the product. Done in a manner attractive to the customer, the initiative may slow investment by the customer in in-house capability and prevent a specialist product from becoming yet another 'me too' commodity-type product

7. To progress and manage the launch of the product to the marketplace
8. To continue to enhance the reputation of the company for high-technology, value-for-money products and services, fit for the purpose for which they are sought
9. To hand over the product to an established product group manager within six months of launch without a hiccup in external or internal relationships and results

### Generating ideas

The ongoing search for new product/service ideas is a vital product management task in all companies, and in all industries. The product teams that survive the 1990s will be those with:

- An extensive enquiring network of contacts
- A steady flow of new ideas or information that is likely to stimulate new ideas
- A creative and lateral thinking process of challenging, massaging, tearing apart, and joining of half-ideas to establish product/service options that are distinctive
- An objective process for the evaluation of options for product improvement or new products to ensure that scarce resources are focused on a few potential winners rather than a fragmented allocation of resources across a myriad of mediocre products.

The accountability for establishing an effective and productive search programme varies from industry to industry, from company to company. Typically, in consumer products industries it rests with the new product manager or the product development manager. In industrial products companies the person accountable will be the product manager, the new product manager, the product development engineer or business unit manager. In the financial services sector, the product manager is accountable for the enhancement of personal, corporate or specific technologically based services, for example credit cards. Regardless of title, the accountable manager needs to establish the network or sources of potentially useful ideas, half-ideas and information that trigger, reinforce, confirm or even question earlier ideas. Ideas will come from internal and external sources.

### Sources of product innovation

In the 1990s, as in the 1980s, there is likely to be no shortage of world-wide opportunities. The constraints on seeking out and exploiting the opportunities will continue to be largely a people problem rather than a financing problem, as outlined in Fig. 3.3.

In areas such as new materials, the early generation of artificial intelligence, biotechnology, fibre optics, process intensification, and so on, there have been many advances in technology which are not yet widely incorporated into new products, manufacturing processes or new high-technology methods of product distribution.

Numerous sources of innovation exist, including:

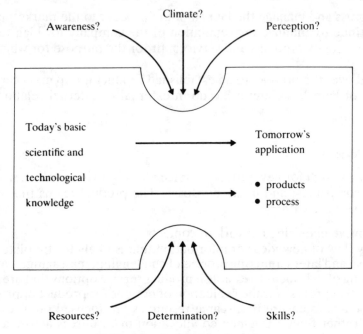

**Figure 3.3** A critical bottleneck

- Previous generations of innovation with lateral thinking: the processing of fibre optics in Japan was derived from fine ceramic technology; the windmill for electrical power; cotton shirts to replace synthetics
- Previous managers' ideas: the archives may have useful disregarded or missed ideas as a result of organizational changes, mergers or technological myopia
- Accidents: bakelite and penicillin founded new industries — it will happen again
- Competitors: you may be able to make a success of their near-misses
- The national technology base: a tour round universities and technological institutes
- Suppliers' technology which could accelerate step changes in design
- New legislation, stimulating products that are safer to use and more environmentally safe
- Cooperative research
- New perspectives or insights into potential applications of technology
- World searches for seedcorn innovations for licensing or 'me too' products
- A look at the do-it-yourself attempts of householders to invent new gadgets.

Figure 3.4 illustrates typical starting points for establishing or updating the idea/ information network. It is presented as an audit questionnaire to stimulate an open, objective and extensive review.

Having decided on whom to involve, the product manager needs to decide how to tap and involve the potential sources. The approaches available include:

1. *Personal visits/discussions* to selected individuals or organizations, the

**Figure 3.4** Review of sources of product ideas

| Are the following sources likely to have useful product/ product technology knowledge, awareness and ideas? | *Yes Probably* | *No Unlikely* | *To what extent are sources currently exploited?* | | | *Future source priorities (H,M,L)* |
|---|---|---|---|---|---|---|
| | | | *Regularly* | *Occasionally* | *Rarely* | |

A. *External sources*
    1. Suppliers
    2. Customers
    3. Competitors
    4. Competitors' salesmen
    5. University professors
    6. Research institute professors
    7. Market research firms
    8. Patent office
    9. Licensing agents
   10. Idea exchanges
   11. Inventors
   12. Design houses
   13. Trade associations
   14. Exhibitons
   15. International literature
   16. Others?

B. *Internal sources*
    1. Research and development
    2. New engineering graduates
    3. New marketing recruits
    4. New salesmen/ engineers
    5. Non-executive directors
    6. Executive directors
    7. Territorial managers
    8. Market research manager
    9. New science graduates
   10. Buyers
   11. Manufacturing managers
   12. Production foremen/ shop floor
   13. Designers
   14. Service/commissioning engineers
   15. Marketing managers
   16. Others?

purpose being either a general exploration or to seek information in a specific predefined area.

2. *External market or technological surveys* of a network of carefullly selected individuals or organizations, in order to explore patterns, trends and potential changes in needs and perceptions. The survey should be designed and managed internally or externally by an experienced consultancy firm. In either case the product manager would be wise to use the internal service available from the market research manager to achieve a time- and cost-effective professional result.

3. *Suggestion schemes* open to all staff, with perhaps a token reward for each idea and major awards for the idea of the quarter.

4. *Visit reports* from all directors, managers and sales engineers making visits to foreign territories or major domestic customers or potential customers.

5. *Exhibition reports* from all persons visiting trade exhibitions and shows.

6. *Conference/seminar* reports from persons attending marketing or technical events, including the graduates still keen to attend events of their respective professional institutes so as to maintain personal professional development.

7. *Product strategy sessions* involving the total product group team, as already discussed in Chapter 2.

8. *Product circles* involving a selected mix of the manufacturing personnel concerned with the direct production, commissioning and servicing of engineering products: this might include the skilled shop-floor and service technicians, who may have valuable ideas for improving both the current and next series of products. This concept is elaborated in Chapter 7.

**Table 3.1**   Product technology strategy session for product 'X'

*Objectives*
1. To provide an enriched technological input to strategic planning at divisional and product group level
2. To share information, views and vision in an objective non-competitive environment
3. To involve a balanced mix of internal and external persons with appropriate market, product, process and technological knowledge and experience
4. To develop the strategic capability of product managers

*Participants*

| *Internal:* | Divisional managing director | (1) | |
|---|---|---|---|
| | Design and development managers | (4) | |
| | Manufacturing managers | (2) | |
| | Market research manager | (1) | |
| | Product managers | (2) | |
| | Advanced development manager | (1) | ..........Total 11 |
| *External:* | Research institutes | (3) | |
| | Suppliers' technical directors | (2) | |
| | Customers' development managers | (2) | |
| | University professors | (2) | |
| | Industrial economist | (1) | |
| | Process leader consultant | (1) | ..........Total 11 |

*Process*
   Pre-work questionnaire
   Two-day strategy session
   Write up and issue results to all participants

9. *Quality circles,* the forerunner of product groups, normally involving the junior staff associated with either the production of a specific component, subassembly or product, or the provision of a specific service. This concept is also elaborated in Chapter 7.
10. *Technology strategy sessions,* involving an invited group of 16–20 internal and external experts, to identify the most significant current and future technical and technological knowledge, trends, capabilities and breakthroughs related to a specific product group.

Table 3.1 illustrates the organization of a typical technology strategy session by an international engineering company, which had decided that:

● It was possible to establish a club of like-minded persons to share knowledge and views, provided it did not involve disclosing competitive secrets
● Managers and technologists at each stage in the product/technological value chain were concerned about the impact of new technologies on trading patterns, and the dangers of losing business as a result of technical breakthroughs, as illustrated in Fig. 3.5
● An uneconomic idea yesterday may be an economic winner tomorrow. The product technology matrix (Fig. 3.6) provides a framework for an analysis and discussion that can be radical in opening up new technological opportunities.

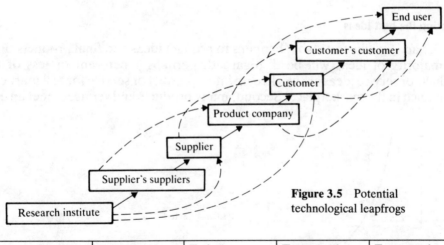

**Figure 3.5** Potential technological leapfrogs

| Source or user? | Technology available used? | Yesterday's | Today's | Tomorrow's 'known' | Tomorrow's 'possible' |
|---|---|---|---|---|---|
| Research institutes | | | | | |
| Suppliers | | | | | |
| Ourselves | | | | | |
| Customers | | | | | |
| Competitors | | | | | |

**Figure 3.6** Product technology matrix

Such a matrix can be revolutionary in opening up new technological opportunities. An uneconomic idea of yesterday may be tomorrow's economic winner. Six important time parameters impact the evolution of the matrix. These require recognition and management by the product management team.

1. *Recognition time:* the timing of the evolution and awareness of the exploitation value of emergent scientific knowledge and ideas.
2. *Response time:* the time delay between the initial recognition and the start of active innovation to translate the idea into a usable and useful technological innovation.
3. *Elapsed time:* the time to develop an application of the idea to a marketable product or service.
4. *Launch timing:* the timing of the launch of the new idea or application internally to the product group and company, and externally to the marketplace and customers.
5. *Expansion time:* the time and timing required to develop and exploit additional applications by innovative marketing of a product or service from the launch market niche to a broader market base; and by expanding a pilot application in a prototype or new product design or manufacturing process to other key areas.
6. *Obsolescence timing:* the critical timing of step changes in product and process technology and design.

### Selecting the best ideas

Figs 3.7 and 3.8 illustrate what happens to product ideas and final products. First, the majority of ideas will be disregarded; perhaps 1 per cent or less of new products or service ideas are worked up into a product or service for test marketing and launch in the marketplace. Second, many products and services meet an early

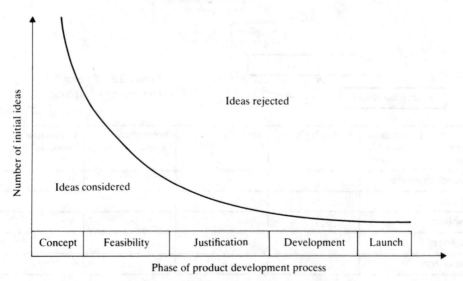

**Figure 3.7**  Screening out of product ideas

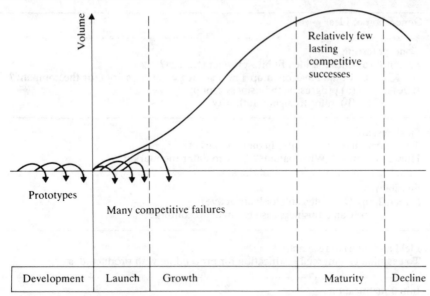

**Figure 3.8**   Market success of products

competitive death, never to be seen outside the test market area, the new product shelf of the supermarket, a national exhibition or trade show.

Each failure represents a significant wasted investment, and reductions in the return on investment, cash flow and worth of a product group or business unit. Each success represents in most cases the result of an objective approach which is both creative and commercial from the initial product concept to product launch. A typical screening process is outlined in Fig. 3.9.

**Managing the product development process**

The product manager will be involved in directing, maintaining and controlling a product development process directly on a personal basis, or indirectly via a product development manager or engineer or a project manager appointed to manage a specific product development programme. The product manager's task is to ensure that a project planning and control process is established, and that the product development programme runs to plan or, with a little luck, ahead of plan. A typical process is illustrated in Fig. 3.10.

The final 'go/no go' decision needs to be based on a number of interrelated factors that affect commercial viability:

- *Technical factors:* can the product be made and will it work reliably?
- *Economic factors:* can the product be marketed at an acceptable cost to the customer, and at a price that at least meets the company's profit and cash-flow demands?
- *Political factors:* will the company be allowed to sell the product? Will there be restrictions on components, additives or operations?
- *Social factors:* does the product meet an emergent life-style or social need? Is it a six-month or a six-year product?

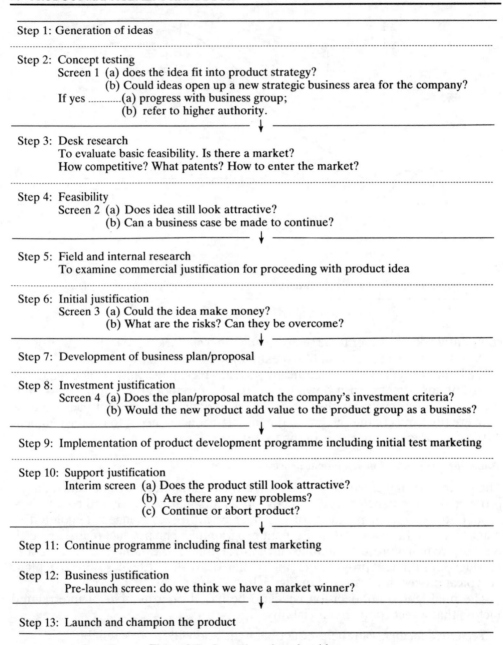

Step 1: Generation of ideas

Step 2:  Concept testing
    Screen 1  (a) does the idea fit into product strategy?
              (b) Could ideas open up a new strategic business area for the company?
    If yes ............(a) progress with business group;
              (b)  refer to higher authority.

Step 3:  Desk research
    To evaluate basic feasibility. Is there a market?
    How competitive? What patents? How to enter the market?

Step 4:  Feasibility
    Screen 2  (a)  Does idea still look attractive?
              (b)  Can a business case be made to continue?

Step 5:  Field and internal research
    To examine commercial justification for proceeding with product idea

Step 6:  Initial justification
    Screen 3  (a) Could the idea make money?
              (b) What are the risks? Can they be overcome?

Step 7:  Development of business plan/proposal

Step 8:  Investment justification
    Screen 4  (a) Does the plan/proposal match the company's investment criteria?
              (b) Would the new product add value to the product group as a business?

Step 9:  Implementation of product development programme including initial test marketing

Step 10:  Support justification
    Interim screen  (a) Does the product still look attractive?
                    (b)  Are there any new problems?
                    (c)  Continue or abort product?

Step 11:  Continue programme including final test marketing

Step 12:  Business justification
    Pre-launch screen: do we think we have a market winner?

Step 13:  Launch and champion the product

**Figure 3.9**   Screening of product ideas

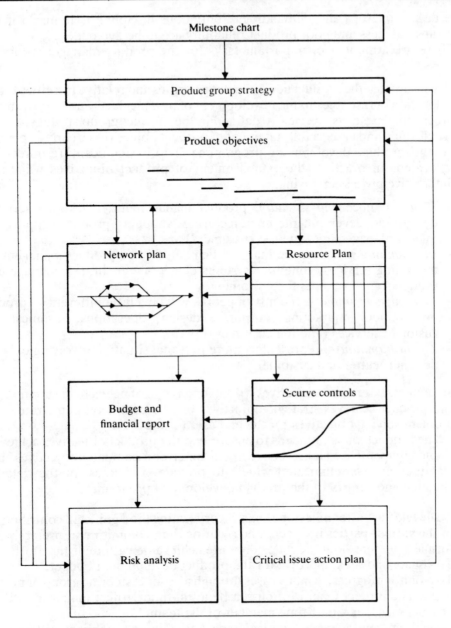

**Figure 3.10** Product development planning and control process

The task is onerous and demanding. Continuous discipline is required if cost overruns, lateness and poor product reliability are to be avoided.

There are a number of important tasks for the product manager within the process.

1. To ensure that the product development priorities and relative priorities for the allocation of resources to the development of new products and improvements to existing products are clearly defined in the product group strategy.
2. To develop and agree a full statement of product objectives as early as possible in the product development programme before significant resources are allocated. In practice, the establishment of product objectives will be an interactive process involving:

    - *In a manufacturing situation:* product management, marketing services, design and development, manufacturing, suppliers product support and quality management (and the customer?)
    - *In a banking situation:* the main participants will be product management, marketing services, computer systems development, branch management (and in some instances the customer)
    - *In a railway company:* the mix of people will be a little different — product management, marketing, corporate design, operations, technical and customer services (and the customer?)
    - *The fashion house:* represents a more personal situation involving only the designer, cutter and customer

    Statements of product objectives will cover a range of needs to ensure that the end product achieves strategic objectives for the company, and strategic or problem-solving objectives for the end user (Table 3.2).

    The product manager needs to ensure that the product objectives achieve a viable competitive balance between customer and company objectives, and that they are communicated widely to provide guidelines for the detailed planning and control of the product development programme.

3. To develop a master milestone chart incorporating the significant contributions of the various parties involved, and securing their commitment, preferably by formal signature, that the milestones are achievable with realistic effort.
4. To collate and seek approval for the product development budget.
5. To monitor progress, in many cases through a product steering group or project team. The project team is often run by a full-time project manager with the product manager a part-time member of the team.
6. To maintain and manage a critical issue action plan to highlight and progress the resolution of issues that could put the planned new product or improved product at risk — a vital task after the establishment of product objectives.
7. To develop and update a product risk analysis to record and analyse anticipated problems. Typical formats are illustrated in Figs 3.11 and 3.12. The risk analysis should explore all aspects and stages of the product development programme, but especially those areas which involve new technology, novel solutions, styling moves, first times, changes, more complexity than previous

**Table 3.2.**   Framework for statement of product development objectives

| | |
|---|---|
| *A.  Customer-related objectives* | |
| Operational objectives | Focused on a specific range of user needs in terms of performance, weight, size, quality, aesthetic styling, maintenance periodicity, operating costs, user friendliness, etc. |
| Technical objectives | Focused on the need to meet specific engineering standards, shelf life, test certification, quality assurance plans, overcome known technological risks, etc. |
| Economic objectives | Focused on the achievement of price, warranty demands, delivery dates, cost of spares, cost of manuals, training, etc. |
| Political objectives | Focused on local content, sourcing of components and materials, etc. |
| Legal objectives | Focused on the need to satisfy product liability and safety legislation, etc. |
| *B.  Company-related objectives* | |
| Profitability objectives | Focused on developing a product that will attract premium prices, enable reductions in cost to be achieved over previous product, and achieve positive cash flow at an early stage |
| Design standardization | Focused on the desire to utilize reliable cost-effective and competitive aspects of previous designs and processes of manufacture |
| Innovative objectives | Focused on the desire to introduce and evaluate new competitive product features, materials, methods of assembly and packaging, etc. |
| Marketing and publicity objectives | Focused on the desire for a product that will enable the image of the product group and company to be raised |
| Follow-on order objectives | Focused on the need to develop a related service, product compatibility, etc., that builds in the potential for achieving customer loyalty |
| Systems objectives | Focused on the desire to introduce and evaluate new planning and control procedures |

| Product-critical issues | Issue no.    : |
|---|---|
| | Issued date : |
| | Issued by    : |

| No. | Critical issue | Action required | PR | By whom | Timescale 19 | | Review notes |
|---|---|---|---|---|---|---|---|
| | | | | | | | |
| | | | | | | | |

**Figure 3.11**   Product development programme product X

|  | Technological problems | Manufacturability | Emergence competitive products | Etc. |
|---|---|---|---|---|
| What could go wrong to put the project at risk |  |  |  |  |
| Probability of problems (H, M, L) |  |  |  |  |
| Likely cause of problems |  |  |  |  |
| Preventive action possible |  |  |  |  |
| Probability of success (H, M, L) |  |  |  |  |
| Cost/benefit |  |  |  |  |
| Contingent plans required |  |  |  |  |

**Figure 3.12**  Product risk analysis

    programmes, or new people, new suppliers, new customer groups or territories.
8. To arrange a post-launch evaluation meeting to ensure that lessons learnt are taken into account in developing future products.

In some cases the above tasks can be managed on a personal basis. In other more complex situations, particularly in the larger company, the project will be progressed by the product manager and/or supporting project manager through a variety of development reviews including: project reviews with the total product team; design reviews with the design team; design make reviews involving design and manufacturing; and supplier customer reviews, introducing and evaluating features, prototypes and initial units or batches with selected customers.

### Relating products to customers

World-wide, product managers are finding that customers are becoming more selective in the quality of products and services they are prepared to purchase. Customers are demonstrating a willingness to look for:

1. Cost-effective basic or commodity products
2. Value-for-money, fun or feel-good products
3. Products with a profit-effective and attractive total product package
4. Expensive image products with important status, luxury or novelty added values
5. Products that enhance lifestyle

As a result, many customers have lower thresholds of product or brand loyalty, a trend which it is the job of the product manager to reverse.
    Product managers have the task of ensuring that:

1. Products and services achieve a basic fitness for purpose and give the customer a perception of added value for money

2. Product design and development decisions can be backed by market research and technological surveys
3. The company does not resort to 'me too' products with little or no distinctive competitive benefit in the eyes of prospective customers
4. Value for money does not slip between one series model and the next as a result of in-fighting among design, manufacturing, marketing, finance and customer service
5. Profit-effective options for product packages are explored
6. A realistic balance between proven market needs (market pull) and proven technological possibilities (technology push) is achieved
7. If customers only want to pay for a basic commodity product, with no service and no frills, that is what they get
8. The requirements of consumer protection and product liability legislation are evaluated and taken seriously
9. The company's needs for profit, return on investment, cash flow and growth in value of the product group as a business are met
10. The product, and visual dimensions of advertising, packaging, distribution vehicles, shop merchandising displays and catalogues minimize the need for tough sales negotiations

In achieving these tasks the product manager needs to decide on how best to harness the combined skills of conceptual designers, style and aesthetic designers, engineering designers and manufacturing process designers. A clear brief is required in all cases with a clear link between the focus of design and product group strategy.

Design and the quality of design are at the heart of achieving an effective competitive mix. They are important to all products and services; as important to speciality chemicals, restaurants, and engineering products as to *haute couture*. Each uses technology through design to create better-looking, durable, value-for-money, profitable products and services.

In some situations, new products are developed as a cooperative venture between a company and an important customer; each partner contributing market, application, technological and design know-how. Initially, the customer desires a unique product, and may assume that he has sole right to design. The product manager and sales force may wish to exploit the product on a wider basis, to satisfy broader market needs and speed the recovery of the development expenditure. This may raise ethical as well as patent or copyright issues. The product manager, therefore, needs to clarify short- and longer-term objectives as part of the contractual arrangement with the initial customer.

### The importance of design

Design is important both to customers and to product managers. The shirt, drought-resistant plants, fast-track office blocks, the credit card, Concorde, and designer shoes are all design breakthroughs which opened up new market and personal opportunities for product managers, product development managers and designers.

**Figure 3.13** Link between design quality and product group strategy

Design is an important element of the competitive mix for both consumer and industrial customer. The consumer customer will be concerned with enhanced lifestyle, personal experience, image and self-confidence at an economic first-time cost. The industrial customer will be concerned with the possibility of improving competitiveness and productivity, enhancing the corporate image and an economically attractive life-time cost.

The product manager has the task of ensuring that competitive opportunities are not lost and that all aspects of design quality are identified and assessed. Fig. 3.13 provides a conceptual framework for establishing a link between product strategy and design. The 14 total design quality factors listed apply to a wide range of products, as illustrated in Table 3.3.

Design quality sells; it is recognized and acknowledged by customers. Overdesign results in overelaborate, heavy, expensive, or low-margin products; underdesign results in shoddy, low-margin, expensive products. Achieving the right balance depends on communication from the customer to all functions within the company. The product manager has the critical job of managing this interface and ensuring that appropriate product and service specifications are established, communicated, applied, and not compromised by a lack of commitment.

The management of the design process requires:

1. That the product development team includes an appropriate mix of industrial

**Table 3.3**   Applications of total design quality factors

| Factor | Shoes | Personal loan | Commuter train |
|---|---|---|---|
| Styling | Visual impact of the shoe | Visual impact of the brochure | Internal/external visual impact |
| Simplicity | Good fit | Customer-friendly forms | Ease of operation |
| Serviceability | Heel bar needs | Computer | Ease of maintenance |
| Security | Non-slip | Reliability | User safety |
| Systems compatibility | Matchability | Computer-linked with other products | Matches railway infrastruture |
| Standardization | Components | Form design | Components |
| Sensitivity to environment | Water resistant | Control of papers | Noise/pollution |
| Effectiveness | Comfort/durability | Customer time | Operation performance |
| Economy | Initial cost | Interest/fees | Life-time costs |
| Energy efficiency | Stitching/welding | Computer power | Motor power |
| Elegance solution | Visual | Ease of use | Engineering |
| Ease of manufacture | Product | Installation | Components/products |
| Expected quality | Product life | Speed of response | Life comfort |
| Ease of use | Comfort | Availability | Ease of access |

(style) designers and engineering designers at each stage of the product development programme.

2. That individual design is applied to the product itself, packaging, merchandising standards, brochures, manuals and such like; all are part of the vital customer experience.
3. That the design approach of competitors is identified, analysed and understood in competitive terms.
4. That step changes in technology are based on a balance of styling, strength, serviceability, manufacturability, reliability as well as cost factors and customer demands.

For instance, the timely introduction of new plastics into shoes has achieved at various times competitive advantages in terms of price, waterproofing, extended sole life, weight, airflow, comfort, shape, designer colours and designs.

Such step changes in technology have implications for:

- *Industrial designers,* in terms of new forms, shapes and images for products, packaging, and merchandise displays
- *Engineering designers* in terms of strength, weight and durability
- *Process designers* in terms of process productivity, costs and flexibility

For the product manager, changes in technology can result in exciting new products; reduced costs that enable increased margins to be achieved; new forms of product differentiation that increase the probability of a product's being successful in the marketplace; but also some downside risks while designers, developers and producers get used to a new technology.

The product manager is accountable for ensuring that design opportunities and risks are reviewed in an objective commercial manner; and that all concerned remember that increased sales begin on the drawing board.

### The political dimension of product design

The product manager and product design and development team need to be constantly and increasingly aware of political decisions, laws and regulations that

**Table 3.4**   Typical political initiatives affecting design and development of products

| Initiatives related to | Likely impact Positive | | Negative |
|---|---|---|---|
| Banned ingredients | ● | or | ● |
| National/international engineering standards | ● | or | ● |
| Patent laws | ● | or | ○ |
| Quality liability legislation | ○ | or | ● |
| Product quality, safety and labelling regulations | | | ○ |
| Local content requirement | ● | or | ● |
| Pre-testing/authorization of products or components | | | ● |
| FDA approval of products for human consumption or use | | | ● |
| Environmental/emission controls | ● | or | ● |
| Maximum lorry gross weights | ● | or | ● |

affect the design and marketing of products and services. Examples of these kinds of political initiatives are listed in Table 3.4.

The likely impact of each political issue from the point of view of the product manager, directing the design and development of a group of products, is also indicated. For competitors, the impact may be the same or reversed, particularly in the home or favoured domestic markets such as the EEC.

Political issues affecting the marketing of products will be covered in Chapter 4.

## Managing the launch

The product development programme is well under way, on time, within budget, and prototype tests are promising. The product manager has a product to launch. He now has the vital task of masterminding the planning and implementation of a product launch programme that is timely, has impact and gives the product a fair chance of survival in a marketplace that tends to remember launch failures better than successes.

The purpose of a product launch is to demonstrate to important potential customers that the company has a product ready and available to meet selected and anticipated needs of those customers at an appropriate time for the customer and at a realistic price. The launch is an opportunity to position the product, the brand and the company firmly in the eyes of customers and in many cases the public at large. Unfortunately, the purpose is not always met for a number of reasons, illustrated in Table 3.5.

## The launch team

Major launches deserve the formation of a properly resourced product launch team, comprising the product manager, marketing services, advertising agent and public affairs. The mission of the product launch team is to plan and implement the

**Table 3.5**  Factors affecting a product launch

| Success as a result of | Failure caused by |
| --- | --- |
| 1. Clear target markets | 1. Lack of discipline and poor coordination of functions |
| 2. Clear objectives – customer related | 2. Resources insufficient for size of launch market |
| 3. Timing | 3. Inadequate launch stocks |
| 4. Cohesive programme, underwritten and supported by all functions | 4. Production capacity insufficient to meet early demand |
| 5. Well-briefed sales force, with time allocated to new product | 5. Price set too low; sales generated but no cash flow |
| 6. Anticipation of competitors' strategy | 6. Promotional material late |
| 7. Risk analysis on launch plan at an early stage, updated and managed throughout programme | 7. Key buyers at a competitive launch |
| 8. A product launch team | 8. Product manager attempting to do everything |

actual launch. The task comprises a pre-commitment feasibility/justification phase and a post-commitment implementation phase.

The initial task will be to develop and cost a launch plan for approval. An effective plan will define:

1. The target customer groups.
2. The target audience for a launch event, including end users; buyers; media able to influence product preferences and likely to provide free editorial; suppliers and employees who need to be rewarded for effort to-date and motivated to maintain day-to-day support for the product; and, with industrial products, government departments and banks.
3. The selected launch date, and benefits of that date compared to other dates considered. Consideration will include timing of conferences, exhibitions and shows, availability of important persons and, most important, a guarantee that the fully proven product will be ready to wear, use, taste, see or test.
4. The style and scale of launch, elected to match the objectives of the product group, corporate style of company and lifestyle of the planned audience. The launch must be something that is remembered; something that stimulates customer interest and potential loyalty from day 1; something that can demonstrate on post-launch evaluation a bottom-line return.
5. The location of the launch.
6. The outline programme.
7. A budget for the expenditure to be incurred, and indication of agreed split of funding between the product group, corporate public affairs, possibly suppliers, and companies where a multiproduct launch is planned.
8. A risk analysis demonstrating a thorough evaluation of the competitive downside risks and an objective response.

In most cases the product manager will need to seek approval for the programme and budget from higher authority. Guidelines for such submissions are discussed in Chapter 5. Once approved, detailed planning for the external launch can start in earnest. Table 3.6 provides a basic checklist of issues for consideration.

The externally focused launch must be a success, but so must be the internal launch to ensure that all functions, departments and individuals that have impact on the success of the product are aware of what is happening and the support required.

1. Manufacturing needs early warning of the product, volumes anticipated, quality standards, special launch packs and samples, the need to build up launch stocks, etc
2. Distribution needs to be warned of warehouse and physical distribution needs
3. Customer service department needs to be briefed
4. Staff unions and associations need to be advised and consulted to achieve commitment to and support for the new product
5. Field sales and telephone sales teams need product and sales skill training to support the new product or service

**Table 3.6**  Outline checklist for planning of product launch

1. *Target audience*
   1.1  Priority potential customers, domestic and international
   1.2  Target distribution channels, domestic and international
   1.3  Influences of buyers — governments, media, banks
   1.4  Persons to commit — employees, trade unions, suppliers

2. *Logistics*
   2.1  Guest lists
   2.2  Despatch and follow up of invitations
   2.3  Travel, hotel arrangements for VIPs
   2.4  Product security
   2.5  Guest security
   2.6  Presentation packs

3. *Key dates*
   3.1  Invitation
   3.2  Rehearsal
   3.3  Press review
   3.4  Product launch — public announcement, press release

4. *Design event*
   4.1  Venue
   4.2  Style/format programme
   4.3  Timetable
   4.4  Supporting display, exhibition, videos, etc.
   4.5  Selection VIP launch pad
   4.6  Staff briefing and training
   4.7  Security
   4.8  Catering
   4.9  Linguistic service
   4.10 Announcement of initial orders

5. *Budget*
   5.1  VIP quest costs
   5.2  The event cost
   5.3  Supportive advertising and promotion
   5.4  Sales brochures
   5.5  Samples
   5.6  Product training

6. Product support team needs to be warned of merchandising, commissioning and potential servicing demands
7. All staff like to know of new company successes, so a special edition of or editorial for the company newspaper or journal needs to be prepared in advance

Product launches are by nature multifunctional, multidisciplined events. The product manager's task is to ensure that professional coordination, cohesive focus and commitment are available and achieved.

### The need for continuous customer feedback

Once launched, the ongoing success of a product or service depends on the continuous satisfaction of customer needs in the eyes of customers. It is therefore important that the product manager establishes a cost-effective product tracking and reporting system to identify what is happening after the launch. The system needs to provide feedback on:

1. Unexpected successes and applications — information that will assist in fine-tuning marketing decisions related to market segmentation and promotion
2. Current and potential customer complaints, in order to identify the need to consider product modifications, or restrictions in recommended use and applications
3. Distribution handling problems which might suggest the need for improved packaging and labelling
4. Comments by customers on features they would appreciate on a later model, in addition to the welcome improvements designed with the current product
5. Customers' comparisons between the products and services last launched and the products and services offered by competitors

This feedback will come from:

1. Customer complaints, either through original correspondence or complaints summaries prepared by the customer service organization
2. Field reports from salesmen, providing feedback on what is occurring at the interface between salesmen and buyers
3. Field reports from service engineers, providing feedback from the user or maintenance staff on issues related to operation and ease of preventive maintenance and repair
4. Reports from the telephone sales staff on direct or indirect comments made by customers when phoning for repeat orders
5. In retail organizations, reports on customer reaction to new merchandise from shop assistants
6. Formal market research by outside research organizations. Relevant approaches include face-to-face interviews, postal questionnaires and telephone interviews with customers
7. Vital personal visits by the product manager to key customers. This is discussed in detail in Chapter 4

Each source will provide valuable product intelligence. The product manager needs to use the information intelligently and aim to ensure that short-term problems are resolved speedily; that emergent problems are watched carefully; that repeat problems are avoided on subsequent designs; and that successful features are built on as fundamental strengths in specifying future designs. Continued good design and development will give customers products that provide the performance and image they want, and sometimes more than they expect: the perception of added value for money. This will have other positive effects:

1. Customers are satisfied with the purchase
2. Customers are more likely to come back for a repeat or follow-on order, and give referrals to new prospective customers

3.  Payment for the product or service, if invoiced versus cash payment, may be speedier, without the need for reminder and without negotiations over a 5 per cent warranty retention
4.  Reduced marketing and sales efforts will be needed for the next order
5.  Customers' loyalty thresholds are raised, resulting in an extension of the product life cycle at a time when many product life cycles are shortening

---

**Chapter 3 – Key point summary**

*Managing the product development process*

1.  Establish a customer-focused product development team
2.  Search wide for product ideas
3.  Be creative in developing product concepts
4.  Ensure tough commercial objectivity in evaluating product concepts
5.  Establish clear product objectives as the focus for design and development
6.  Don't forget the customer:
    meet needs with competitive differentiation
7.  Manage the product development programme and market launch professionally

# 4. Product managers as marketing managers

**Product managers' key task**

To establish the marketing concept in all functions impacting the commercial success of the product range. To prepare and implement competitive marketing strategies to improve sales, margins, market share, customer loyalty, cash flows and the productivity of the sales process

### The nature of the marketing task

Marketing is defined as the corporate activity associated with, first, the identification of current and potential national, international, industry and specific customer needs in those priority business areas and territories defined by the overall strategy of the company, and second, the development and promotion of products and services which meet those needs in a manner acceptable to the customer, at a realistic price and which will produce a profit when provided through cost-effective, consistent and reliable methods of sale and servicing devised and supported by the market function.

Marketing starts and finishes with the customer. The need is basic; businesses are about products and markets, and marketing is about the process of matching the two at a profit. Yet around the world there remain many frustrated buyers, and many unprofitable products.

Successful marketing requires a commitment at all levels to an agreed definition of what is entailed. Marketing cannot be restricted to a single management function or a single operating level: every member of the staff, from junior to general management, needs to know what it's all about, and the part that he or she can play. In particular, perhaps, the individual must remember that selling is a fundamental part of marketing: the best marketing plans can be diluted, or worse, by poor face-to-face selling.

The concept of marketing is not new; as far back as the seventeenth century the Mitsui family established a merchant business that in time became the Mitsui empire of manufacturing, financial services, trading and retail activities. The empire was founded on the principles of product management, designing products that matched customers needs, developed productive sources of manufacturing, market segmentation, professional promotion, pricing and customer service. A picture that we again recognize as Japanese. In 1856 George Rae in the UK described in *The Country Banker* the challenges of opening new banks and branches, the launching of new services and other basic ingredients of what is now referred to as effective marketing. Unfortunately, the UK banks do not have the worldwide market shares of a decade ago.

Ford achieved early success through product development with the Model T, but later found that promotion and hard selling tactics were also essential to sell against competitive products that, among other features, were not all black. Motor manufacturers have since become as enthusiastic for the marketing concept as such leading consumer industry exponents as Mars, Procter and Gamble, and Unilever. In such market-orientated companies, marketing becomes an engrained attitude of mind shared by most people in the business.

The identification of customer needs, product group strategy and the development of products and services have been discussed in Chapters 2 and 3. This chapter builds on that base and concentrates on the role of the product manager in three important areas: first, in establishing a market-led culture in the company; second, the development of product marketing strategies; and third, the implementation of marketing strategies in a manner that supports the sales force of the industrial company or branch network of the bank in the face-to-face sale of products and services. An appropriate balance of theory and practical guidelines is provided for the active product manager and persons studying the topic for the first time.

### Evolution of the product management marketing concept

Marketing theory and practice have evolved around six central themes; these are reviewed below to provide a background for considering action when preparing product marketing strategies.

*The product concept*
The product concept assumes that potential customers will respond to good products and services which are reasonably priced, and that little company marketing effort is required to achieve satisfactory sales and profits. It is a questionable concept, but still followed by some professions and by small companies that have a long-standing record for excellent specialist products and services, limited desire for growth, and considerable repeat and referral business. Such companies spend little or nothing on any form of promotion or direct sales and believe that their products and services still have a relatively long and stable potential in the marketplace; and that the customer will pay for an elegant technical solution to a problem, whether it be a new machine, a legal problem, or securing a one-off fashion item for Ascot.

If appointed, the product manager's role would be mainly that of a product development manager or product process engineer, and providing after-sales support.

## The selling concept

The selling concept assumes that potential customers must be persuaded to seek out and purchase the company's products by substantial investments in sales and promotional efforts. The desire for growth and sales productivity often leads to a decision to opt out of low market share and low-growth markets. The consumer goods industries are typical, often striving for significant short-term increases in sales volume through a large and effective sales force, which in turn is motivated by monetary rewards linked to sales volume, often without sufficient regard to the profitability of sales. The marketing mix concept of 'product, price, promotion and place' emerged from the selling concept.

Selling is focused on today's customer; a concentration on individual repeat customer versus selective market segmentation.

Market demand will be stimulated by an emphasis of product features and benefits through advertising, sales promotion, special offers, discounts, customer service, face-to-face selling or, increasingly, telephone and direct mail. From a planning point of view the level of demand may be managed in an attempt to smooth fluctuating sales levels and achieve a consistently high utilization of manufacturing and servicing capacity.

The product managment role would tend towards that of a market manager or brand manager.

## The marketing concept

The marketing concept evolved from the selling concept as companies discovered the need to establish a market-driven ethos in all functions. This has been followed by many engineering companies and food-processing companies requiring close cooperation among marketing, product development and manufacturing. The concept assumes that a company must determine the needs, wants and value of a target market, and then design and adapt services, products and the organization structure and culture to meet those needs more effectively than competitor companies. Much effort will be spent in developing information systems for market analysis, planning and control, and in directing the definition and selection of target market segments.

Profit planning and detailed action planning are seen as important and are focused on managing the product–market–customer mix to achieve profitable volumes and market shares at levels of risk acceptable to the company as a whole. Resources are allocated to an ongoing analysis of the competition and on monitoring longer-term market trends, opportunities and threats as vital inputs to strategic planning.

Comprehensive strategic planning for new products, services and markets is a normal feature of companies believing in the marketing concept. The concept was also behind many of the drives for corporate excellence, customer service and total quality that became popular in the 1980s.

In such companies the product management role would evolve towards that of a full product manager, with the task of coordinating product development, marketing and sales support, with a move towards appointing business unit managers with direct line accountability for the profits of a product group. In such situations product managers have a significant and vital role to play in establishing a market-led culture in all functions across the company.

*The societal marketing concept*

The product, selling and marketing concepts had become recognized theories by the 1970s. In the following 20 years they provided theoretical guidelines for many companies and product managers. However, in this period three new concepts emerged.

The first of these, the societal marketing concept, emphasizes the need for a company to aim at satisfying the needs of the customer, public, employees, suppliers, shareholders and other important social and political stakeholder groups as the way to achieve long-term corporate image, profit and responsibilities. It was developed in the mid-1970s by socially minded companies in the USA, Europe and Japan. Such companies build into their product planning a constant search for:

- Better products in terms of appeal and benefit to the customer, user friendliness, reduced adverse effect on the environment through pollution, garbage, noise, and ethical promotions
- Better methods of manufacture that create less pollution, and practical improved working conditions for employees
- Product groups that have cash- and wealth-creating capacity, to enable the company to sustain steady improvement in the total investment return to shareholders

The electronics, chemical, health care, financial services and property industries have been firm supporters of the concept. Promotions often have a social responsibility appeal and, in many cases, companies demonstrate willingness to scrap products that are not in the best interest of the customer and society, sometimes accepting liability for mishaps by making out-of-court settlements.

Product managers are in an ideal position to utilize the power behind this concept and build in social responsibility at the third dimension in business planning (see Fig. 4.1).

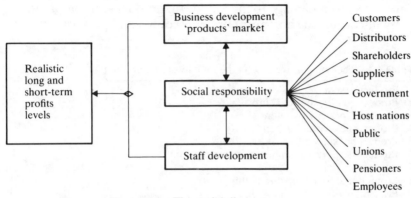

**Figure 4.1** The social dimension

*The competitive mix concept*

The second new concept to emerge, that of the competitive mix, recognizes the importance of establishing the marketing concept as an important element of corporate culture, the resistance of many managers to giving up functional power, and the competitive demands of the marketplace for a multifunctional response. The competitive mix concept assumes that potential customers will respond increasingly to value-for-money products that are either market/customer-led or technology-led provided that they are promoted through appropriate marketing and sales techniques. In the 1980s many companies have grasped the concept and inevitably more will follow in the 1990s.

The competitive mix concept goes beyond the selling concept and marketing concept and provides useful guidelines for the product manager. Typical management behaviour in competitive-led companies include the following:

- The customer is seen as number one
- A belief that customers buy satisfaction, not products *per se*, and that competitiveness is achieved through the competitive mix discussed in Chapter 3 and repeated in Table 4.1 for convenience
- Marketing is focused on achieving improvement in the productivity of the sales process
- Managers and staff at all levels in the organization are stimulated to recognize that competitiveness is about value for the customer's money, and that all have a role to play in contributing ideas for improved product design, productivity and promotion
- Marketing strategies are developed within the framework of an overall marketing strategy
- A recognition that the marketing concept of a market pull strategy is not the only viable business strategy
- Increased emphasis on product strategy, technological innovation, management of technology and industrial design
- A careful balance of product research and development between a short-term market orientation and long-term state-of-the-art developments for tomorrow
- Competing on product value in terms of aspirations, quality, design, technology, application and strategic needs
- Avoidance of serious damage to the long-term product and comparative quality images by ill-conceived short-term price discounts and promotions

**Table 4.1**  The competitive mix — the nine lives of a product

1. Product design
2. Product quality and reliability
3. Product productivity potential
4. Prompt delivery and dependability
5. Product package
6. Product support in commissioning/application
7. Product servicing and spares
8. Promotional follow-up and reality
9. Price reduction through discount

– Time allocated to auditing and developing the capabilities and resources required to achieve the timely implementation of strategic decisions

In essence the competitive mix concept is at the heart of effective product management; the third marketing concept to become prominent in recent years and discussed below.

The five concepts outlined so far provide a framework against which a product manager can evaluate the position in the company and product group and the current and future needs. The product manager can then plan to move towards the most relevant aspects of the concepts while recognizing that they are not precise theories but provide practical guidelines which have evolved with time.

*The product management marketing concept*
The product management marketing concept assumes that the dedicated management of strategically important products and services is more likely to improve product competitiveness and financial results than more traditional marketing and sales functional structures. The full implementation of the product management concept requires:

1. Dedication, innovation, creativity, dynamism and a challenging spirit
2. The implementation of the competitiveness mix concept
3. An organization culture in harmony with the marketing concept within the product group and, if possible, the company as a whole
4. Increased attention to the development of detailed product strategies and plans
5. The establishment of product management teams as product-based centres of excellence and expertise, with tentacles into relevant functions and territories.
   Recently one senior group described the product manager as a friendly octopus, extracting information, searching the company crevices for opportunities to improve products; moving stealthily in the marketplace to identify tasty market segments, and squeezing them to increase market share
6. Close links with territorial teams in priority markets through information flows, direction and support
7. Balanced and integrated product development and product process development plans
8. A focus on the early identification and resolution of internal conflicts that could harm product success
9. Leadership through product champions

**Focus on improving sales productivity**

The main marketing task of the product manager is the use of marketing knowledge, experience, techniques and skills to improve the productivity of the sales process.

In most companies, the active selling time of a salesperson visiting customers to sell is of the order of 8–16 per cent. The balance of the time is spent in a variety of ways, illustrated in Fig. 4.2. International analyses by authorities such as Heinz Goldman indicate that this picture applies to most, if not all, product and service industries and industrialized markets.

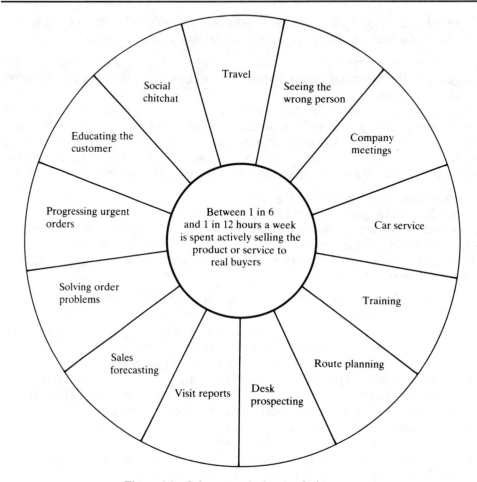

**Figure 4.2** Sales person's time analysis

The sales general manager or territorial manager has the task of organizing and motivating the sales team to increase the time spent with the customer, and providing sales skills training to ensure that the time with the customer is exploited to the full.

The product manager has a vital and full role in both directing and supporting the sales force. It includes securing improvements in the product or service package, the introduction of new products or services, the organisation of product briefings, the focus of the sales force on those markets most in need of the company's products and services and improving the image customers have of the product or service package by effective promotion and customer service support. The aim is to ensure that the sales force can spend less time thinking about where to sell, what to sell, how to sell and whether the customer will get what was ordered when required, and can concentrate on servicing satisfied customers.

Five characteristics of customers are common worldwide.

1. Whether buying an inexpensive commodity product or a *haute couture* dress, customers buy satisfaction
2. The satisfaction is inspired by the total product service package offered (see Fig. 4.3).
3. Customers pay the price for wrong buying decisions as well as for the product
4. Customers and buyers are less likely to shop around if they get value for money; an experience above their expectations; quality standards at a price related to life-time costs (except in a pure commodity market with no product differentiation)
5. Many industrial and private customers may be willing to replace a lower priced widget, hotel room, computer terminal, computer software or garment of clothing with one providing a surprise: enhanced performance, image, quality, pre- and after-sales service at an incremental or indeed significantly higher price. In all industries there are examples of one company charging too much,

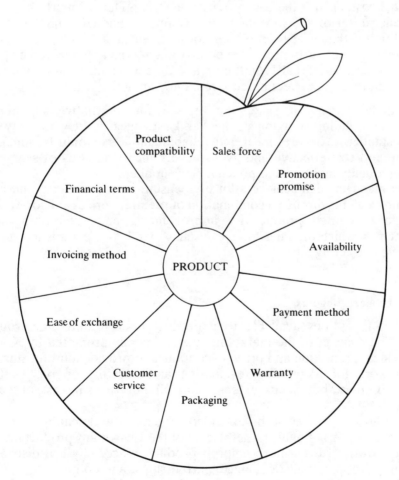

**Figure 4.3**  A product/service package

one charging and securing the premium price, one playing it safe by discounting and another charging suicide rock-bottom prices

Grasping the market opportunities implicit in these five statements has been, and will remain, the only way of achieving the vital 80 per cent repeat business and significant new customers, year after year. Missing such opportunities — not currency rates or government policy — are at the root cause of

- The decline in world share for many UK manufactured goods over the last 15 years parallel with a weakening pound. It is difficult to remember that just prior to the first oil crisis and entry into the EEC, the pound was worth twice as many Dutch guilders as it is today
- The growth in the share of US and UK consumer purchases secured by Japanese products, designed with the customer in mind at attractive prices, when the Yen had never been stronger
- The growth in German international sales of products strong in life-time cost, if not initial cost, against the background of a strong Deutschmark
- The penetration of US-style fast food chains in the UK and Far East, in competition with perhaps complacent local restaurants
- The growth in the sale of processed poultry and red meat pioneered by product champions such as Bernard Matthews, at a time when farm shops were on the increase and the high street butcher remained an active trade

Increasingly, buyers are shopping around for alternative suppliers and experiences, including sourcing in the Far East, because of what they see as declining standards. Secure, local and reliable suppliers would be much more acceptable and cost-effective and avoid buyers incurring costs of seeking out, evaluating, quality auditing and policing new suppliers.

Product managers can achieve a lot by focusing on these needs, and chasing profit improvements through a combination of premium prices and lower costs as a result of sustained productivity improvement, and establishing a firm environment in which the sales force can sell. A vital start point is to establish a competitive marketing mix.

**Managing the marketing mix**

The marketing options available to a product manager are numerous and complex. The concept of the marketing mix, originally promoted by Kotler — product, place, promotion and price — continues to provide a useful start point and framework for identifying, evaluating and deciding on profit-effective marketing options, but needs extension in all but the simplest of decision situations.

First, Kotler's 4 *P*s need to be extended to match the demands of the more competitive and international marketplace. For the 1990s many product managers find a framework of 8 *P*s more helpful: product, place, physical distribution, promotion, price, paternalistic finance, partnerships, and politics.

Second, the decision-making process, although led and coordinated by the

**Table 4.2** Contributions to the management of the marketing mix

*TYPICAL CONTRIBUTION*

| Aspect of marketing mix | Product (group) manager | Marketing services group | Sales force |
|---|---|---|---|
| Product package | Definition of product and management of product development programme | Market research support | Market intelligence on customer needs and competitor activity |
| Priority markets | Choice of priority territories, market segments and customer groups | Market research support | Choice of priority customers within segments |
| Physical distribution | Choice of profitable and secure direct or indirect distribution channels | Advice on historic, current and future options, and company practice in other product groups | Personal sales activity and sales support to appointed agents and distributors |
| Pricing policy | Definition and communication of policy guidelines for product pricing, discounts and trade terms | Advice on compatibility of proposed policy with general company policy of other product groups selling to the same or similar customers and markets | Sales to specific customers at net prices within policy guidelines |
| Promotion | Development of corporate promotional programmes and guidelines for local promotion by regional sales force and foreign subsidiaries | Support in development and implementation of promotional programmes | Use of promotional activity to improve productivity of sales activity plus local promotional activity where appropriate |
| Paternalistic finance | Definition/development of financial packages to aid product sales | Assistance in development and servicing of financial packages | Objective use of financial packages to secure difficult but strategic sales |
| Partnerships | Consideration and establishment of collaborations to secure accelerated development of product range or market for products | Support in analysis, negotiation and servicing | Possibly assistance in choice and support to established collaborations |
| Politics | Consideration of opportunities for obtaining government support for products in terms of trade barriers, national standards quality awards, etc., to raise or overcome import barriers | Support in identifying, evaluating, lobbying and negotiating political support | Support to product managers in implementation of policy |

product manager, is in practice shared with other members of the total product management team, as illustrated in Table 4.2.

The application of the marketing mix is not an exact science and requires commercial creativity and judgement for success. There are many ways of cutting the cake, as illustrated in Fig. 4.4. In practice the product manager and support team need to consider the following questions:

- What marketing mix has been used in the past? How successful was it?
- How successful is the recent mix likely to be under anticipated market conditions for both new and existing products?
- What would happen if nothing were changed?
- What marginal expenditure would be required to change buyer behaviour significantly?
- What new creative options should be evaluated and tested before making major changes in the mix of expenditure?
- How sensitive is volume for the best and worst products in the product range to variations in price and the level of promotion?
- What changes would competitors find most difficult to follow?
- What aspects of the marketing mix of competitors are the most difficult to match?
- What changes are customers looking for and why?
- What risks are associated with planned changes in the marketing mix?
- Who in the company is able to contribute to the analysis and decisions required?
- How can they be best involved?
- How can the impact of changes be measured and monitored?
- Who must be committed to the decisions to secure successful implementation?
- How will commitment be most easily achieved?
- What marketing mix will best stimulate profit and cost-effective improvements in the productivity of the sales force? This is discussed in more detail in Chapter 6

The above analysis and subsequent decisions are fundamental to the development and implementation of a marketing plan that is both competitive and profitable. In total it represents the most important task performed by many product managers. It is rarely an easy task to find the mix that creates the greatest market leverage for the least expenditure for each phase of the product life cycle.

Fig. 4.5 illustrates a number of important variations, relating the balance between product development and marketing to the type of product managed by the product group.

### Product differentiation

An important dimension of the product/market matrix is product differentiation. The objective of product differentiation is to establish products which are different, distinctive (or even unique) in the way they match customer needs compared to previous own products and services, and the current and anticipated products of competitors.

| Marketing mix sub-options | | Extent of use in 1980s | Extent of success | Options to be considered for 1990s |
|---|---|---|---|---|
| Product package | ○ Product development | | | |
| | ○ Product acquisition | | | |
| | ○ Special packs | | | |
| | ○ Customer service | | | |
| | ○ Credit terms | | | |
| | ○ Credit cards | | | |
| | ○ Spares | | | |
| | ○ Training | | | |
| | ○ Warranty | | | |
| Place/physical distribution | ○ Market research | | | |
| | ○ Segmentation | | | |
| | ○ Distributors/agents | | | |
| | ○ Retailers | | | |
| | ○ Stocking | | | |
| | ○ Direct mail | | | |
| | ○ Telephone sales | | | |
| | ○ More salesmen | | | |
| Promotion | ○ Advertising | | | |
| | ○ Brochures | | | |
| | ○ Exhibitions | | | |
| | ○ Demonstrations | | | |
| | ○ Competitors | | | |
| | ○ Public relations | | | |
| Price | ○ Reduction | | | |
| | ○ Discounts | | | |
| | ○ Term contracts | | | |
| | ○ Volume rebates | | | |
| | ○ Company discounts | | | |
| | ○ Reductions for reduced service level | | | |
| Partnerships | ○ Franchising | | | |
| | ○ Licensing | | | |
| | ○ Joint R&D | | | |
| | ○ Joint promotion | | | |
| | ○ Joint marketing | | | |
| | ○ Distributors | | | |
| Paternalistic finance | ○ Trade investments | | | |
| | ○ Government grants | | | |
| | ○ Government loans | | | |
| | ○ Interest free finance | | | |
| | ○ First £10 in account | | | |
| Politics | ○ Lobbying | | | |
| | ○ Local content | | | |
| | ○ Intermediaries | | | |
| | ○ Re-exports | | | |
| | ○ National Design Awards | | | |

**Figure 4.4**   Example of checklist to aid allocation of product marketing budget for the 1990s

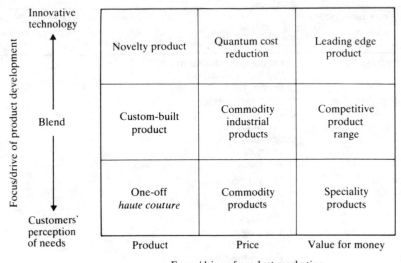

**Figure 4.5** Important variables in the marketing mix

In practice, the range of options for differentiating one product (or service) from another is extensive. Some of the major factors of differentiation are:

– Physical characteristics
– Technical performance
– Styling
– Physical packaging
– Brand name
– Advertising
– Pricing
– Range available
– Sourcing
– Safety
– Local content
– Environmental control
– Interface/compatability with other products
– Method of sale
– Method of distribution
– Speed of availability
– Packaging of all services directly or indirectly provided with product or service

Therefore, product managers need to make choices; choices that are objective and commercially viable. The starting point is to decide why it is necessary to differentiate in relation to each product and market under consideration to achieve the most profitable balance between product differentiation and market segmentation.

The product manager will have three main reasons for differentiating products.

1. *To stimulate product preference in the mind of the customer(s)* The objective is to influence the intended customer or buyer; to ensure that when the customer or buyer considers which single product to buy from a range of different products offered by the company and its competitors, he or she consciously or unconsciously perceives differences between the products or services on offer. Such distinction in the product manager's product or service must be sufficiently strong and positive that it influences the final buying decision. This buying decision must lead to customer satisfaction, repeat business and loyalty, whether the product be clothes or aircraft.

2. *To distinguish the product from products marketed by competitors* In this case the product manager tailors the distinctive features of his product mainly *vis-à-vis* his competitors' products, and does not aim primarily at greater market satisfaction. In practice the product manager's products and competitive products may well have the same performance satisfaction value. The prime objective is to establish a company, product group or brand image or identity in the marketplace.

3. *To serve or cover the market better* This approach recognizes that each customer, or group of customers, represents a different market segment with different needs, calling for variations in products for different applications. In this case the objective is to identify attractive market segments, to follow the market in those segments, and provide the customer with what he or she wants; in other words, to follow the marketing concept. Speciality food products, chemical products, and mass-produced cars are examples of this philosophy.

The need for product differentiation varies from one business to another and depends upon the stage the product has reached in its life cycle. Consumer goods and industrial products call for different forms of differentiation and the solution will be specific to each situation.

Fig. 4.6 provides a checklist for comparing competitive products to establish areas in which

- Competitive products are an equal match
- The product manager's products have a distinct competitive advantage
- The product manager's products are at a distinct competitive disadvantage
- Differentiation may have been expensive through overdesign
- Matches with competitive products may be difficult or expensive to achieve
- Matches by competitors may be difficult or expensive to achieve

Such an analysis can help a product manager and his team select meaningful differences to be emphasized in promotional material, advertisements, product training for the sale force and in face-to-face feature benefit selling by the sales force. The analysis can also be of help in assessing possible and likely moves by competitors who could have made the same analysis.

The form of analysis can be made more complex by weighting the differentiation factors and performance levels in order to calculate product performance indices, and the cumulative level of competitiveness *vis-à-vis* selected competitor products.

In some cases this will be a realistic development, but in many cases the product

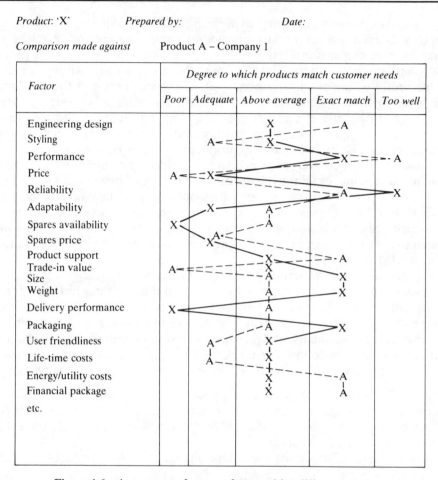

*Product*: 'X'          *Prepared by:*                    *Date:*

*Comparison made against*       Product A – Company 1

**Figure 4.6** Assessment of extent of competitive differentiation

manager will not have the extent of competitor information available to achieve statistical reliability. Nevertheless, there is evidence of more and more companies buying in competing products for a full performance and strip-down evaluation. This provides a vital input to the intelligence base of a product manager.

### Distribution decisions

Distribution decisions concern the choice of how products or services will be transmitted from company to customer. The decisions need to be made at three levels.

The first of these concerns the markets in which company representatives will present products and services directly to the customer, whether face-to-face, by telephone, telex or fax; and the organization structure supporting this function. Table 4.3(a) illustrates the alternatives available to the company and group product manager.

**Table 4.3**  Distribution choices

| (a) *Company distribution channels* | (b) *Third party distribution channels* |
|---|---|
| 1. Local subsidiary | 1. General agents |
| 2. Local associate company | 2. Dedicated agents |
| 3. Local branch | 3. Distributor |
| 4. Permanent sales force | 4. Merchant house |
| 5. Regular sales visits | 5. Licensing-out |
| 6. Occasional sales visits | 6. Franchise |
| 7. Opportunistic sales visits | 7. Joint venture |
| 8. Wait for enquiries and respond effectively | 8. Brokers |
| 9. Telephone | 9. Mail order |
| 10. Do nothing | 10. Direct mail company |

(c)  *Decision matrix*

Product group:
Territory:

| | | | Options | |
|---|---|---|---|---|
| *Selection criteria* | *A3* | *A4* | *B5* | *etc.* |
| 1. Forecast net margins | | | | |
| 2. Importance of market | | | | |
| 3. Ease of control | | | | |
| 4. Ability to handle product launches | | | | |
| 5. Experience of products | | | | |
| 6. Overcomes political barriers | | | | |
| 7. Handling seasonal variations | | | | |
| 8. Extent of dedicated resourcing | | | | |
| 9. Capacity for growth | | | | |
| 10. etc. | | | | |

The second decision level concerns the markets in which the company and product group will be presented by a third party in selling and responding to customers' buying enquiries and requests. Table 4.3(b) illustrates a range of practical possibilities in both national and international markets.

These two decisions are interrelated, and choices need to be considered objectively, as illustrated in Table 4.3(c). The decision needs to be made in relation to:

– high-priority markets, where direct sales and distribution will often be the preferred solution
– medium-priority markets, where a combination of own and third party distribution is often the profit-effective solution
– low-priority markets, where the profit-effective solution needs to be a low-cost solution, for example, do nothing, opportunistic visits or good agents who will dig out the occasional windfall order

Once the most productive distribution structure for making sales, taking orders, displaying and demonstrating products and services has been decided, the third decision required is the choice of a cost-effective method of distribution. Typical

**Table 4.4**   Distribution choices

| Warehousing | Movement | |
|---|---|---|
| Own company | | |
| Agent | Airfreight | Motor cycle |
| Cash and carry | Airship | Pipeline |
| Contractor | Barge | Postal service |
| Delivery trucks | Buyer | Rail |
| Distributors | Cable TV | Satellite |
| Mail order house | Cycle | Ship |
| Wholesaler | Foot delivery | Standard van |
| World Trade Centre | Helicopter | Telephone |
| Cash | Horse and trap | Truck |
| Retailer | Launch | Vintage van |

options are listed in Table 4.4. A decision matrix, similar to that illustrated in Table 4.3(c), will aid the decision process, whether the decision is made by an individual manager or a group. All options are real and in current use by product managers for regular or special feature delivery associated with a product launch or mega order.

The possible combinations of distribution channels (Table 4.3) and methods of distribution (Table 4.4) offer many opportunities for creative promotional programmes.

**The advertising and sales promotion task**

The key tasks in the area of advertising and sales promotion are as follows:

1. Defining an advertising and sales promotion strategy, for both the short and longer term, as an integral part of the overall marketing strategy for the product group
2. Fine-tuning the strategy to achieve appropriate compatibility and synergy with the strategy of the total company
3. Planning and organizing the resources, activities and actions required to launch and implement the advertising and sales promotion strategy
4. Preparing a financial budget to evaluate and agree the cost expenditure that can be afforded
5. Managing the budget and action plans in terms of monitoring progress and investigation of unexpected deviations
6. Establishing and sustaining ongoing market research of competitor advertising and sales promotion activity
7. Evaluating the results and the provision of feedback to product managers and market managers of market research, before and after advertising, and sales promotion trials
8. Selecting, planning and evaluation of media
9. Most importantly, selecting an advertising agency to supplement and support the in-company resources available to the product group(s)

In a small company, the product group manager himself may do the job of managing advertising and sales promotion as well as recruiting, directing and supervising the external agency. In a large multinational company, the product group manager is likely to have the support of a fully staffed advertising and sales promotion department within the overall structure of the marketing function. However, the wise product manager would not completely delegate the choice and supervision of the agency in respect of work for the specific product group.

### Balancing promotional efforts

The forms of promotional effort will vary from industry to industry, product to product and company to company. However, there is a general trend in the mix of promotional effort for consumer products and industrial products (see Fig. 4.7). At the one extreme, the product manager marketing through direct mail or mail order will place a heavy emphasis on major advertising campaigns, with a significant public relations image-building programme, catalogues or brochures, but with relatively little bulk direct selling, except perhaps for a small amount of follow-up telephone selling. At the other extreme, the high-technology engineering product or system will require a major personal selling activity to help potential customers assess their needs, to develop specifications and to keep close to customers to secure repeat business, and less relative emphasis on advertising.

*Personal selling*
Personal selling includes the face-to-face activities of sales engineers, as well as the activities of account executives, salesmen, telephone salespeople, product

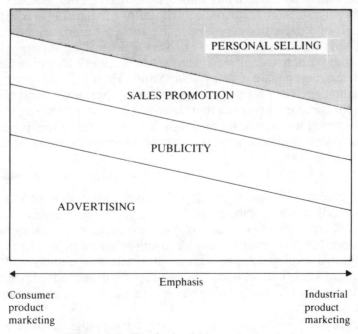

**Figure 4.7**   Emphasis within promotional mix

specialists and service engineers. The product manager needs to ensure that action has been taken, or is planned, to improve sales skills, product knowledge, personal appearance, quality of advice and customer support, and with the objective of stimulating customers to buy from a professional sales team.

*Sales promotion*
Sales promotion expenditure includes brochures, leaflets, samples, product launches, calendars, diaries, exhibitions, workshops, customer visits, product label and packaging design. The product manager needs to establish specific objectives and quality standards for such activities and to ensure that a positive image is not negated by poor or inadequate direct or indirect publicity.

*Publicity*
Two aspects of publicity need to be examined. The first of these is the direct publicity planned for the product or brand, and umbrella company publicity in the form of press releases, articles, editorials, radio and TV features and interviews, general customer visits and entertainment, in-company and customer bulletins, newspapers and journals, trade association involvement, social responsibility donations, and the annual report. The product manager, except in the smallest company, is unlikely to handle all these activities directly. Therefore, the product manager needs to establish a working relationship with the public affairs department and ensure that the product group or brand features prominently in corporate public affairs by feeding success stories, pictures for the annual report, and a continuing information update.

The second aspect of publicity is indirect publicity. This includes how well enquiries and complaints are handled; ease of visitor car-parking at company sites; the customer friendliness of reception staff; the customer orientation of the switchboard; and the attitude of delivery drivers. The product manager is unlikely to manage the above activities directly, but who else does? Negative impressions in these areas can soon negate a well-planned and expensive sales promotion and advertising campaign. The product manager should, therefore, audit and become aware of current company practices and customer attitudes, and suggest changes to appropriate senior managers. Increasingly a 'Customer is King' programme or 'Five-Star Customer' initiative features in corporate promotional strategies, as will be discusssed in Chapter 7.

*Advertising*
Advertising includes all ways of making the company and/or product known: written media, billboards, radio, television, in-flight commercial tapes on the entertainment channel, stickers, and so on. Two aspects are important to the product manager. First, the corporate advertising programme at a local, national, territorial or global level which provides an umbrella image and reputation with product links and benefits. Second, the product or brand advertising commissioned by the product manager directly or through a sales promotion and advertising department.

The focus of promotional activity, particularly advertising, needs to be carefully considered.

- Is the primary focus to be on current, past or potential customers?
- Is the company, product group, brand or specific product to be promoted?
- Is the emphasis to be on current or new products? At what level of awareness should the promotional message focus, what objectives need to be achieved?

The level of promotional focus is elaborated in Table 4.5 and illustrated in Fig. 4.8.

Having established the level of sales promotion and advertising required, the product manager then needs to establish a message or messages with a high probability of impact in stimulating potential customers to enquire, buy or buy again. There are many options. To illustrate, should the emphasis of the message communicated stimulate the potential for value for money, improved performance, enhanced status or security, a one-off bargain opportunity, a low price and therefore low-cost purchase, a new mood, a new experience, a new lease of life, environmental protection, not being left out, being seen as out of touch, wealth creation or reliability?

The product manager will be wise to seek professional advice and support in

**Table 4.5** Level of promotional focus

| Level | Description of focus | Typical situation |
|---|---|---|
| 1. | Focus on companies or persons who are unaware of a specific product, technology or the company, to stimulate an initial interest, a desire to find out more, to obtain information | Launch of an entirely new product, or product group aiming to expand into new industries or territories |
| 2. | Focus on companies or persons who are probably aware of the company's type of product or technology, but have not yet tested or purchased the product, to stimulate a desire to know more, to go and see, test and evaluate a new product possibility | The launch of a competitive product or product group with innovative features, technology or pricing. Product may be a replacement product, addition to product range or company's first entry into an established market |
| 3. | Focus on companies or persons who are knowledgeable about the company, specific products or technologies, and have already used or evaluated other companies' products, to stimulate a desire to include a new option in the decision process, and make a definite enquiry | Current, new, replacement, in-fill or range-extension product |
| 4. | Focus on companies or persons who have already indicated a preference for purchasing from the company by an initial purchase of the product, or by previous purchase of other products within the brand, or products from other divisions or product groups, to stimulate a repeat or extension purchase | Current, new, replacement, in-fill, or range-extension product |
| 5. | Focus on current repeat purchase companies or persons to establish and reinforce long-term product or brand loyalty | Current, new, replacement, in-fill, or range-extension product |

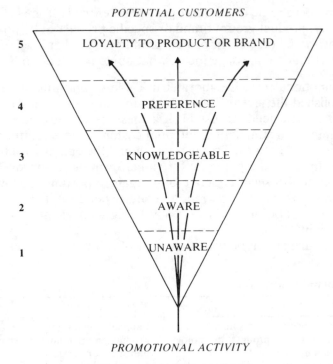

*POTENTIAL CUSTOMERS*

**Figure 4.8**   Level of promotional focus

these areas from the sales promotion and advertising department and/or an external advertising agency. However, before approaching the professionals, the product manager should evaluate the present performance of sales promotion and advertising activity.

A starting point for the analysis necessary before deciding on priority areas and internal and external improvement objectives is provided in Table 4.6.

### Advertising and sales promotion support

The implementation of the advertising and sales promotion element of the marketing strategy can range from the placement of one or two advertisements in specialist trade journals, to a razzmatazz programme to support the launch and growth phase of a new major consumer product such as a newly formulated global soft drink in a highly competitive marketplace.

In a basic situation the advertising and sales promotion tasks may be performed by the product group manager alone or with in-company support from the advertising and sales promotion department. In a more complex situation the task will be managed by a triad: the product manager, the advertising and sales promotion manager, and an external advertising agency.

The choice of approach is a critical one and needs to take account of a number of factors:

**Table 4.6** Evaluation of quality of product group image to customers/potential customers

| Image-builder | Current quality of impact in relation to product group X | Assessment of competition range | |
|---|---|---|---|
| | | Company R | Company S |
| Company name | 5 | 4 | 5 |
| Brand name | 2 | 4 | 3 |
| Product name | 5 | 5 | 4 |
| Stationery/letter style | 3 | 4 | 3 |
| Product literature | 3 | 5 | 4 |
| Product packaging | 5 | 4 | 3 |
| Product cleanliness and wrapping | 4 | 4 | 4 |
| Product labelling | 4 | 4 | 3 |
| Price list | 3 | 5 | 4 |
| Product manual | 3 | 3 | 3 |
| Direct mailshot | 4 | 4 | 4 |
| Press release | 3 | 4 | 3 |
| Exhibitions | 4 | 4 | 3 |
| Works visits | 2 | 4 | 3 |
| Product launches | 4 | 5 | 3 |
| Samples/giveaways | 3 | 3 | 4 |
| Customer reception | 3 | 4 | 3 |
| Customer telephone handling | 3 | 4 | 3 |
| Customer query handling | 3 | 4 | 3 |
| Customer deliveries | 3 | 3 | 3 |
| Annual report | 2 | 4 | 2 |
| Company magazine | 3 | 2 | 4 |
| Company notice board | 2 | 3 | 2 |
| Trade associations | 4 | 3 | 4 |
| Social responsibility donations | 5 | 2 | 3 |
| Directory entries | 2 | 4 | 2 |
| TV advertisements | 3 | 4 | 3 |
| Radio advertisements | 2 | 3 | 2 |
| National press | 4 | 4 | 4 |
| Trade press | 4 | 3 | 4 |
| Total score | 100/150 | 113/150 | 98/150 |

Rating Scale: 0–5; 5 equals competitive excellence.

1. The importance of promotion and advertising in the marketing strategy for the product group
2. The strengths, weaknesses and loading of the in-company advertising and sales promotion department
3. The extent to which a global view of advertising and promotion can be taken in respect of the specific product group and customer base
4. The company policy related to the role of headquarters-based versus territorially based managers in commissioning advertising and sales promotion activity.

## Selecting the advertising agency

The selection of an agency is an important decision and, if successful, a decision that does not need to come up too often. Having found an effective, well-

**Table 4.7**   Typical criteria for selection of an agency

1. Proven creative talents that achieve results in related markets
2. Reputation for achievement of deadlines and tight management of expenditure
3. A stable core team of professionals with excellent new recruits
4. No major conflicting accounts
5. Reputation for understanding and responding to real client problems
6. Willingness to spend time finding out about the company, product group and target customer groups
7. Secure, with no history of competitive leaks
8. Strong financial position
9. Full range of services offered

motivated and creative agency, product managers tend to stick with the partner they know works.

Situations vary widely. In one company the product group manager may be required to use the services of an international agency with which the company works world-wide. In another company the product group manager may have the authority to select and use a network of local agencies covering the territories in which the product group operates. In a third company, the product group manager may manage an international motherhood campaign and merely provide guidelines within which local territorial general managers will directly commission and manage advertising and sales promotion in their local market. However, there are common guidelines for selecting an advertising agency, as illustrated in Table 4.7.

In many cases the product manager will continue to use an existing agency. In other general or specific situations the product manager may want to share work between two agencies or consider in the medium term a switch of agencies.

The product manager needs to shortlist candidates against the needs of the product group and then visit the agencies at their offices to gain a feel of their philosophy, structure, culture and motivations. Visits can tell more than setting up competitive presentations.

Visits may reduce the shortlist from six down to two or three candidates. The final candidates can then be asked to make a formal presentation against a common brief indicating how they consider they match the needs of the product group, and their ability and dedication to allocating good people to the assignment.

An important decision will concern the role of the agency. For instance, will all advertising and promotional tasks be assigned to the agency? Will the agency function as a sparring partner to enable in-house activities to be strengthened, with only selected tasks being assigned to the agency? Will the agency only handle media orders, or will the agency also act as a creative adviser? The product manager needs to examine the scope and capability of the in-company department and external agency before reaching a decision.

A major agency will be able to provide the following services independently or as a total package.

1. Marketing services: advice on the focus and balance of marketing strategy
2. Creative services: advice on the form and content of advertisements and promotional material
3. Media services: advice on forms of media and booking and negotiation
4. Production services: project management of a campaign to achieve agreed budgets and deadlines
5. Public relations advisory services: advice and support in the general area of public relations

### Establishing an effective working relationship

A successful company–agency relationship depends on six important factors.

1. A clear understanding of the services and support available from agencies in general
2. A clear statement of the support required by a specific product group
3. An objective selection of advertising agencies to provide the support
4. A professional briefing of the agency by the product manager; where appropriate in association with the promotion and advertising manager
5. Understanding and agreement of the nature and balance of company and agency roles
6. Openness and trust as business partners

### The effective briefing

What constitutes an effective brief from a product manager to the selected agency? This question was put to the chairman of a growing agency. What follows is based closely on his 20 years' personal day-to-day contact with clients.

The briefing should be aimed at specific members of the agency:

- An account manager will be most interested in discussing product group business strategy, market statistics and financial results
- The creative team will be impatient to conceive new concepts, visions, logos and material
- The production manager will be determined to progress the client's affairs in a productive and professional manner

Its objective is quite simply to inform and inspire the agency team.

The contents will include:

1. *Introduction*
   - Background to the company, the product group and the product management team
   - Reasons for choice of agency to establish empathy
2. *The product or service*
   - Initial introduction to the product or service
3. *The market*
   - An overview of the competitive marketplace

4. *Target groups*
   - The planned strategic positioning of the product in the marketplace by segment and customer group
5. *Product or service needs*
   - Competitive differentiation, and indication of extent and speed of repositioning planned
6. *Pricing policy*
   - The balance of price and promotion currently planned
7. *Distribution channels*
   - From company to consumer or user
8. *Advertising and promotion needs*
   - Review of previous campaigns, the objectives, successes and failures, previous agencies, continuing contracts, etc.
   - Focus of new campaign, theme, seasonal impacts, regional, national or international focus
   - Objectives to be achieved, for example:

     - % improved customer awareness
     - % increased market share
     - % new positioning of the product in the marketplace
     - % coupon returns
     - % increased enquiries/orders
     - % switch from old to new product

   - The target groups for advertising and promotion within the overall target market; including what is known about the buying behaviour, demographic and psychological characteristics
   - The competitors' products, market position, strengths and weaknesses
   - What has to be communicated and achieved; perhaps the most difficult part of the brief. This point is expanded upon below
9. *Support required*
   - A clear statement of what the company plans to do; what the agency is being asked to do and how individual and joint actions will be monitored and evaluated
10. A clear statement of *what is not required*: particularly important in briefing a full service agency
11. The planned *budget*
12. *The product group team*
    - Prime contact regarding contracts
    - Contact(s) for information
    - Contact(s) for approvals
13. *Management of contract*
    - Progress reports and review meetings
    - Invoicing requirements

Naturally, the extent of the briefing in time-scale and content will depend on previous knowledge and experience of working together. In practice, the brief will be added to and refined as a result of an ongoing series of discussions. However, these discussions are no substitute for a thorough initial presentation, followed up with a written brief.

In many cases the brief will need to be discussed and cleared by the product group manager with the marketing manager or director prior to the verbal briefing.

After the briefing the marketing problem of the product manager becomes an advertising problem. A good briefing ensures that the agency focuses on the problem immediately, with the product manager in control. A poor briefing can result in misunderstanding, a false start, wasted effort and money, and the external agency taking over the initiative — potentially a disaster situation.

To avoid conflicts later, the terms of reference need to be agreed in writing, together with a specific scale of charges and budget for an agreed period. In particular the balance of emphasis between the following levels of public affairs and advertising need to be clarified: Corporate image-building — to make the company more prominent in the minds of persons influencing buying decisions; broad image-building — to reinforce the name and reputation of the brand in the minds of persons making or influencing buying decisions; product image-building — to establish and reinforce the name, promise and good reputation of the specific product in the minds of persons and prospective buyers to influence and stimulate buying decisions.

## Product briefing

The agency's task is to make the product the champion or hero in a current or potential buyer's mind. In principle, the more the agency knows about a product, the more likely the agency is to come up with a winning campaign. The product manager needs to ensure a thorough briefing by providing an initial contents briefing, and following this up by providing background reading material and visits to the company and customers to see the product being produced and used.

The contents briefing needs to focus on factors such as the composition, the function, the use, and the range of colours. It needs to provide consumer message guidelines to the agency, as a framework for the creative team to work within, but not as a straitjacket. The product manager must focus on useful objective statements and not attempt to anticipate the agency's creative efforts. For example, he might brief the agency as follows:

*Product A* Product manager briefs agency that the consumer needs to be aware that: 'Our peanut butter contains the most peanuts', but need not make comments such as 'The TV shot should incorporate a cascade of peanuts'.

*Product B* Product manager briefs: 'We give a five-year guarantee on the paint work of our cars', but not 'Grandpa should be seen sitting inside the car informing the family that he has been driving the car all his life'.

The product manager needs to focus on useful objective statements and not attempt to anticipate or outgun the agency's creative efforts.

The objective statements should expand the agency's understanding of the product in terms of its structure, function, method of use, atmosphere creation, and so on. A weighting of statements can be particularly helpful to the agency. For example, product content ('our chocolate bar contains the most nuts') may carry a weighting of 50 per cent, product function ('our chocolate bar is a typical snack') 25 per cent, and product positioning ('campaign should convey the product in a youthful modern atmosphere') 25 per cent.

A detailed analysis of the competitive strengths and weaknesses of the product is an essential base for the above contents briefing. An experienced product manager may prepare the contents briefing independently, the less experienced in association with the selected agency.

The agency's role is twofold: to assist the product manager, via the agency's in-house experience and systems, to prepare a thorough product briefing; and to translate the product briefing into effective advertisements and promotional material. The product manager states the content of the message, the agency gives it form and impact.

### Agency fee structures

It goes without saying that the agency needs to be rewarded equitably for the services provided, no more and no less. A number of fee structures are in general use. The basis of all of them is an accurate and comprehensive agency cost accounting system.

When the cost-plus fee structure is used, all services provided by the agency are charged on the basis of an agreed tariff incorporating agreed profit margins, for example, overheads plus 25 per cent, or below-the-line and media plus 15 per cent; it is the client who carries the risks.

One way of sharing the risks between client and agency is to use a fixed percentage fee structure, whereby a fixed profit percentage is agreed in advance, expressed either in terms of capitalized turnover (usually around 4–5 per cent) or of gross income (usually around 20–25 per cent).

If a flexible profit percentage fee structure is used, however, then it is the agency which carries the risks. This structure involves the agreement of a percentage profit range, calculated on capitalized turnover and typically amounting to 3–5 per cent. If the agency makes less than 3 per cent profit, it receives a top-up payment from the client up to the 3 per cent mark. If, on the other hand, the agency's profit is greater than 5 per cent, then it reimburses the client so that it is left with 5 per cent profit.

Forecast profit and loss accounts can assist the client and agency to compare and decide on the most equitable basis of fees prior to finalizing a contract. The profit percentage systems have the advantage that how income is generated is relatively unimportant to the agency, so the client can expect objective, unbiased media advice.

However, one area can create confusion: the fees for media buying and broking. Media buying is the negotiation of tariffs with the media by the agency. Normally the agency receives a discount of 15 per cent. In this case the agency media buyer is acting in the name of and under instructions of the advertiser.

Media broking is different and occurs in two forms. In the first, the media purchase is negotiated separately by the advertiser, not via the agency, and the discount goes to the advertiser. In the second, a media broker buys media space

**Table 4.8** Example of agency fee structure costings

| | £ | £ |
|---|---|---|
| 1. *Income* | | |
| Media expenditure | 500 000 | |
| Negotiated purchase price | 425 000 | |
| Surplus | | 75 000 |
| Below-the-line expenditure | 800 000 | |
| Negotiated purchase price | 680 000 | |
| Surplus | | 120 000 |
| Charge for direct costs (incurred for concept, creation, copywriting, etc.) | | 250 000 |
| Gross profit (and the base for the calculation of capitalized turnover) | | 445 000 |
| 2. *Costs* | | |
| Cost of payment for direct hours | 200 000 | |
| Overhead costs | 20 000 | |
| Cost of payment for direct hours (contracts, marketing, production, etc.) | 110 000 | |
| Total costs | 330 000 | |
| 3. Net profit | | 115 000 |
| 4. Capitalized turnover $= £445\,000 \times \dfrac{100}{15} =$ | £2 966 000 | |

5. *Examples of calculation of agency profits*
   (a) Based on fixed percentage of 4.5% of capitalized turnover, the agency should be allowed to achieve a net profit of £133 500.
   In this case the advertiser would supplement the net profit (3) up to £133 500 in total.
   (b) Based on a flexible profit range of 3–5% the agency would receive no top-up payment since $\dfrac{£115\,000}{£2\,966\,000} \times 100 = 3.9\%$.

and time and attempts to sell this at discounted prices within a widely fluctuating international media market. Which approach to use needs to be discussed and agreed between the company and agency before commencing a campaign.

The advertiser can expect to receive agency profit and loss accounts itemizing and substantiating the agency's gross income from media and non media (below-the-line activities); the agency's costs based on agreed hourly rates and invoices; and profit margin calculated on capitalized turnover (capitalized turnover = gross margin $\times 100/15$). The 15 per cent represents the agency commission on advertising and related services.

An example of agency costings is provided in Table 4.8 by way of illustration.

**Evaluating the work of the agency**

The advertising agency has prepared the printed brochures, placed the advertisements on radio and television, but has it had the planned impact in the market place? It is important to attempt to measure the effect of the campaign and to establish whether the agency made a positive contribution to championing the product or service. Measures may include:

1. A simple count of the number of returned coupons
2. A market research survey comparing the post-campaign situation with a base measurement commissioned before the campaign in terms of consumer product knowledge, attitudes to the brand, and brand image
3. Shelf-count turnovers after and before the campaign by the company merchandise department or external agency
4. A measurement of the trend in enquiries and orders for existing and new products
5. Measurements of changes in market share
6. Did the campaign make the task of the sales force easier and enable productivity to be improved?
7. Have there been spin-off benefits to other products or product groups?

### The international promotional dimension

Three problems face product managers in considering how to provide promotional support to the international sales force, agent network, or multinational network of subsidiaries and associate companies. First, much sales promotion and advertising is not internationally transferable. In spite of discussions of globalization of products, few products and their promotional and advertising support are truly global. Advertising culture and humour are different from one EEC country to the next, for example. Second, there are variations in the level of corporate accountability delegated to territorial managers. Third, there is a diversity of agency support available.

The product manager has a number of choices in deciding how to tackle the problem most effectively:

1. Organize a world-wide product group strategy review, lay down marketing strategy guidelines and allow each international subsidiary and associate to produce local marketing strategies, assisted in planning and implementation by locally selected national marketing and advertising agencies or the local branch of a big-name multinational
2. Establish the policy guidelines at the centre, test in the national market and then require international subsidiaries and associates to implement the tested corporate formula using the local offices of a company-nominated multinational agency
3. Commission an international agency to assist with the development of a world-wide marketing strategy and supervise the implementation via the local branches of the agency, or increasingly through third party agencies to avoid a conflict of interest. The trend is starting to blur the traditional distinctions between international marketing consultancy companies and international marketing and advertising agencies

The product manager needs to choose between the options on the basis of:

1. The relevant international experience of the agency
2. The extent to which the common language for customers of the specific product group is English or American English

3. The balance of accountability between product group managers and territorial managers
4. Success rate with current and previous approaches
5. The difficulty of achieving consistent translations of messages and manuals; this is often more difficult with high-technology engineering products than with consumer products

### Pricing options

The aim of pricing is to charge for a product at a level that satisfies four sets of needs in parallel:

1. The end customer's need for a cost of purchase that represents value for money
2. The middleman's need for commercially attractive financial returns in line with the effort and expenditure required to introduce, push and support a product in the marketplace
3. The salesman's desire for a price that eases the sales process in comparison with competitors' products
4. The basic product manager's objective of improving profits, return on investment and cash flow by maintaining premium prices that reflect the value for money of the total product and service package available from the company

The feasibility of meeting these multiple objectives will be directly related to:

1. The competitive differentiation of the product or service
2. The extent of competition in or likely to enter the market
3. The market share the product or service holds
4. Whether the product is a price-insensitive commodity sold to customers with a strategic need or a price-sensitive commodity product meeting operational needs
5. The professionalism of the sales force, whether the typical salesman is a seller or order-taker and whether the sales force is fully briefed and committed to the product strategy and provided with up-to-date product training.

In all markets there is a highest price and a lowest price and a wide variety in the middle, as illustrated by Fig. 4.9.

The product manager needs to establish a feel for the price-sensitivity of the marketplace in order to decide which end of the spectrum to play and how and when to move within the spectrum to achieve or maintain a competitive position (see Fig. 4.10).

In an international auction house, the product manager responsible for auctioning old masters is fortunate to manage products that are distinctly price-insensitive. The presentation of the masterpiece, the promotion and customer invitations to bid can be carefully geared to increasing the previous best world prices. The volume of product is limited and the number of potential customers, although relatively small in number is growing, assisted in some cases by a paternalistic tax regime.

The product manager in the oil products business in 1988 operated at the other extreme: a relatively stable total market, excess world-wide capacity, and

Competitive product strengths, value for money, demand, rarity, limited customer choice

Overcapacity, commodity least-cost purchases, multiple customer choice

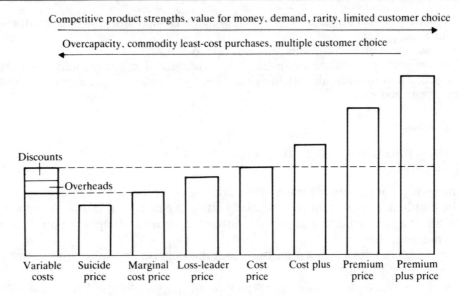

**Figure 4.9**   Range of prices recognizable in the marketplace

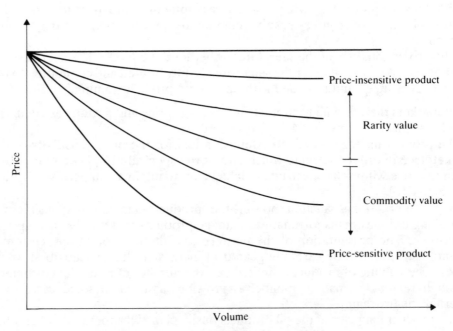

**Figure 4.10**   Variations in price sensitivity

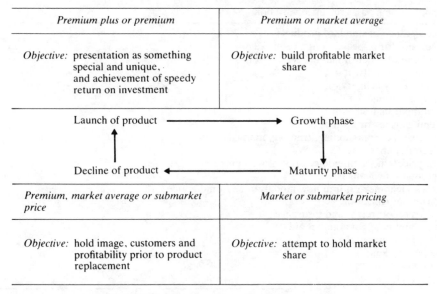

| Premium plus or premium | Premium or market average |
|---|---|
| *Objective:* presentation as something special and unique, and achievement of speedy return on investment | *Objective:* build profitable market share |

Launch of product ⟶ Growth phase

↑ ↓

Decline of product ⟵ Maturity phase

| Premium, market average or submarket price | Market or submarket pricing |
|---|---|
| *Objective:* hold image, customers and profitability prior to product replacement | *Objective:* attempt to hold market share |

**Figure 4.11**  Product life cycle pricing strategy

customers buying on price for forward stockpiling, trading in their own right, or immediate use. Only in very specialist markets with special blends, technical support, stockbuilding and secure pipeline supply, was any sort of premium price in relation to competitors possible.

The primary aim of the product manager is to be in the position of marketing superior products which achieve premium prices because of demand for added value or at worst average market prices. A move towards marginal cost price will generally be a recognition of product management failures.

There is no common formula or practice. The typical product manager's job is situated somewhere between the two extremes illustrated above, and he faces the task of establishing a competitive pricing structure appropriate to the type of product and position of the product in the life cycle (see Fig. 4.11).

The pricing strategy prepared and communicated by the product manager as a guideline for regional and territorial sales forces will need to include:

1. The company-recommended price list
2. The validity dates
3. Guidelines for variations (see Table 4.9)
    (a) Premiums for special requirements
    (b) Discounts for special situations
4. Authority levels for agreeing to variations

However, what is a loss-leader price in one segment of the market may be a premium price in another segment. In practice, many markets stratify over time, as illustrated in Fig. 4.12. This phenomenon needs to be analysed and forecast by the product manager in positioning the product, the promotion and the price structure in each situation.

**Table 4.9**   Some bases for price variations

 1. Acceptance of standard products
 2. Demand for a special design or packaging
 3. Volume of order or cumulative 12-month purchase
 4. Long-term contract
 5. Emergency delivery
 6. Barter arrangement
 7. Multinational account
 8. Semi-finished or kit part order
 9. Provision commissioning, training, manuals
10. Currency changes
11. Oil price/other commodity price movements
12. Interest rate changes
13. Stock clearance prior to new models or seasonal goods
14. Customer collection
15. Inclusion of freight and insurance
16. Availability of government aid
17. Free issue material
18. Repeat orders
19. Non-seasonal orders
20. Immediate delivery

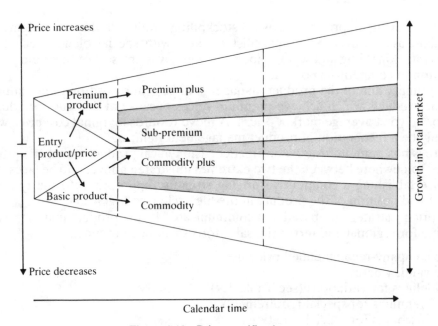

**Figure 4.12**   Price stratification

The issue of price stratification highlights the close interrelationship and delicate balance between all the elements of marketing strategy.

Pricing is a complex issue, one at the heart of corporate business beliefs, behaviour and accountability. The product manager needs to ensure that territorial sales teams recognize the importance of correct pricing in generating not only sales volume but profits and cash flow. This is discussed in Chapter 6.

**Paternalistic finance**

The availability of finance at more competitive terms than those available from banks and shareholders has become an important factor in the buying decision in many markets, particularly in industrializing countries characterized by:

– Shortage of hard currency
– Desire to buy at lowest total cost including interest on funds tied up in the purchase
– Determination to obtain up-to-date technology at low cost
– Limited allegiance to previous suppliers or a specific nation

Products sold to such markets will include power stations and chemical plants, aircraft and railway equipment, infrastructure and health services, machinery and vehicles. Sales in such situations are likely to be achieved where the product package offer includes:

– A product fit for the purpose for which it is sought
– Interesting technology
– Reliable delivery once an order is placed
– Technology transfer through training, commissioning and consultancy
– A fixed or strictly controlled price
– Protection from fluctuations in exchange rates
– Long-term financing at preferential rates of interest with, in some cases, an initial interest-free period
– Access to government aid programmes

Product managers involved in such situations need to support the sales force by:

1. Maintaining an up-to-date analysis of the competitors interested in each significant international market, the ability of the competitors to offer low-interest and long-term loans, and the policy of the national governments of the countries in which the competitors have major manufacturing units in respect of indirect and direct aid programmes
2. Ensuring that the company has appointed a manager to search out and secure the maximum government and international aid available for the product group in the form of soft loans, project finance and export credit guarantees in each country in which the product group manufactures

Paternalistic finance is also becoming a factor with private customer products offered by companies exporting from a low-interest, hard-currency country such as Japan. Japanese cars sold in Europe with no- or low-interest loan facilities can put considerable pressure on the product package offered by domestic manufacturers.

Paternalistic finance is a political issue which will not impact all product managers. However, there are a large number of political issues which will be of importance.

**Table 4.10** Typical political initiatives affecting the marketing of products

| Initiatives related to | Likely impact | | |
| --- | :---: | :---: | :---: |
| | Positive | or | Negative |
| Competition rules, price fixing | ● | or | ● |
| Market dominance/monopoly situations | ● | or | ● |
| Truthfulness of advertising | ● | or | ● |
| Banned advertising messages | ● | or | ● |
| Requirements for local content | ● | or | ● |
| Restrictions on foreign shareholding | ● | or | ● |
| Diplomatic relations | ● | or | ● |
| Separation of customs ports and entry facilities | ● | or | ● |
| Subsidized prices | ● | or | ● |
| Quota/tariff barriers | ● | or | ● |
| Religion of country of source | ● | or | ● |
| Requirement to re-export | | | ● |
| Resale price maintenance | ● | or | ● |
| Exclusive dealing | | | ● |
| Control on interest rates | | | ● |
| Price freezes or controls | | | ● |
| EEC single market (1992) | ● | or | ● |
| Import taxes and sales taxes | ● | or | ● |
| Export of sensitive technology | | | ● |
| Registration of freight transporters | ● | or | ● |
| Government aid and soft loans | ● | or | ● |
| Patent and copyright | ● | or | ● |

## The political dimension

There are many political initiatives that affect the marketing decisions made by a product manager in relation to both the development and marketing of a product. The initiatives related to the design of products and services have been discussed in Chapter 3. Some of the more important initiatives related to the promotion, advertising and sale of products are listed in Table 4.10. Wise product managers will make their own checklist, and update and review it regularly to ensure that they are sufficiently informed and knowledgeable to assess the impact of political influences on products territory by territory.

To ensure that the information base is up-to-date, the product manager needs to ensure two things. First, that a network of internal and external contacts feeds updated information on changes and new political initiatives on a daily basis. Second, that the total product team, full-time and associate members, are kept aware of the political dimension by the same sources of information, via internal summary notes or personal updates by the product manager at planning sessions, review meetings and training sessions.

The impact of the initiatives needs to be assessed in updating product business strategies, product marketing strategies and specific actions such as imminent and recent product launches. The impacts need to be appraised from both the company viewpoint and the viewpoint of the competition.

At best, political initiatives will give products a new image of quality and value for money. The case for new national quality standards saved the Austrian wine industry from disaster.

At worst, political initiatives will ban specific products and/or components of products, or close market borders permanently, such as the US ban on the export of sensitive technology to the Eastern bloc.

In most cases, political initiatives protect markets from some competitors, but only until the more innovative and aggressive find a competitive hole in the fence, as in the case of Japanese cars and electronic products.

Political issues are important to all product managers, but especially to product managers planning to globalize products. There are five particularly important questions:

1. What political dimensions represent market opportunities?
2. What political dimensions represent market threats?
3. What government aid could be made available to support significant product sales?
4. What political lobbying is desirable to improve the probability of active aid/support?
5. What national and international collaborations could accelerate moves into important export markets, particularly for globally acceptable products?

### Managing the trend towards global strategy

Globalization became a popular word during the 1980s as Japanese and other companies attempted to increase their penetration of foreign markets against a background of stagnant or slow growth of domestic markets. Similarly, Europeanization is becoming a key word as companies start to plan for the single European market in 1992. However, few companies have yet achieved full globalization in terms of a product that can be sold in all significant markets, with exactly the same specification, finish and packaging and with exactly the same advertising and sales promotion. Before considering common global strategic thrust, as opposed to a number of coordinated regional or national strategies, the product manager needs to assess in detail whether and where a move towards globalization is feasible. As a starting point the following questions need to be asked:

1. Will a standard product meet customer needs in all priority markets?
2. What are the cost benefits of total standardization, taking into account the cost of new facilities and the closure of old ones?
3. Is a standard product, based on the best of today's designs, the right answer or should globalization be the focus of the next generation of products in order to achieve the following?
   ● Establish a product with new competitive features that will secure or retain a significant share of the domestic market against foreign attempts to fragment the market
   ● Build volume fast to achieve cost benefits, and investment repayment speedier than historically
   ● Attack the foreign markets of global competitors where their products are vulnerable

● Import a product for the domestic market from an overseas subsidiary such as the growing trend from the USA to Japan
● Attack the domestic markets of national company competitors who may find it difficult to generate the cost benefits to defend in an aggressive manner
4. What form of national or international collaboration would enable a significant European or global market force to be established speedily and profit-effectively?

**Product collaborations**

Product strategy reviews (see Chapter 3) need to examine possibilities for both national and international collaboration from three points of view. First, what form(s) of collaboration present significant opportunities to the product group in terms of enhanced competitive advantage? Second, what form(s) of collaboration present significant opportunities to competitors, and hence significant threats to the product group? Third, what internal barriers would have to be overcome to secure and implement a market collaboration?

Internally the situation will require:

● Clear corporate strategic guidelines, as discussed in Chapters 2 and 5
● Effective working relationships with territories, as discussed in Chapter 5
● Effective working relationships with manufacturing, as discussed in Chapter 7

A wide range of possible forms of collaboration exist, as shown in Fig. 4.13.

Collaboration may be vertical between suppliers, manufacturers and distributors, or horizontal between competing manufacturing or service companies. Two multinational companies might, for example, compete fiercely with each other in one product group, but in another product group:

● Service each other's exported products in the home market

| | | Strategic priority of product/market | | |
|---|---|---|---|---|
| | | Low | Medium | High |
| Company's technological capabilities | High | License out product know how or sell product as a business | License out or subcontract manufacture | Independent leadership or joint product development |
| | Medium | Phase out or sell business | License out, joint marketing, or shared product improvement | Joint marketing and/or product development, or merger |
| | Low | Don't start or abort | Buy product in, with technology transfer | Buy product in, license in technology or acquire competitor |

**Figure 4.13** Typical forms of international collaboration

- Represent each other in selected markets
- Jointly exploit selected new markets
- Cooperate in research and development or license know-how to each other, to reduce the joint investment
- Cooperate in the design and development of a new product, for both national and global markets, to speed a step change in product concept and/or technology
- Each produce a subsection of the total product range to share investment in manufacturing facilities
- In a service industry, transfer resources within a common professional labour pool to use scarce resources most productively

In each case the objectives are enhanced national and international competitiveness.

Collaboration requires disciplined management, with the product manager frequently playing a major liaison and coordinating role.

---

**Chapter 4 – Key point summary**

*Product managers as effective marketing managers*

1. Recognize that marketing begins and ends with customer value for money
2. Manage the objective mix in a profit and socially effective manner
3. Focus on improving the productivity of the sales process
4. Evaluate and balance all aspects of the marketing mix
5. Establish an effective working relationship with the advertising agency
6. Manage towards premium prices and market share
7. Recognize the importance of global collaboration

# 5. Product managers and board decisions

> **Product managers' and corporate managers' key task**
> To establish a strategic approach to the direction, management and administration of all decisions, plans and actions affecting the competitive success of strategically important products and services

### Links with corporate strategic decisions

The introduction and operation of product management will be affected by six types of corporate strategic decision, made by or requiring the confirmation and agreement of the board of directors.

The first type of decision concerns the future strategy of the company, with special regard to the relative importance of current and new business areas and product groups for future investment and, in some cases, divestment. This will dictate the level of investment in working and fixed capital likely to be made available to a specific business or product group and the difficulty of making a case for future investment.

The second type of decision concerns the future organization of the company: the form of structure, especially the relationship between divisions, territories, functions, subsidiaries, business units and centralized or decentralized product management; the forms of product management selected as the most effective for each specific business and product group; and the level of accountability allocated to different parts of the organization and their designation as a financial unit as illustrated in Table 5.1. In a large company there is likely to be an objective but complex matrix of all four types of unit. The product manager needs to be aware of the financial power bases within the matrix to secure support for the development of the product group.

The third type of decision concerns the power behind the decision to manage the business with a product management structure. When the ownership of product management is visibly in the hands of the chief executive as an important

**Table 5.1**  Types of financial unit

| Type of unit | Accountability | Typical titles |
|---|---|---|
| Revenue centre | Generation of revenue but with limited influence over the total expenditure required to achieve revenue | Area sales force or branch office |
| Cost centre | Control of total costs and minimization of unit costs but with limited impact, if any, on revenue | Functional departments or works |
| Profit centre | Excess of revenue over costs, return on investment and cash flow; decisions to trade off promotion to increase sales and costs; sales to other parts of the company at equivalent outside prices | International subsidiary, business unit or product group |
| Investment centre | As above, plus total accountability for return on investment, financial gearing and the negotiation of funds; can take decisions on expansion, replacement or disposal of assets | Legal company, the parent group, major subsidiaries or associate companies |

corporate initiative, product management will normally have more support than if it is seen to be only an important feature of the organization structure of the marketing department.

The fourth type of decision concerns the board-level decision as to how the company's planning process will be structured and implemented. To be fully effective, product management requires the support of a planning process with the following features:

1.  A planning philosophy that requires the planning sequence shown in Fig. 5.1.
2.  An interactive cascade process as illustrated in Fig. 5.2.

The process provides for:

(a)  Product strategy reviews to be organized within a framework of planning guidelines emanating from level 1 and 2 stategic planning.
(b)  Product strategy reviews to highlight strategic options for consideration at level 1 and 2.
(c)  Product strategies to provide direction and coordination of level 3 strategy reviews and operational plans related to the product group.

The fifth type of decision concerns the decision-making process for presenting product strategies, investment proposals and budgets for approval.

In a company with a single or small number of product groups it will be normal for the product group manager to present and discuss plans with directors.

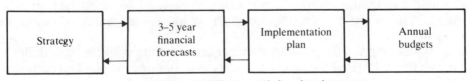

**Figure 5.1**  Framework for planning process

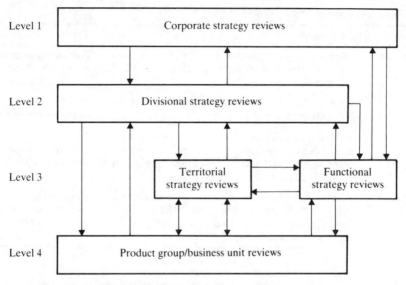

**Figure 5.2**   Strategic review process

However, large multinationals with a large number of product groups face a major procedural issue: how to review plans from a hundred or more product groups parallel with the review of territorial and functional plans without the process becoming purely a bureaucratic paper exercise?

The following process provides a solution for many companies:

1. The product manager prepares his product strategy, annual plans and budget and reviews them with the marketing director, territorial managers, and corporate product development and manufacturing
2. The product manager then submits his product plans to senior corporate management for review, comparison with territorial and functional plans to check for compatibility and areas of conflict, and comparison with plans submitted by other product managers to assess and finalize decisions on priority corporate investments
3. Senior managers take account of product management inputs when fine-tuning the corporate strategy and preparing global financial forecasts
4. The product manager is advised of any revisions required to make the product plans compatible with corporate investment plans
5. The product manager makes an annual presentation of his product strategy, five-year financial forecasts, detailed implementation plan and budget for two years to senior management. A session that allows senior management to evaluate the quality of product managers assigned to important product groups, and allows the product manager to judge the quality of corporate support

   This session gives the product manager the motivation and responsibility to take on the full role of the product champion in fighting market and corporate battles, and in turning his plans into results

The sixth and last type of decision concerns the corporate personnel decision taken in respect of the quality of product manager to be appointed, the training and development programme, the career structure and the philosophy for sharing the gains from improvements in the productivity of product groups. These decisions are discussed in detail in Chapter 9.

There are dual obligations related to the six decisions. First, the obligations of senior management to communicate the decisions to provide policy guidelines for product managers and associated managers. Second, the obligation of product managers to ask questions and find out.

### Preparation and presentation of investment plans

World-wide, managers operate in an increasingly competitive environment; product managers particularly so. It is an environment which requires a competitive approach to project appraisal to ensure that appropriate investments are made both in product/market developments and in process and productivity initiatives. The aim of senior managers and directors will be to facilitate the timely, competitive implementation of changes in products and market sectors. But what is project appraisal? To the product manager, the project appraisal process will normally be divided into three phases:

1. Identification of potential areas for capital or revenue investments designed to improve product performance, productivity and competitiveness
2. Evaluation of options and the identification of preferred investments prior to allocating significant resources and funds
3. Ongoing post-authorization appraisal to check that the project remains viable at the stages of design, development, prototype, pilot, and after; positive decisions are required at each stage in terms of whether to continue, accelerate or abort the investment

Effectively managed companies ensure that at each phase of a key project an appropriate multifunctional blend of knowledge and experience is involved. The product manager is likely to lead or be a member of a team of managers who between them will plan and revise all aspects of the project, technical, financial and commercial.

Running a company has always been a risk business, not least in the competitive environment of the 1990s. The business climate is characterized by:

– Significant overcapacity
– Ongoing uncertainty over the timing of orders
– Pressures on prices, quality and delivery
– Competition from countries rich in natural resources
– The entry of the Far East into new industries and markets from a highly productive work-force base
– World-wide access to 'micro-chip' control technology
– Rescheduling/cancellation of projects by developing countries as a result of currency crises
– The challenge of process plant intensification (performing unit operations at greatly increased efficiency or speed)

- Political constraints on free trading
- Wrong project selection or ill-timed investments in relation to competitors' actions and the state of the market
- Poor project definition against corporate business objectives and the state of the art in related technology
- Cost overruns due to initially unclear objectives and *ad hoc* modification
- Financial criteria for project authorization met by adjustment of costs through either overambitious estimates of the level of probable revenue and cost saving opportunities, or unrealistic assessments for the financial implications of the risks associated with anticipated market conditions and the ability of the company to implement the project on time

In many industries, the rationale for a project could be supported in the 1950s and 1960s by extrapolation of customer demands under relatively stable market conditions with a manageable degree of competition. In the 1970s the concept of portfolio management was readily grasped by many companies. The rationale for projects became the desire to build market share based on volume production and low price. Later management research demonstrated that such strategies would fail unless significant investment in technological support was sustained, and in the late 1970s the traditional rule of thumb of cost × scale 0.6 broke down. This and the need for flexibility has led to an enthusiasm for plant intensification, a competitive move as important as cost-effective plant debottlenecking in the 1960s.

Such changes in the fortunes of customers have significant implications for product management teams. Not only are many customer demands at a stable or lower and fluctuating level but their technical needs are changing. A broader range of international competitors diligently seeks out such opportunities as occur. New products, however innovative, have difficulty in finding effective distributors in already saturated export markets.

Therefore, the information on which decisions are made needs careful preparation, evaluation and processing. Opportunities are being more carefully scrutinized and risks evaluated in greater depth.

*A strategic process*
Fig. 5.3 outlines a practical approach to establishing a competitive basis for project appraisal linked to the corporate strategy of a business. This scheme helps with the process of improving competitiveness in two ways: externally, by stimulating a broad-based identification and evaluation of market-related investment opportunities and the various ways in which the opportunities could be exploited; and internally, by ensuring that several investment opportunities are evaluated and ranked against one another, rather than each option being evaluated in isolation.

Project appraisal is no longer essentially a financial analysis exercise. A broader general management approach is now essential, one which balances potential opportunities with the risks implied in competitors' and customers' strategies, trends in process and material technology, and social and political changes, as illustrated in Table 5.2.

The successful presentation and implementation of investment proposals

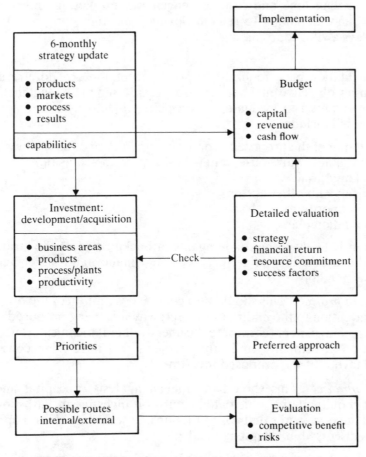

**Figure 5.3**  Strategic processing of investment proposals

**Table 5.2**  Trend in project evaluation criteria

| Criteria | 1960s | 1970s | 1980s | 1990s |
|---|---|---|---|---|
| Financial objectives | ● | ● | ● | ● |
| Added shareholder value | | ○ | ● | ● |
| Sales priorities | ● | ○ | | |
| Marketing strategy priorities | | ● | ○ | ○ |
| Corporate strategy priorities | | ○ | ● | ● |
| Degree of competition | ○ | ○ | ● | ● |
| Customer options | | ○ | ● | ● |
| Alternate technology | | ○ | ● | ● |
| Risk analysis | ○ | ○ | ● | ● |

○=some emphasis  ●=major emphasis

require more than time and cash. Management, marketing and technological capabilities, and the ability to remain flexible, are important, and the product manager plays a vital coordinating role.

## Documentation

The documentation pack required to present a major expenditure project for approval in an objective manner, and to provide senior management with the information required to evaluate the proposal objectively and reach a speedy decision, should include:

1. A description of the proposed product group initiative, be it a new product, a new plant, a new warehouse, a new business or an acquisition
2. Financial appraisal
3. Comparison with other options
4. Risk and opportunity analysis
5. Implementation plan

This decision is likely to be made against a background of the strategy of the business, the availability and likely cost of finance and other requests for significant expenditure.

*Description of project*   This should be a concise description of the project paying particular attention to the nature of project; why it is being proposed; objectives that it is designed to meet (corporate, business-related, technical, time-scale, cost and return on investment); and other projects that have been considered but rejected in favour of the proposed investment.

*Financial appraisal*   This should include an analysis of capital and revenue investment requirements; anticipated return on investment; cash-flow requirements; and the best- and worst-case situations, based on a risk and opportunities analysis, as discussed in Chapters 2 and 8.

*Comparison with other options*   Is the best project being submitted? Have other options been explored; are there other ways of tackling the specific market opportunity and productivity problem or other discrete opportunities? Has a narrow view of how to implement the corporate strategy been taken; has there been sufficient creative and lateral thinking? Have the opportunities inherent in changes in technology and emergent customer needs been fully explored? How do the potential benefits and risks of the proposed investment compare with other possible options? Such questions need to be asked before financial resources are allocated to a project. When answers are provided, the decision process is speeded up and senior management is more informed as to the detailed opportunities facing the business. Inevitably, this results in a greater commitment and the knowledge that real and realistic investment proposals are being submitted.

*Risk and opportunity analysis*   Perhaps inevitably, the initial financial forecasts for a project are often based on middle-of-the-road or overoptimistic assumptions. It is therefore important that a thorough analysis be made of both opportunities and risks.

1. The opportunities that could occur for improving the financial performance of

the project need to be analysed in respect of the probability of being able to take advantage of the opportunity, the actions that would have to be taken to take advantage of the opportunities and a realistic assessment of the financial benefit of taking advantage of the opportunity.

Opportunities could include speeding design by 'licensing in' or using an outside design house, modifications to specification to enable wider market needs to be met, or reducing the sophistication of the project.

2. The risks or potential problems that can be anticipated need to be analysed in terms of the probability of the risks surfacing, the preventive action that could be planned, a realistic assessment of the total degree of financial risk and the degree to which this could be dissipated.

Such analysis allows the financial implications of the project to be objectively assessed and fine-tuned.

*Implementation plan*   An outline action plan for the duration of the project should be made, indicating key milestones, key potential problem points, critical dates and major human resources that will be required (e.g. project manager, designer). This will enable those reviewing the project to assess the chance of successfully implementing the project on time and within estimated costs, and the potential impact on other projects also requiring key human resources during the period of the project. Examples of action plans and risk analyses are illustrated in Figs 3.11 and 3.12 in Chapter 3.

Senior management faces the task of evaluating projects with short- or medium-term positive return on investment and cash flow; product and process development initiatives; and new capital investment versus productivity investments for existing facilities and products. The process outlined provides a basis for a consistent open-minded, objective and relatively unbiased approach.

A product group's results will be much influenced by the quality of its investment decisions and proposals. Preparing for professional project appraisals is therefore a vital product management task.

### Business plans

Product managers prepare business plans for three main reasons:

1. To prove the business viability of the product group, or specific new products, or potential product acquisition to themselves and the product team
2. As an integral part of the documentation required to support major investment proposals, including acquisitions to corporate management or the board of directors
3. In requesting final approval to proceed with an acquisition, the development of a new product range or business area

In many multinationals the process outlined in Fig. 5.3 will be applied phase by phase, with provisional and updated proposals submitted at a number of significant milestones, a fully substantiated business plan being required at the final decision point. The phase by phase approach to authorizing investment was

**Table 5.3**   Typical business plan format

| Content | Inclusion in | |
|---|---|---|
| | concept proposal | full proposal |
| 1. Definition of scope of business unit/product group and relationship to remainder of company | ○ | ● |
| 2. Primary business objectives: | | |
| (a) Financial objectives | ○ | ● |
| (b) Market customer objectives | ○ | ● |
| 3. Business strategy | ○ | ● |
| 4. Five-Year financial forecast: investment required, profit, return on investment, cash flow, sensitivity analyses | | ● |
| 5. Action plan for preparing full proposal if concept proposal is accepted in principle | ● | |
| 6. Risk analysis and critical issue action plan | | ● |
| 7. Supportive appendices: market analysis, competitor analyses, risk/opportunity analysis on financial forecast, forecast balance sheet | ○ | ● |

Code: ● Full statement        ○ Outline statement

discussed in Chapter 2, in relation to the management of the product life cycle, and in Chapter 3 in relation to the progressing of product development programmes.

The preparation of business plans creates a conflict: on the one hand, the product manager may be tempted to present every item of information and argument available to support the case; on the other hand, senior management do not have the time to read and evaluate in detail proposals running to hundreds of pages, but do require the presentation of a case that is strong on analysis, argument and commercial viability.

The solution is to establish and agree corporate guidelines for the preparation and presentation of business plans to achieve strategic objectivity, brevity, ease of evaluation, separation of the proposal and supportive analyses, a balanced evaluation of commercial benefits and risks. A format used by a number of companies as an integral part of their product management planning and control process is illustrated in Table 5.3.

## Product group acquisitions

There are seven main reasons for strategic acquisitions:

1. The decision by the board of directors to diversify into a totally new business area
2. To speed entry into a new market for current products and services
3. To speed the replacement of a product range by a product range based on the next generation of technology, where a competitor or supplier of the technology is ahead of the design and development capability of the acquiring company

4. To reduce the extent of competition in strategically important market segments by buying out a competitor and thus immediately increasing market share, customer base and the opportunity for productivity improvement
5. To buy in products that will enhance the competitiveness of a product range by either extending the range or filling important gaps in the product range
6. The acquisition of important suppliers or subcontractors to ensure continued security of supply and control over supplies to competitors
7. The acquisition of distribution outlets such as an agent, retail chain or carrier to improve the security and profit-effectiveness of the distribution network for a product range

A new product or new business manager would in many companies be involved in identifying type (1) acquisition candidates. Product group managers may consider types (2)–(7) as part of product strategy reviews in association with strategic planners and corporate management. Typical decision criteria for the identification, evaluation and selection of acquisition candidates are listed in Table 5.4.

**Table 5.4** Typical criteria for identifying and selecting acquisition candidates to strengthen the product group

1. Product technology is as good as or better than ours
2. Current products would provide useful range of fillers and/or extenders
3. Good complementary customer base
4. Would open up new applications
5. Would open up new international markets
6. Would prevent a potentially damaging strategic alliance with a competitor
7. Good potential profitability
8. Would enhance cash flow
9. Return on investment equal to or greater than internal rate of return on new product development
10. Complementary management, technical and sales team

However, many acquisitions, like newly launched products, do not achieve the potential assessed at the time of purchase, and the cause can frequently be traced to three factors:

1. The poor quality of pre-acquisition analysis and a 'buy' decision based on ill-founded information
2. The failure to direct and manage the acquired business in the first year, including the failure to integrate it into an existing product group structure where this exists in the acquiring company
3. The failure to find out immediately after the acquisition whether and why the 'buyer' was correct in having higher expectations for the value of the ongoing acquired business than the seller

The basic problems arise from the different perceptions of the managers from the buying and the selling company on issues such as:

– The strategic purpose of the acquisition
– The commercial product group benefits of the acquisition

– Emphasis on early asset stripping with insufficient parallel attention to maintaining and building on the customer base
– Confusion over staff security and career potential
– Indecision over whether to retain, merge or cease the existing corporate and territorial product management organization structure of the acquired company

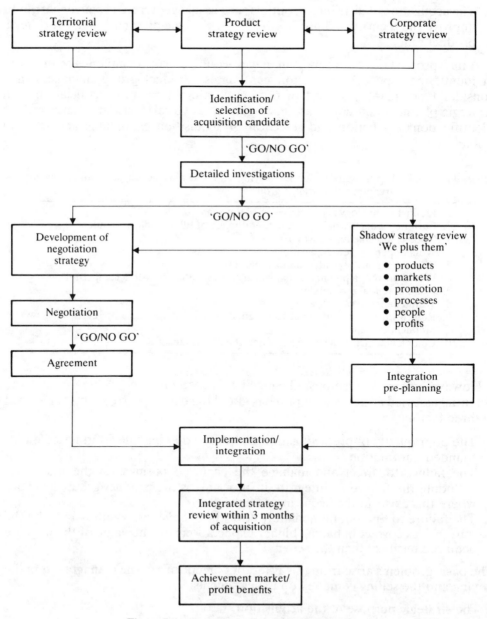

**Figure 5.4**   A product group acquisition process

- Slowness in achieving cost-effective integration and rationalization of territorial, functional and corporate staff
- Most importantly, a failure to establish strategic direction, motivation and control of merged companies and product groups within a matter of months

Fig. 5.4 outlines a planning process that aims to minimize the cause and effect of the above potential problems. The process is derived from, and therefore compatible with, the strategic planning processes described in Chapter 2.

### Divestment decisions

As part of the annual strategy review a number of divestment decisions may need to be considered by directors and product group managers.

In each case an objective evaluation of divestment options is required. Table 5.5 illustrates the approach of a company in the electronics industry as part of an annual strategic review.

The product in product group A is no longer compatible with the mainstream strategy of the company, which has been unsuccessful in selling the business at a premium to generate cash for reinvestment in tomorrow's strategic business. Selling to a national, international or multinational company, seeking expansion in a specific market, has been considered and more recently a fashionable buyout to the local team has been investigated. The product managers now face the choice

**Table 5.5**   Evaluation of divestment candidates

| Decision criteria | | Comparative evaluation of product groups (H, M, L) | | | |
|---|---|---|---|---|---|
| | | A | B | C | D |
| 1. Does not fit into best strategic options for the future | | M | H | M | H |
| 2. Business diverts attention of key executives/technologists away from turnround/development of main 'core' businesses | | M | M | H | H |
| 3. Retention will continue to require significant group support | | M | M | H | H |
| 4. Divestment would stop cash outflow from operational losses or non-strategic expenditure | | L | M | H | H |
| 5. No significant product/customer overhead synergy with other parts of group | | M | H | H | M |
| 6. Profitable growth in medium-term doubtful | | L | H | M | H |
| 7. Ready buyer likely to be available | | L | M | H | L |
| 8. Premium above book value likely | | M | M | H | L |
| 9. Divestment less expensive than liquidation | | M | H | H | L |
| Summary | H | 0 | 4 | 7 | 5 |
| | M | 6 | 5 | 2 | 1 |
| | L | 3 | 0 | 0 | 3 |
| Relative attractiveness as a divestment | | 4 | 3 | 1 | 2 |

of accepting the challenge of a new perhaps accelerated career in a new parent company, or seek a career move into another part of the present company.

The products in product group B are unlikely to be profitable in the short-term. They are a mix of non-competitive products past their peak in the product life cycle and expensive to support, and several newer products with cost structures considerably over original forecasts. In the medium-term they are unlikely to achieve planned levels of profit, cash flow and even break even.

Product Group C consists of a number of products under development for the longer term. The decision to develop them was made five years earlier under less competitive market conditions. Over the last two years costs have escalated and the anticipated launch date delayed. The products are now seen as a future millstone around the neck of the product manager, and the only realistic option would be to abort the development programme or drastically rethink the product designs.

Product group D has excellent products today but is overshadowed by imminent technological breakthroughs and replacement products. In this situation the company and product manager need to consider carefully whether to continue in the market until the threat is real and then cease an involvement in that market, or accelerate the development of a new 'me too' product to enable an early but natural changeover from today's to tomorrow's generation of products.

As a result of the strategic review the products in product group C were sold off to a foreign company; product group D was closed down; product group B was subjected to closer scrutiny by outside consultants and product A was turned round as a useful add-on product to a strategically important product group.

Product managers need to develop decision matrices appropriate to their own specific situation. It is a tough process of analysis and decision-making and should be undertaken in an unemotional and business like manner. There are few second chances to deal with disaster situations.

---

**Chapter 5 — Key point summary**

*Product managers and board decisions*

1. Ensure strategic direction and priority for product managers
2. Establish a participative and integrative strategic planning process
3. Demonstrate ownership of product management
4. Make investment appraisal strategic, objective and realistic
5. Require business plans to support major investment
6. Evaluate product group acquisitions on the basis of ongoing strategic business
7. Establish disciplined divestment analysis and decision-making

# 6. Product managers, customers and the sales force

**Product managers' key task**

To provide strategic direction and support to regional and territorial sales forces to secure both increases in profitable sales and improvements in the productivity of the sales process

### The relationship between product manager and sales force

The relationship between the product manager and the sales force is critical to the performance of the company, the success of a product range, and the profit-effectiveness and survival of a product management structure. The product manager needs the right kind of relationship in order to be able to operate, be accepted and supported as a product champion.

The product manager has a joint accountability for profit contribution with the sales manager, but he has no direct authority over the sales force. He has to use the skills of leadership, strategic direction and persuasion to achieve acceptance and commitment to the implementation of specific guidelines, plans, actions and requests.

Unfortunately, many product managers do not have a good relationship with the sales force for a number of reasons, and resort to two courses of action that result in product management becoming just another overhead rather than a vital stimulator of profits.

First, product managers resort to seeking support and authoritarian action from the marketing director to get ideas through to the sales force, a course likely to cause more long-term harm than good if used too often. Second, product managers retreat, go on the defensive and manage from the apparent safety of a headquarters-based administration-style product manager. The safety net is likely to be short-lived. Good ongoing working relationships are likely to be based on a trust and respect relationship, built on an understanding and acceptance of mutually compatible and supportive roles and the practical relationship between marketing and sales within the sales process.

### Customer buying decisions

With customers becoming less loyal to consumer brands, industrial products and services and financial services, there is an increasing need to explore the decision-making process adopted by major customers.

The changes in loyalty arise from a number of trends, including increased consumer personal purchasing capacity, increased buyer purchasing power and targeting of purchase cost targets, the wider range of products and services offered as a result of the internationalization of markets, fluctuation in exchange rates, government pressures for local content and the impact of international collaboration, mergers and acquisitions of product ranges and competitive patterns.

The following questions provide a starting point for analysis:

– Who uses the product or services?
– Who specifies the product or service to purchase?
– Who decides on the companies and products to shortlist?
– Who triggers decisions to establish dual or multiple sourcing?
– Who controls the cost policy in respect of trends in prices accepted, target prices/costs or attitude to estimated life-time costs?
– What factors are taken into account in major buying decisions by the customer? Are decisions made by an individual or a buyer panel? Is there a formal vendor rating procedure?
– What are the authority levels of buyers?
– Should the desirable size of individual sales be focused within these authority levels or be refocused above these levels to take the buying decisions up to a more strategic rather than operational level?
– Is the tendency to decentralize or centralize buying decisions with major national and multinational customers?

### The sales process

During the 1980s, the accountability of most sales forces has ceased to be confined to sales volume. They now have the strategic task of securing a reliable, growing pattern of confirmed orders that will generate levels of revenue, profit contribution and cash flow that at least match the company's financial objectives. This applies not only to national sales forces but also to international sales forces, international subsidiaries, affiliates, agents and distributors.

The achievement of this task requires that the customer–company relationship is clearly understood and managed in a professional manner. In this the product manager has a significant role to play in ensuring that the customer is satisfied and the sales force and company achieve a succession of good sales. Each party will have a different perspective of what contributes a good sale, as illustrated in Table 6.1.

As the product champion, the product manager has the task of recognizing these differences in basic attitudes, and developing product group strategies and plans that succeed as far as possible in matching customer and company needs through a well-motivated sales force. The task goes further than the basic

**Table 6.1** Parameters of a good sale

| Customer's point of view | Salesman's point of view | Company/product management point of view |
|---|---|---|
| 1. A time- and cost-effective buying process | 1. An easy, speedy sales process | 1. Strategic focus on commercially attractive sources of profit and cash flow |
| 2. Availability of a salesman and support team who understand needs and solve a combination of short-term problem needs and medium-term strategic needs | 2. A continuous flow of leads to good prospects | 2. A focus on priority market segments and major national/international accounts |
| 3. Reliable range of products/ sources available at a profit-effective price in terms of initial life-time costs | 3. Stable range of quality competitive products at a price no greater than those of competitors | 3. A focus on the sale of priority existing and new products, and phasing out of old products |
| 4. Attractive trade terms | 4. Flexibility in discounting | 4. A drive for premium prices and restricted discounts through professional promotion and selling |
| 5. Speedy, undamaged and complete delivery | 5. Delivery from stock or within record time-scales | 5. Behaviour of staff and systems demonstrate that the product and customer are important |
| 6. Prompt, effective and courteous customer service | 6. Effective promotional support and thorough product training | 6. Cost-effective promotional programmes and materials |
| 7. Stability of partnership with proven supplier | 7. An incentive reward system that generates a gross remuneration at least in line with comparable companies | 7. An incentive system focused on the achievement of strategic objectives |
| 8. Extended credit retention for warranty period or incentive for prompt payment | 8. Bonus based on orders not receipts | 8. Prompt payment for goods and services without retention |

marketing task of stimulating market demand and the promotion of marketing support. Product management must continuously stimulate, nudge and persuade all departments in the company, from design through manufacture and distribution, to finance, to give the customer and sales force fair deals; in essence, facilitating decisions and actions towards a progressive improvement in the productivity of total sales activity in both the short and long term. Whether it is successful in this must be judged from the bottom line (see Table 6.2).

Turning financial calculations from theory into practice requires that the company establishes a commitment to the marketing concept outlined in Chapter 5, and the active involvement of the product management team in the process. The

**Table 6.2** Influence of product management on bottom line

|  | Unsatisfactory situation | | Satisfactory situation | |
|---|---|---|---|---|
|  | Product A | Product B | Product A | Product B |
| Nominal sales revenue | 1000 | 1000 | 1000 | 1070 |
| Discounts | 100 | 50 | 50 | 10 |
| Net bookable revenue | 900 | 950 | 950 | 1060 |
| Total costs | 800 | 900 | 750 | 860 |
| Profit contribution | 100 | 50 | 200 | 200 |
| Profit/sales ratio (%) | 11.1 | 5.3 | 21.1 | 18.9 |

|  | | |
|---|---|---|
| **Emphasis on marketing** | *Promotional concept*<br><br>Shaping the customer to the product and company | *Marketing concept*<br>Shaping the organization, product and market response to the customer's future needs |
|  | *Product concept*<br><br>Order taking from the self starter/tied customer | *Selling concept*<br>Negotiation of individual order by pursuasion |

Emphasis on selling

**Figure 6.1** Relationships between marketing concepts and sales process

implications of the marketing concepts discussed in Chapter 4 for the sales process are outlined in Fig. 6.1.

In practice, the product manager attempts to establish an appropriate balance between the basic marketing theories and the achievement of a corporate culture consistent with the marketing concept, in a continuing drive to ensure support to the sales force.

For instance, a product manager employed by a water company would recognize that sales are in general achieved through the product concept for domestic customers and the selling concept for significant industrial users such as the major food processors. Product management will focus on ensuring that the storage, purification and distribution systems have the capacity to meet demand and that customer service departments give a speedy response.

The product manager working for a confectionery company would focus on the promotional aspects of support to the sales force to ensure a sufficient market/customer demand pull through the retail/wholesale distribution chain.

The product manager in a capital equipment or speciality chemical business would focus on establishing the overall marketing concept to achieve an overall company focus on customers' strategic needs, an understanding by all functions of the complex nature of the sales process, and the coordinated multifunctional support required by the sales force to secure major one-off and repeat sales.

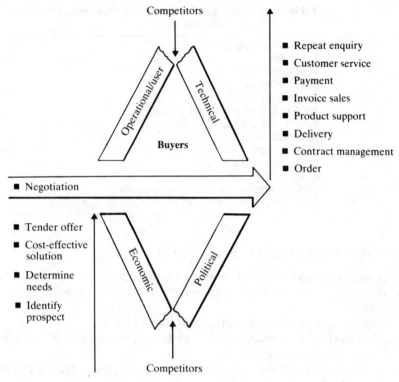

- Repeat enquiry
- Customer service
- Payment
- Invoice sales
- Product support
- Delivery
- Contract management
- Order

- Negotiation

- Tender offer
- Cost-effective solution
- Determine needs
- Identify prospect

Competitors

**Figure 6.2**  The sales process

In each situation the role of the product manager is a vital ingredient in the competitive success of the sales force. It is therefore essential that product managers strive towards effective working relationships with sales management and the sales force, and the achievement of their respect and support. Such respect and support are most easily achieved by visible productive support to the sales process. The sales process is illustrated in Fig. 6.2. The model can be applied to a wide range of customer–company buying situations in both industrial and consumer markets.

In a buying company seeking to place a major engineering contract, the operational/user buyer could be the operations director accountable for the productive operation of the new facility when built, and concerned about life-time and operating costs; the technical buyer the engineering director concerned about protecting engineering standards; the political buyer the chairman sensitive to purchasing internationally; and the economic buyer the finance director more concerned about initial capital costs and the availability of an attractive financial package to aid the profit-effective funding of the project. Jointly the four buyers would have contributed to the preparation of a final tender document and would again jointly be involved in evaluating tender offers against a range of selection criteria. An example of these criteria is given in Table 6.3.

**Table 6.3** Typical buying decision criteria for capital plant and equipment

Capacity and performance
Flexibility
Unit operating costs
Delivery dates
Product support
Quality history and accreditation
Extent of unproven technology
Aesthetic design
Capital cost
Estimated life-time cost
Financial package available
Performance guarantees and warranties
Reliability of project/contract management capability

The product manager might be involved in:

1. The commissioning of market research to identify the trends in customer needs and demands, and the scale and pattern of current emerging international competition
2. The concept design of a competitive product range
3. The preparation of product design briefs that combine market needs with reliable technological options
4. The preparation of product promotional material that reflects the implication of points (1), (2) and (3)
5. Membership of project teams for the design and development of prototype products
6. Briefing sales engineers on the best potential prospects and likely needs and timing
7. Membership of and support for the tender preparation teams for larger orders
8. Development of the total product package combining products, total engineering system, product support, customer service and financial packages

For the family unit purchasing a package holiday, the marketing company is constituted by the travel company and local travel agent who jointly put together a tender offer. The operational/user buyers will include all members of the unit: the father who wants to play golf; the son who would like some nightlife; the mother who would like a quiet break with good local shops; and the daughter who wants the romance of the beaches. Before a buying decision is made, demands and wishes will be balanced, modified and blended as a result of the various economic, political and technical decisions: the mother may be concerned that the holiday fund should not be depleted before the end of the holiday; son and daughter may have clear positive or negative attitudes to potential host governments; father may be concerned that the demands of all family members should be accommodated.

The product manager is involved at two levels: first, in developing holiday products attractive to mature families, preparing eye-catching and easy-to-use brochures, analysing past holiday complaints and aiming to improve the quality of future offerings and experiences, and designing a discounted repeat business booking scheme to secure a committed customer base; second, in developing products that are attractive to the travel agent in terms of merchandizing, ease of processing quotations, orders, payments, resolution of customer queries and problems; launching of the product range to the travel agents; commissioning national advertising campaigns; organizing product training sessions for travel agents, and incentive reward programmes for the most successful agent. At both levels the product manager might commission market research to aid the decision-making process.

A hotel management team seeking to purchase a new computer system, will each have unique needs: the front office manager user, with concerns about the extent of retraining of staff involved and the ease of operation; the accounts department user requires compatibility with the existing system to facilitate transfer of the existing data base; the systems development manager, the technical buyer, typically concerned with the reliability, service back-up, the technology base, speed of obsolescence, and compatibility with retained systems; and the general manager, the economic buyer, with concerns about the direct and indirect benefits of the investment in terms of profit, cost control and customer service. One of the managers may be the political buyer, demanding that a national company's product be selected.

Hopefully, the product manager will have been involved in becoming familiar with the specific needs of the hotel industry, to ensure that the product package — software, technical support, back-up facilities, user friendliness of the system — matches the expectations of major hotel groups; and the product package is supported by internationally attractive and dependable promotional material.

### Managing sales forecasts

The provision of timely product management support and support from functions such as product design and development, manufacturing, delivery, commissioning and servicing requires that realistic and current sales forecasts are prepared and updated regularly.

In practice sales forecasts range from a mathematical extrapolation of recent trends in orders to a more complex customer by customer, product group by product group forecast based on the best knowledge of the sales force and the product management team.

Fig. 6.3 illustrates a form of customer forecast that stimulates a number of questions aimed towards realism, accuracy, a focus on selected priority sales prospects and hence an increase in the probability of achieving specific targeted orders. This is, in essence, a strategic approach, applying the strategic planning concepts, described in Chapter 2, at a micro level. The approach is applicable to a wide range of consumer and industrial products and service product groups.

Fig. 6.4 illustrates an alternative format, similar in some ways, but recognizing the need to identify the specific persons likely to influence the eventual buying decision and their specific needs, viewpoints and preferences. The approach is particularly applicable to companies selling customized capital equipment and systems in an internationally competitive market and major service contracts.

*Country*

*Product group*

| Potential customer | Potential purchases | | Probability of order being placed | Our previous success rate | Competitors' strengths and weaknesses | Our strengths and weaknesses | Current probability of order | Action to improve probability |
|---|---|---|---|---|---|---|---|---|
| | *19—* | *19—* | | | | | | |
| | | | | | | | | |

**Figure 6.3**  Customer forecasts

*Country*

*Product group*

| Key potential customers | Potential purchases | | Economic/ political buyers and needs | Operational/ technical buyers and needs | Competitors' strengths and weaknesses | Our strengths and weaknesses | Customer sales strategy |
|---|---|---|---|---|---|---|---|
| | *Yr 1* | *Yr 2* | | | | | |
| | | | | | | | |

**Figure 6.4**  Customer strategy

In many situations product sales forecasts are prepared and processed as follows:

1. Individual salesmen prepare and submit sales forecasts monthly to their territory, national or area marketing or sales manager, depending on company structure
2. The territorial, national or area marketing or sales manager then collates inputs and prepares a consolidated statement with adjustments based on an

overview of specific customer situations and general trends in the market. The forecasts are then forwarded to the appropriate corporate marketing department, product group or business unit manager for collation to present regional or world-wide situations as most relevant

Forecasts provide vital inputs to

- Product manager-led reviews and updates of product strategy, and annual objectives and plans
- Product managers, as the basis for quarterly reviews of underlying trends with territorial managers
- Those involved in manufacturing, to enable them to update future production plans
- To design and development teams, to facilitate resource planning in line with future contract and product development demands

The product manager has a vital coordinating role in ensuring that product sales forecasts are prepared, communicated, understood and acted upon in an objective manner. The exact role depends on whether the product manager is based at headquarters with a national or international coordinating role or within a foreign subsidiary, or affiliate with a national role and operational link to a headquarters based product group manager.

### Relationships with regional sales teams

The organizational relationship between product managers and regional sales teams is illustrated in Fig. 6.5. The relationship with sales forces in foreign subsidiaries will be considered in the next section.

The organization structure is representative of the situations in many national companies with a product management structure, and also within individual major foreign subsidiaries or affiliate companies. Variations in exact reporting relationships do exist in practice, but do not affect the fundamental contribution of each of the managers illustrated.

The most important roles of the participants in the partnership between product managers and sales teams are typically as follows:

1. *Sales team*
   (a) The generation of growth in sales volume, with a sales mix that reflects the company's product priorities, at margins that reflect a professionalism in selling and the quality of the product or service package on offer to customers
   (b) The securement of a substantial proportion of repeat business from satisfied customers
   (c) The establishment of new customers within strategic market segments taking advantage of the company's promotional activity, and referrals from satisfied customers
   (d) Reporting on current and potential customer and product needs and problems, and the current and emergent activity of the competition

2. *Regional sales managers*
   (a) The direction, motivation and day-to-day management and support of the sales team
   (b) The personal handling of major regional or national accounts
   (c) Ensuring that the sales team understands and supports the company's overall marketing strategy and, in particular, the market strategy for each product group
   (d) The development of a sales team that is professional in terms of appearance, sales skills, product and company knowledge
   (e) The preparation of regular sales forecasts for personal use and use by the sales manager, marketing director and product managers
   (f) The provision of visible support to the product managers through agreement to the product management concept, regular market reports and sales forecasts, and inviting product managers to make presentations to sales team sessions
   (g) Dedicated support to product managers in the launch of new products and in taking unsuccessful products out of the market with minimum disruption to customer relations
   (h) Together with the personal function and product managers, the development of a sales incentive scheme focused on the achievement of a realistic balance between increased sales, increased margins, mix of existing and new product sales, mix between existing and new customers, and reduction in overdue customer accounts

3. *Product managers*
   (a) The provision of clear strategic guidelines in terms of the market segments and specific major customers likely to offer the most significant sales potential
   (b) The development, launch and ongoing market support of a range of continuing and new products with significant competitive advantages
   (c) The provision of product promotions support to establish a product image and customer pull to secure an improvement in the cost-effectiveness of sales
   (d) Pricing guidelines that are realistic and saleable, provided the sales manager ensures that the sales skill and product knowledge of the sales team are among the best in the target markets and industries
   (e) The joint development with the sales manager of a product sales budget, as illustrated in Fig. 6.6
   (f) The provision of professionally presented product group briefings, bulletins and reports

4. *The marketing services manager*
   (a) The provision of support to the product managers in terms of the arrangement and progression of product launches, promotional material, advertising schedules, exhibitions and other marketing initiatives
   (b) The coordination of advertising agency activity to ensure a balance of priorities between product groups

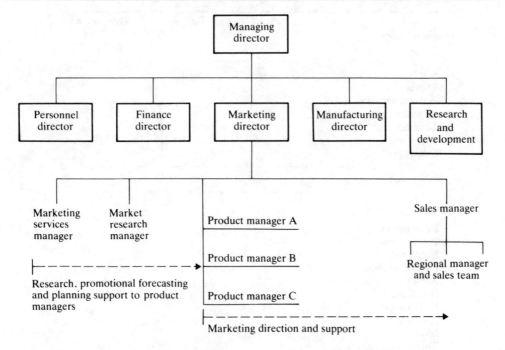

**Figure 6.5**   Typical organization structure

(c) The collation and communication of market statistics relevant to each product manager including comparisons between product group results

5. *The market research manager:* the commissioning, implementation and reporting on market research requested by product managers in relation to the market and competitiveness of existing products and the potential market and competitiveness of possible and planned products

It is important that mutually supporting roles are clarified at an early stage in the introduction of a product management organization. In practice, the quality of the working relationships will depend substantially on six factors:

1. The clarity and realism of the product strategy for each product group
2. The coordination and integration of the implementation plans of the various product groups to ensure that the workload on the total marketing department is realistic and resourced, and that the objectives and priorities communicated to the sales force are realistic. Depending on the structure of the marketing department the marketing director and marketing services manager or equivalent have an important role in ensuring that sales plans and priorities are not confused by too many conflicting requests and initiatives from product managers
3. The careful phasing of new product launches both within and between product groups

| Direct sales | Product group budgets | | | | | | Total region | |
|---|---|---|---|---|---|---|---|---|
| | A | | B | | C | | | |
| | $ | (%) | $ | (%) | $ | (%) | $ | (%) |
| Staff | | | | | | | | |
| Travel | | | | | | | | |
| Accommodation | | | | | | | | |
| Subsistence | | | | | | | | |
| Telephone | | | | | | | | |
| Secretarial | | | | | | | | |
| Stationery | | | | | | | | |
| (a) | | | | | | | | |
| *Promotion* | | | | | | | | |
| Entertainment | | | | | | | | |
| Promotions | | | | | | | | |
| Exhibitons | | | | | | | | |
| Demonstrations | | | | | | | | |
| Advertisements | | | | | | | | |
| Brochures | | | | | | | | |
| Data sheets | | | | | | | | |
| Articles | | | | | | | | |
| Models | | | | | | | | |
| Throw-away gifts | | | | | | | | |
| Diaries/calenders | | | | | | | | |
| Other | | | | | | | | |
| (b) | | | | | | | | |
| (a)+(b) | | | | | | | | |

**Figure 6.6**   Allocation of sales budget

4. The quality of sales forecasts and competitive intelligence fed back from the sales force
5. The quality of product briefings by product managers to the sales force
6. The calibre of product managers appointed to manage product groups. Product managers will need to gain the respect of the sales force not by virtue of their status, rank or education but through demonstrated professionalism, sustained support, knowledge and realistic plans and ideas

**Relationships with international subsidiaries**

Effective working relationships are as critical in multinational companies but often more difficult to establish. A typical organization structure for product management in a multinational company is illustrated in Fig. 6.7.

Six common problems occur that can only be resolved with forethought and careful planning by senior management in support of product managers. The problems and solutions are outlined on page 154.

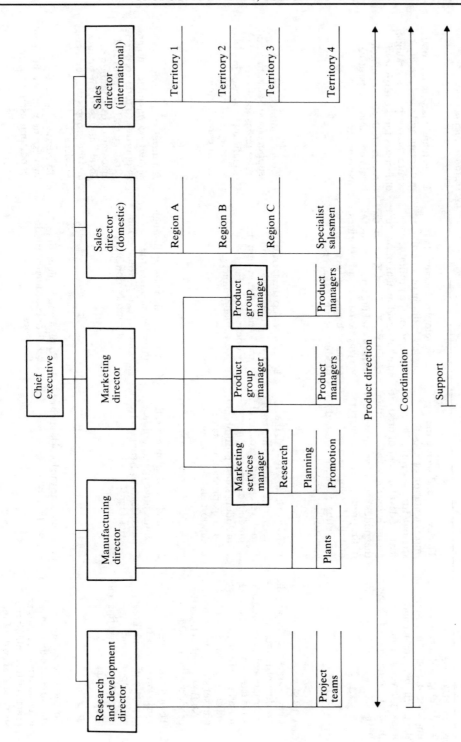

**Figure 6.7**   Illustrative multinational product management structure

**Table 6.4**   Comparison of roles of typical product and market managers

| 1. *Product group manager* | 2. *Product manager* | 3. *Market manager* | 4. *Territorial general manager-based internationally, running a foreign branch, subsidiary or regional sales activity* |
| --- | --- | --- | --- |
| **MAIN PURPOSE** To develop and secure the implementation of a strategy for the profitable product and market development of product group X on a worldwide basis | To develop and secure the implementation of a local strategy for the profitable market development of product group X for the territory within the guidelines to overall strategy of the product group manager, and the development and marketing of locally sourced compatible products | To develop and secure the implementation of a local strategy for the profitable market development of product group W, X, Y and Z within the territory taking into account the varying demands and priorities of the strategies of corporate product group managers | To plan and manage the total marketing and sales activity to secure the company's strategic objectives for the territory through products that match local needs and competitive environment |
| **KEY TASKS** 1. Lead, direct and support the product group team, international marketing and sales executives in planning for and achieving an improving trend in sales, market share, profits and cash flow secured from the product group worldwide | 1. To work closely with the corporate product manager to develop and agree local product business plan, including sales, profitability, pricing, promotion, sales support and sales activity | 1. To develop the territory's total product sales and marketing plan within the guidelines of strategies of individual product groups | 1. To lead, direct, develop and support local marketing and sales teams to secure significant increases in volume, market share and profit contribution |
| 2. To audit and analyse worldwide competitive opportunities and threats with support from international marketing and sales managers | 2. To audit and analyse local competitive opportunities and threats with support from sales team | 2. To plan and manage through the sales manager the achievement of volume and profit contribution objectives | 2. To develop local business strategy compatible with and supportive to total corporate strategy that identifies and maximizes exploitation of local business opportunities for the group's products and services |
| 3. To audit, report and encourage changes in international attitudes and practices that inhibit the successful growth of the product group | 3. To manage the local launch of new products | 3. To plan and implement a series of coordinated product launches | 3. To advise corporate management of new business opportunities in the region |

4. To plan and secure directly or by persuasion the type and extent of product/market support required by foreign sales operations

5. To plan, agree and progress with research and development a product development programme to secure a competitive flow of improved and new products

6. To budget for and secure corporate product promotional programme and provide guidelines for local promotional activity

7. To develop and implement personally, and through local managers, a comprehensive product training programme

ACCOUNTABILITY
*Worldwide*
Margins
Profit
Return on capital employed
Cash flow
Market share
Market volume of product group as a business

---

4. To provide territorial sales support in terms of customer support

5. To collect, collate and communicate market intelligence in order to identify local opportunities and assist product group manager to assess priorities and changes in developing and updating product strategies and plans

6. To budget for and secure local product promotion within corporate product group and local promotional guidelines

7. To develop local product training and support programme with support from product group manager

*Local*
Margins
Profit contribution
Market share
Volume

---

4. To coordinate requests for product support for corporate and local resources

5. To collect, collate and communicate market intelligence to assist both the territorial general manager and product group manager

6. To coordinate planning and implementation of local promotional activity in balance with corporate promotional support

7. To assist in development and implementation of marketing and sales training and development programme

*Local*
Volume
Market share
Margins
Profit contribution

---

4. To ensure that product managers receive a regular flow of competitive intelligence

5. To cooperate with, take benefit from and support activities of corporate and local product managers

6. To budget for and manage combined local promotional programme

7. To direct and supervise the development and implementation of local training and development programme for marketing, sales and customer support staff

*Local*
Profit contribution
Cash flow
Return on capital employed
Market share new and old products
Sales volume new and old products

*Problem 1*
Confusion between accountability of product manager and territorial management for market strategy, budget and sales plans
    Typical solutions are to:

(a)  Establish an integrated planning and control system as outlined in Chapter 2
(b)  Emphasize product managers global coordinating and support role and local
     management direct management role
(c)  Establish comprehensive territorial budgets.

*Problem 2*
Territorial managers resent authority of product managers to explore, evaluate
and comment on the financial implications of local marketing and sales decisions
and actions
    Typical solutions are to:

(a)  Emphasize product managers global coordinating and support role
(b)  Ensure that product managers are well selected and trained to enable them to
     secure respect rather than conflict

*Problem 3*
Conflict over timescales and contents of plans
    Typical solutions are to:

(a)  Establish different time perspectives, e.g. product management five-year
     strategy and forecast with three-year action plans and budget, and territorial
     time perspectives as three-year strategy and forecast with one-year action
     plans
(b)  Involve territorial manager, locally allocated sales executive or product or
     market manager in product group strategy sessions

*Problem 4*
Confusion over the parallel roles of worldwide product managers and territorial
product or market managers
    Typical solutions are to:

(a)  Develop, communicate and reach agreement on job descriptions along the
     lines of Table 6.4. Emphasize that all four jobs have a common purpose — to
     ensure the future commercial success of strategically important product
     groups
(b)  Ensure equitable job gradings that support achievement of corporate
     objective and typical career paths

*Problem 5*
Poor feedback of market intelligence from sales force to product managers
    Typical corrective actions are to:

(a)  Discuss needs and likely sources, and benefits to the sales force of allocating
     time and effort to the task
(b)  Develop a standard market intelligence report form

*Problem 6*
Inadequate allocation of sales resources to product range where territories allocate salesmen to sell a number of product groups in parallel
Typical corrective actions are to:

(a) Negotiate allocation of realistic sales time to product group in line with company objectives, profit contribution of product groups and quality of sales support provided by product managers
(b) Product managers to develop and aid implementation of comprehensive product training for sales force through product briefings, training sessions or distance learning manuals

**Sales training**

The effective training of salesmen, sales engineers and account executives will include five areas of knowledge, the balance between them varying according to the nature of the product and market for the product.

1. *Sales skills:* the development of the planning and interpersonal skills associated with identifying prospects, establishing contact, achieving a sale and maintaining the ongoing commercial relationship and empathy important to achieving the repeat and expanded sales essential to a secure market share
2. *Sales administration:* the development of understanding and acceptance of the company's policies and practices related to sales forecasts, reporting of orders, processing expenses and other administrative matters
3. *Product knowledge:* the development of awareness, understanding and commitment to current and new products and services
4. *Competitive knowledge:* the development of a deeper awareness and understanding of competitors, the strengths and weaknesses of their products, their marketing strategies, customer base, and so on
5. *Market awareness:* the development of awareness and understanding of the nature of marketing, the marketing strategies for specific products and the market/product support available from the product management team

The territorial sales manager or marketing manager will normally be accountable for areas (1) and (2). The others are essentially joint tasks of the product manager and territorial manager.

In situations where territorial sales teams, subsidiaries or affiliate companies are accountable for the sale of a number of product ranges, each competing for time and attention, it is important that the product manager takes the initiative in establishing timely training needs analysis; and arranging timely product briefings for new products and services prior to and in follow-up to launches.

A typical training needs questionnaire designed for self-analysis by sales engineers in a capital engineering product situation is illustrated in Fig. 6.8. With minor modifications this questionnaire is applicable to a wide range of situations.

Company.
Self-review of sales training needs
Analysis completed by:

Territory:
Date:

| | Level of personal needs | | | Current level of knowledge/ability | | | | Personal view of priority training needs for 19— |
|---|---|---|---|---|---|---|---|---|
| A. *Product range training needs* | *High* | *Medium* | *Low* | *Nil* | *Poor* | *Satisfactory* | *Excellent* | |
| Product A | | | | | | | | |
| Product B | | | | | | | | |
| Product C | | | | | | | | |
| Product D | | | | | | | | |
| Product support services | | | | | | | | |
| Financial packages | | | | | | | | |
| B. *Sales skills needs* | | | | | | | | |
| Sales prospecting | | | | | | | | |
| Call planning | | | | | | | | |
| Face-to-face selling skills | | | | | | | | |
| Identification of customer needs | | | | | | | | |
| Preparation of formal offer | | | | | | | | |
| Presentation of formal offer | | | | | | | | |
| Negotiation | | | | | | | | |
| Sales forecasting | | | | | | | | |
| Budgeting | | | | | | | | |
| Licensing/collaborations | | | | | | | | |

Reviewed by:
Date:

**Figure 6.8** Example of sales training needs analysis

## The sales force as a source of information

In addition to the provision of sales forecasts, the sales force should be an important source for the product manager of vital up-to-date information about competitors. The sales force is the only part of the organization structure in regular contact with current and potential customers of the company and specific product groups, and the customers of competitors and their specific competitive product groups.

Motivated sales professionals become very aware of the field information important to product management decisions and plans and provide regular and timely market intelligence. This might include:

● Ideas for new products or services or improvements to current offerings
● Changes in customers' strategies and supply demands
● Samples of competitive products and literature
● Changes in customers' end products and the potential implication for own products
● Lists of current, potential and competitors' customers
● The level of activity of competitors and the front-end focus of their marketing strategies and initiatives
● Changes in competitors' product packing and distribution, and customers' vision of product strengths and weaknesses
● Special promotional campaigns, particularly those focused on prices, volume discounts and low-interest customer financing
● Views on current and potential market trends, opportunities and threats

However, the extent to which such information is retrieved varies considerably.

Fig. 6.9 illustrates an analysis carried out by the product management team of a company in a specialist product business. The relationship between the product managers and sales force was good. Most sales engineers included competitor reports in their monthly sales report pack. One copy of these went to the territorial sales manager for information and to provide vital inputs to decisions related to territorial sales strategies, customer strategies and sales forecasts. Another copy went to the most appropriate product manager. Cumulatively the returns provided a vital input to product strategy reviews to which selected sales engineers were invited.

However, in one of its competitor companies, the reverse was true. The relationship between the product manager and sales force was poor. Requests for information were ignored or poorly completed. The territorial sales manager took the attitude that his team was there to sell short-term and that any intrusion into a sales engineer's time was an excuse for an extra hour in the office and non-productive. Product managers were not welcome at territorial sales events and customer visits rarely aranged for product managers. Luckily there was a way out.

After much effort the product group manager of a new product range, vital to the company and vital to the territory's medium-term success, secured a platform at a quarterly sales meeting to present his product range. He used the opportunity to provide a product briefing commencing with the product strategy and concluding with a detailed briefing on the product's competitive features and benefits, but with an indication of missing links in current competitive

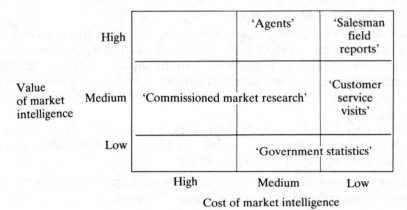

Figure 6.9 Relative value of market intelligence

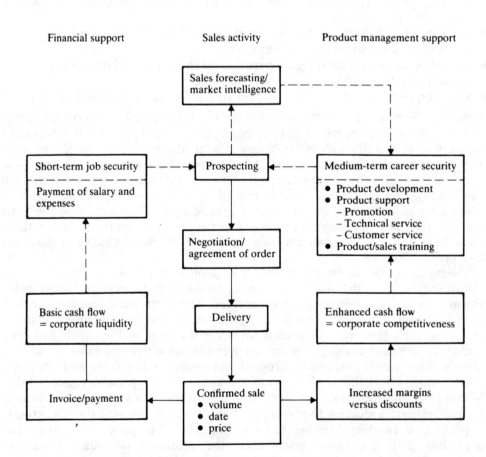

**Figure 6.10** Practical relationships between sales and product management

intelligence; presented a model illustrating the copartnership between product management and sales, as illustrated in Fig. 6.10; and concluded by asking for any up-to-date market intelligence overnight, issuing a basic questionnaire along the lines of Table 6.5.

The seeds were sown. Half the sales engineers responded well; the others were embarrassed by their apparent lack of market knowledge at a post-breakfast debriefing. Over the next year the basis of a productive intelligence network was established. The product manager started to receive more information and more accurate forecasts. The sales engineers had accepted their role as local marketing engineers and the associate status in the product management team referred to in Chapter 1.

**Contacts with customers**

Two important tasks of the product manager have been previously highlighted; first, ensuring that current and future products and services match the current and

**Table 6.5**   *Sales force market intelligence – a first step*

To: Sales engineers                                                                                    Date 2.1.--

From: Product manager/sales manager

To enable us to establish a better understanding of the marketplace for product group X please complete this short questionnaire and return for collection prior to the product briefing at 10 a.m. on 6.1.--

1. What is the most significant piece of market intelligence that you have picked up in the last month related to

   (a) your competitors:
   (b) your customers:

2. Excluding ABC products, *what* is the most successful product in your marketplace?
   Who sells it?
   When was it launched?
   Why is it successful?

3. What specific, or type of, product, if launched within two years would be most beneficial to you in expanding sales with

   (a) current cutomers

   (b) new customers

4. Which customer presents the greatest potential for growth in 1990 in your marketplace?

   What support would be helpful in ensuring that you obtain this additional business (e.g. technical service, packaging, product training etc.)?
   If this support were provided, what level of business from this customer can we expect:

   (a) Within one year?
   (b) Within two years?

future needs of the most significant buyers in selected market segments; second, that there is a company-wide customer-focused process of design, manufacture, distribution and post-sale service and support. It is therefore vital that product managers allocate time to visit strategically important customers at their premises, and customer groups at important conferences and exhibitions.

The choice of customers to visit should be made in conjunction with the regional, national and territorial sales managers, against the following criteria.

1. Significant existing or potential customers
2. Customers for whom the company's products/services are of strategic importance, that is, critical to their future plans
3. A mix of well-satisfied customers and disgruntled present and past customers
4. Customers who have ideas for new products or product improvements
5. Customers who are possible partners in the development, evaluation and full-scale testing of products, prior to general launch in the marketplace
6. A mix of customers that will provide a balanced view of the international competitiveness of the company's products and services
7. Companies able and willing to discuss the competitive merits of both the product manager's products and competitive products in an objective manner
8. A mix of end-use and middleman customers, that is, distributors and agents

Senior management need to recognize that a desk-bound product manager at company headquarters will be at best an administrator, and that product champions will only emerge when product managers have the close understanding of markets that comes from contact with end-user customers. Money and time need to be budgeted towards this end.

---

**Chapter 6 – Key point summary**
*Establish good working relationships with the sales force*

1. Make the sales force associate members of the product management team
2. Establish mutually supportive working relationships
3. Communicate and understand each other's job descriptions, accountabilities and plans
4. Jointly develop an understanding of the buying process affecting the product
5. Establish regular strategic sales forecasts
6. Integrate product group and territorial market planning
7. Support comprehensive sales training
8. Use the sales force as a vital source of competitive information
9. Establish the profit and cash-flow accountability of the sales force
10. Visit future customers

# 7. Product managers and manufacturing

**Product managers' key task**

To establish effective working relationships with the manufacturing team to ensure that the team is aware of and responsive to the manufacturing implications of the product strategy; committed to the timely delivery of reliable products with the planned quality and cost structure, in the planned volume and sequence; and dedicated to customer-orientated commercial behaviour

## The need for effective relationships

The product manager is dependent on the manufacturing function for the manufacture of products of the right aesthetic and engineering quality, at the right cost, in the right quantity, packed and labelled in the right way, in the right sequence and at the right time. A close working relationship between the product management team and the manufacturing function is therefore vital. Without it a well-researched and designed product could become a disaster before even reaching the marketplace.

The development of a close working relationship depends on a number of factors.

First, it depends on the development of a manufacturing strategy that supports, and is complementary to, the product group strategy, as illustrated in Fig. 7.1 and Table 7.1. The manufacturing manager will be accountable for the preparation of the manufacturing strategy. Product managers have the responsibility to ensure that the manufacturing strategy reflects both the strategic and operational needs of their respective product groups, and to identify commercial conflicts of interest that emerge. The key decision as to 'what product is produced where' needs to be a joint product management and manufacturing decision to ensure a balance between total corporate profitability, return on investment and quality of customer service, rather than a decision determined only on the basis of manufacturing costs. Such decisions will be handled more objectively if

**Table 7.1**   Framework for manufacturing strategy

1. *Introduction*
   1.1   Statement product group strategic mission
   1.2   Statement of product/market priorities
      1.2.1  Existing products
      1.2.2  New products
   1.3   Volume trends
   1.4   Competitive trends

2. *Statement of manufacturing mission and objectives*
   2.1   Supportive mission to product group
   2.2   Plant capability and location
   2.3   Process development priorities
   2.4   Computer-integrated manufacturing systems
   2.5   Design, make, buy philosophy
   2.6   Sourcing materials, components, assemblies
   2.7   Supplier/subcontractor management
   2.8   Productivity/cost initiatives
   2.9   Total quality approach
   2.10  Industrial relations
   2.11  Personnel development
   2.12  Stockholding and supply
   2.13  Customer relations

3. *Key financial indicators and ratios*

manufacturing management has taken part in the type of product strategy review discussed in Chapter 2.

Second, it depends on the development and update of a comparison between the competitiveness of the manufacturing plants producing the products for the product group and national and international plants producing competitive products. Comparative studies need to review and assess the reliability of information available from the sales force, market research, technical department, customers, designers, competitors, suppliers, comparative market surveys, technical papers, process patents, and so on. Competitiveness profiles are a useful way of maintaining a summary of competitive comparisons as a focus for analysis and action.

Third, it depends on the development of manufacturing processes in both manufacturing and process industries that match the needs of the product group in terms of:

- Volume needs, now and over the next few years
- Seasonal fluctuations in demand
- The need for flexibility in mix of products produced within the product range
- Quality standards
- Cost trends and the need to maximize the benefit of the learning curve in respect of consecutive batches in batch production or cumulative volume in respect of long-run series or commodity products
- Lead times for introducing new plants
- The need to reduce payback time by controlling investment in new plant, particularly for products with short half-lives

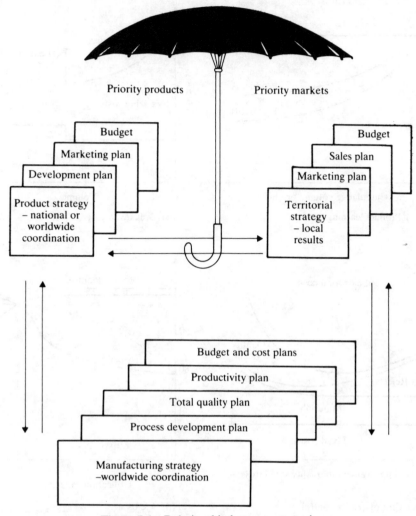

**Figure 7.1**  Relationship between strategies

The process development task is typically handled as a joint project between process development, manufacturing and product development departments through an integrated design–make–buy process. The project team needs to establish a number of important relationships (see Fig. 7.2), and as a result find answers to the following questions.

– What learning curve has been, and could be achieved? What are the implications for product costs and quality?

– What changes in materials, methods and technology are planned, which will require a period of retraining and orientation? What are the short-term cost penalties as well as the long-term benefits?

– Is the lowest total manufacturing cost synonymous with the level of quality required by customers? What premium can be built into prices to compensate and charge for quality added value as value for money?

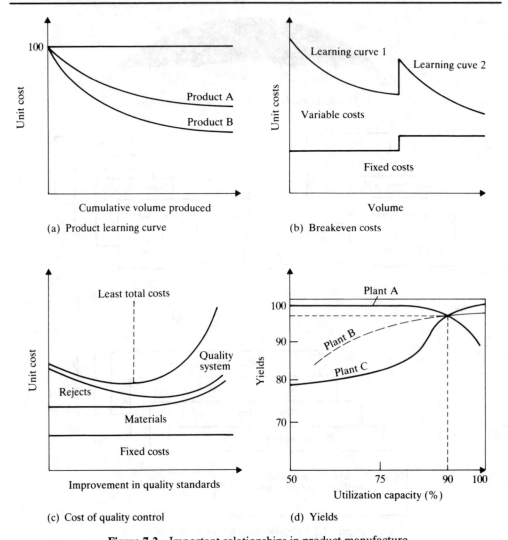

**Figure 7.2** Important relationships in product manufacture

- What yields are achieved at different plant loadings? What yield profile best fits market demands for the product?
- What are the scale effects? Would one large plant or a number of smaller distributed plants be most market- and profit-effective?

The answers will be vital inputs on the nature of the manufacturing unit required (see Fig. 7.3), and the development of best- and worst-case financial appraisals and budgets.

Fourth, it depends on the establishment of corporate or product-led programmes to examine and improve product quality and product productivity. These must recognize that in all cases the customer needs to be seen as number one.

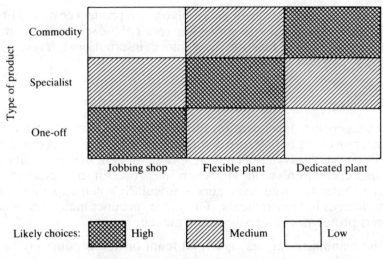

**Figure 7.3**   Choice of manufacturing unit

Finally, it depends on the establishment of mutually agreed standards for customer service and an action plan to secure the benefits.

### The impact of manufacturing processes on product decisions

The product manager with accountability for specifying products and steering the direction of the product development programme, needs to explore and understand the implications of emergent changes in the manufacturing technology affecting the manufacture of the product range.

In the process industry, process intensification and debottlenecking exercises can have major impacts on the sensitivity of production costs to variations in volume, fluctuations in product mix, adjustments to specifications to meet the needs of special customers, and the ability to achieve profit-effective growth.

In the advanced manufacturing industries, the integration of design, component manufacture and assembly achievable through computer-integrated management technology provides a flexibility that allows for profit-effective smaller batches, reduced product and parts inventory, speedier spares service, a wider variety of product specifications and ability to process specials.

In the garment industry in Europe, the introduction of computer-integrated cutting and making-up achieves lower costs than continuing to import garments from the Far East or South America.

As a result of such developments, the product manager achieves the ability to:

– Change designs and series more frequently and with reduced lead times, without incurring high abortive design or changeover costs
– Build and test a number of prototype products cost-effectively, before finalizing product specification; this provides a competitive power far beyond the traditional approach of producing one 'optimized' compromise prototype
– Respond to the different buying behaviours of major international customers

- Make more accurate investment decisions on new product costs and breakevens
- Raise the entry cost of low-cost copies as a result of the scale of investment made by the manufacturing function to achieve international levels of quality, productivity and cost-effectiveness

### Prototype planning

Product managers are dependent on the manufacturing manager for the timely and efficient processing of prototype products, whether a first-off machine tool for a major exhibition, the availability of on-spec samples of new speciality chemicals or a test range of children's wear. However, the processing of specials is a nuisance factor to most manufacturing managers, particularly when unplanned, rushed or subject to changes in requirements. Therefore, product managers need to plan and progress prototypes in a professional manner:

1. Brief the manufacturing manager and team on the product group strategy, including outline plans for the introduction of new or modified products
2. As soon as detailed plans are available, advise the manufacturing manager of the requirements in terms of volume, numbers, tonnes, litres, cans; quality standards (particularly changes required), new components and assemblies to be processed, timing of prototype batches, packaging and labelling needs; and cost targets
3. Prepare a risk analysis in conjunction with the manufacturing manager to ensure joint awareness of any potential problems associated with the agreed plan, resolve the problems and adjust product management objectives realistically, where major constraints are agreed
4. Nearer the date, arrange a briefing of the manufacturing supervisors and shop floor, who will be involved in prototype production, to ensure an understanding of the importance of the new product to the company, and achieve commitment to a special effort
5. Visit the manufacturing unit during the manufacture of the prototype to reinforce belief in the product, and the urgency of success
6. Shortly after the production of the prototype, arrange a debriefing session involving the shop floor and design and development, to gather ideas for improving the design and manufacturing process for the final product prior to full production
7. Provide feedback to manufacturing on the success of the new product via product briefings, success stories in the company newspaper and customer visits by satisfied customers arranged by the sales force

### Productivity potentials

Productivity is a major problem, one that has existed for some time. In recent years, many companies and product groups have without doubt achieved significant improvements, at least in the area of labour productivity. However, for many others, efforts to date will probably not sustain competitiveness until the 1990s, and certainly not through the 1990s. Continued efforts to raise productivity to the highest international standards need to be sustained if an increased share of potentially profitable orders is to be won.

During the late 1970s productivity was seen as a problem of labour rates, and of competing with other national companies. During the 1980s it has been a more fundamental issue: one of international competitiveness and survival. No longer can productivity be seen as merely an operational issue. It has become a critical strategic resource.

First, the strategic decisions taken by boards of directors and product managers in respect of corporate priority market sectors, products, customer groups and new technologies. All have a major impact on the potential for productivity improvement arising from both the potential for increased output or sales and the potential for improved manufacturing productivity.

Second, international competitiveness in the chosen markets, and the ability to fund investments in new product development and new manufacturing techniques such as robots, depend on manufacturing management's achieving ongoing and sustained improvements in total productivity.

Total productivity is a process to which all manufacturing managers and engineers can contribute.

*Six key resources*
Traditionally, many works managers, supervisors and support staff have focused too narrowly on labour productivity. Today, manufacturing managers are generally more conscious of the importance of: added value achieved per employee; value for money and life-time cost to the customer; and delivery performance and technical support to international standards.

Productivity in the 1990s needs to be approached as the management of six key resources: the productive allocation and utilization of managers' time, money, manufacturing space, materials, machinery and manpower in achieving the only output that matters — competitive products and services. The benefits of the broader perspective are:

1. Productivity can be communicated as the foundation for international competitiveness rather than merely as the basis for wage bargaining
2. Managers, supervisors, support staff and hourly-paid employees can more readily recognize their respective contributions to improving the competitiveness of the products and services they produce or provide
3. A productivity improvement programme can incorporate all the functions involved in achieving total productivity in the manufacturing function: conceptual design, manufacturing design, purchasing, production, quality assurance, personnel, accounts

However, there are four basic success factors to establishing such a productivity drive. First, productivity must be seen as an ongoing requirement and not merely as a short-term blitz. Second, productivity improvements must start at the top with senior manufacturing management establishing (a) the urgency of productivity improvements as an essential part of the strategic initiatives of the company, and (b) the priority areas for attack and specific objectives. Third, there has to be a concentrated effort to change attitudes and behaviour not only within the manufacturing function but also within all functions with which manufacturing interfaces. Fourth, there has to be a product group focus to achieve dedication and commitment.

*Measuring productivity*

Six productivity ratios can be singled out which measure the gearing between output or resources generated and inputs or resources consumed. They provide a useful starting point for identifying where the greatest scope for productivity improvement lies.

1. Total productivity, expressed as:

$$\frac{\text{added value}}{\text{salaries} + \text{capital}}$$

This is equivalent to:

$$\frac{\text{sales} - \text{materials/services} + \text{work-in-progress}}{\text{salaries and wage-related costs} + \text{depreciation and revenue investment}}$$

2. $$\frac{\text{Production to quality standards first time}}{\text{Total production}}$$

3. $$\frac{\text{Delivery performance}}{\text{Competitive performance}}$$

4. $$\frac{\text{Direct costs}}{\text{Overhead costs}}$$

5. $$\frac{\text{Land (space) used productively}}{\text{Total land (space)}}$$

6. $$\frac{\text{Production}}{\text{Design capacity}}$$

*The human bottleneck*

The establishment of priority areas and tentative improvement objectives is, however, only the first step; achieving improved productivity involves change. In many cases, what is done and how must change, rather than how much is done by old methods and techniques. Successful change implies gaining the understanding and commitment of managers and supervisors as well as the shop floor.

Major breakthroughs and step improvements in productivity come about not through overdetailed analysis of productivity, but through creative thinking concerned with

- Designing new products for productive manufacture
- Designing manufacturing processes with characteristics that match the demand profile of products; large dedicated capacity plants for commodity products with a high probability of shortage of plant capacity; medium-sized, flexible plants for more specialist, varied product demands; jobbing manufacturing plants or process plants for multirange specialist products or small runs

- Computer-integrated management systems in machine-driven manufacturing plants, process plants and distribution warehouses
- Use of biotechnology versus chemical approaches to products and processes
- Computerization of CAD/CAM designer links with supplier machine tools
- The involvement of the total manufacturing staff in the productivity movement and, at the right time, their close associates: product designers, suppliers, process engineers, planners, cost accountants, project managers and the product manager
- Achieving the compatibility and user friendliness of office equipment and systems to achieve breakthroughs in white-collar productivity in the planning office, in the quality-control laboratory, and on the shop floor

Unfortunately, human nature being what it is, many managers and engineers do not have a natural motivation and curiosity continually to seek out and follow up ways of achieving productivity improvement. Even in busy times, the manufacturing environment creates opportunities for allocating time to 'interesting personal technical' problems rather than 'critical product competitiveness' problems (see Fig. 7.4).

Increasingly, companies are recognizing the benefits of a formalized approach to improving manufacturing productivity. Such an approach can incorporate all the functions associated with the design, manufacture and servicing of specific products and services.

*Guidelines*
The following guidelines are applicable to both large- and small-scale manufacturing activity. They are readily translated into guidelines for productivity improvement programmes in other situations.

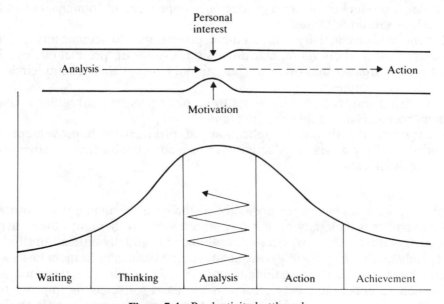

**Figure 7.4**   Productivity bottleneck

1. Analyse recent trends in productivity levels and gain some indication of competitive levels of productivity in the industrial sector
2. Organize a one-day productivity workshop for the 10–20 senior managers and support specialists with the following agenda:

   (a) Review of product group strategy
   (b) Review of implications for manufacturing strategy
   (c) Establishment of priority areas for productivity improvement
   (d) Start to establish action plans for tackling these areas focused on product competitiveness

3. Organize a series of similar workshops for the junior managers and manufacturing support staff
4. Establish specific objectives and action plans for each section in the plant
5. Establish a number of task forces to tackle broader issues. For maximum impact the members of a task force should comprise a mix of production managers and supervisors, product service managers and related functional managers (e.g. design, estimating, etc.). Topics allocated to task forces to analyse on a part-time basis over 6–8 weeks might include:

   (a) Value analysis/value engineering of all aspects of a specific product
   (b) Materials management
   (c) Shop-floor training and motivation
   (d) How to modify products to help customers improve their own productivity

6. Establish a basic skill development programme for junior management within the company
7. Establish a regular verbal communication of key aspects of the product strategy, product results and productivity improvement to managers and all levels of subordinate staff
8. Extend the productivity improvement programme to technicians and key hourly-paid workers via regular discussion sessions or 'product circles'. The latter is a broader and often less emotional concept than quality circles or productivity circles
9. Establish a series of control charts to monitor progress at regular management meetings and display in the plant
10. Incorporate the financial implications of productivity improvement into budgets. Budget via productivity improvement objectives rather than resource allocation

*Productivity audits*
The above guidelines have been presented as the basis for an integrated process. Most companies will already have incorporated some of them into their current productivity efforts. There is, after all, nothing conceptually difficult in thinking about productivity, the difficulty is the action: doing basic management tasks well, keeping things simple. The questionnaire presented in Table 7.2 is designed as an aid to audit recent productivity efforts as the basis for selecting improvement initiatives for the near future. The survival of products and companies in the long

**Table 7.2** Productivity audit

| Question | Evaluation of effectiveness of current process | | | | Areas for priority action in 19— |
|---|---|---|---|---|---|
| | Poor | Fair | Good | Too sophisticated | |
| 1. How effective is the process of incorporating productivity improvement into annual budgets? | | | | | |
| 2. How effective are the productivity ratios used to monitor performance? | | | | | |
| 3. How effective is the process of updating priority objectives and action plans? | | | | | |
| 4. How effective is the process of gaining the commitment and motivation of managers and supervisors? | | | | | |
| 5. How effective is the process of involving other functions (supply, design, sales, etc.) in contributing to manufacturing productivity? | | | | | |
| 6. How effective is the process of generating improvement ideas from the shop floor? | | | | | |
| 7. How effective is the link between manufacturing productivity improvement and development of product group strategy? | | | | | |

term — if not the short term — depends on productivity being seen in the total business context. Product managers need to incorporate an analysis of competitive productivity into their strategic thinking.

Data-processing specialists can do much to improve the way in which information is processed and presented to enable managers to understand where they are and plan ahead effectively. But ultimately business success depends on the dedication of manufacturing management to be as productive in all aspects as the best in the USA, Japan, Europe and elsewhere.

## Management of product quality

Product quality is at the heart of product competitiveness and success. Yet only in the last decade has the quality crusade become truly international. However, even now day-to-day experience demonstrates that attitudes towards quality management and, even more importantly, behaviour at all corporate hierarchy levels, vary from international excellence to national and corporate disaster, as illustrated in Table 7.3.

Historically, the guilds and livery companies of the twelfth and thirteenth centuries established a strict discipline over the work of member craftsmen. In parallel, the merchants of the fifteenth century and earlier funded expeditions to secure new products and exerted discipline and control on both price and quality.

**Table 7.3**   Typical quality attitudes and behaviour

| Approach | Laissez-faire | Inspection | Quality control | Quality assurance | Total quality management |
|---|---|---|---|---|---|
| Attitude | A nuisance factor | Can't trust the operator | Can't rely on line managers | Must have an operation-led system | Strategic corporate initiative vital |
| Behaviour | Crisis management —react to emergencies | Routine task — by junior staff | Administration — check of work management/ authorized by line managers in manufacturing | Introduction of plans, procedures and audits affecting design, supplies, manufacturing, servicing | Involve all functions and levels in integrated culture change programme |
| Led by | Chief executive or product manager by default | Foremen | Quality manager | Design director/ manufacturing director | Chief executive or product champion |

In the eighteenth century wealthy merchants took control of the emergent capital-intensive manufacturing equipment and manufacturing industries, and the role of the craftsmen in setting and maintaining quality standards started a downward trend which continued until recent years.

Since the end of the nineteenth century, research and development of quality practices has been continuously stimulated in many cases by the demands on defence industries and the requirements of new technologies, particularly those related to machining, electronics, power, transport and processing.

Foresighted companies in the USA and Europe recognized the opportunities for improving quality management, but many failed to respond until the Japanese — using hired help from American experts such as Juran and Deming — proved that improved quality and reduced costs and improved delivery performance can be synonymous.

Since the late 1970s, more and more companies have recognized the importance of adhering to international and national quality and reliability, assessment and certification systems such as BS 5750 and ISO 9000.

The actions required in preparation for, and to retain, certifications have proved a useful discipline for many companies, but in many cases do not go far enough in achieving a real day-to-day commitment at all employee levels, at all stages of the product cycle and treating the customer as king; the latter is a concept which has become lost over the years, and is now an issue product managers need to emphasize as an integral part of product strategies, product design briefs and product promotion.

The Japanese are said to have up to a three-decade head start in the learning curve. With much of the Japanese collective and authoritarian approach not directly transferable to countries and companies with more individualistic cultures, companies particularly in the USA and Europe need to establish their own profit-effective approaches towards quality excellence.

Product managers can play an important role in tackling this problem and in

**Table 7.4**  Statement of product-quality objectives

1. To deliver error-free and reliable competitive products or services on time to customers which, at least, match their expectations
2. To deliver products ready for service, complete with instructions, spares and maintenance manuals
3. To achieve recognition by all levels of staff, associated directly or indirectly with the product group, of their personal responsibility for the quality of products and services in all respects
4. Continuously to evaluate and upgrade systems, procedures, practices and services towards total quality in all company activity. To plan for prevention not correction
5. To maintain economic quality systems that meet the requirements of recognized national and international quality standards
6. To ensure customer confidence in total product quality and personal experience of the company achieving repeat orders

stimulating a productive total quality programme by taking the following seven-step approach.

1. Review the strengths and weaknesses of the quality aspects of own and competitive products as an input to product strategy reviews, product development reviews and product differentiation studies
2. Together with the product development and manufacturing members of the product group team, establish a statement of product quality objectives — an example is provided in Table 7.4
3. Initiate an estimate of total quality costs, as illustrated in Table 7.5 for a service and product. Not doing things right first time has become an expensive habit. Wastage in many manufacturing and service industries has been estimated to

**Table 7.5**  Illustrative estimate of total quality costs

| | Product | | Service | |
|---|---|---|---|---|
| | *Typical performance* | *Competitive performance* | *Typical performance* | *Competitive performance* |
| *Sales* | 100 | 100 | 100 | 100 |
| *Source of quality costs* | | | | |
| Overspecification by marketing, sales and design | 10 | 1 | 10 | 2 |
| Design modifications | 5 | 1 | 1 | 0 |
| Scrap/rectification | 2 | ½ | 1 | — |
| Reprocessing | 2 | ½ | 5 | 2 |
| Out-of-stage work | 2 | 0 | 2 | 0 |
| Rejection supplies | 2 | ½ | 2 | ½ |
| Materials handling and storage losses | 2 | 1 | 2 | ½ |
| Quality assurance system | 2 | 3 | 5 | ½ |
| Quality training | 0 | ½ | 0 | ½ |
| Customer support | 1 | 1 | 1 | 1 |
| Warranty insurance/payments | 2 | 1 | 1 | 1 |
| % sales | 30 | 10 | 30 | 8 |

cost 20 per cent of sales value, which represents direct reductions in profit and cash flow.

4. In association with product development and manufacturing, organize a quality strategy session to:

   (a) Review the present state of attitudes, actions and achievements towards competitive total quality standards
   (b) Establish specific objectives and action plans
   (c) Achieve multifunctional understanding, concern and commitment to change

5. Involve representatives of sales, marketing, product management, product development, quality assurance, finance, buying, customer service and manufacturing in the process to lever out interfunctional quality problems and evaluate all issues from design specifications to the attitude of the company telephonist towards customers

6. Follow up by reviewing progress as an agenda item at product group review meetings and when visiting the manufacturing plants

7. Check out customers' perceptions of product quality and the attitude of the company towards customer service and quality when visiting current and potential customers

### Customer service levels

The delivery performance from the manufacturing unit to the customer is a vital aspect of the competitive mix for all products. It is important, therefore, that the product manager, together with the manufacturing team, establishes specific, unambiguous and realistic standards of customer service, which focus on excellence in all respects from initial telephone enquiries to final delivery and support.

Company Q, a producer of bulk liquid products, established the following standards as a starting point. They were quantified and refined as a result of experience and the availability of accurate records and trend analysis.

● Lead times on standard product from order to availability for despatch, e.g. days
● Lead times on special blends, e.g. days
● Delivery reliability, e.g. hours on promised time
● Volumes delivered, e.g. ± per cent of order
● Time to handle customer telephone technical queries, e.g. minutes
● Lead time for samples. e.g. days

Because of conflicting demands, establishing customer service standards is never simple. The customer often wants almost instant service. The sales force wishes to match customers' needs with attractive offers including early, perhaps unrealistic, delivery dates. The product manager knows that not all customers can be satisfied on this basis and the manufacturing manager seeks stability in the pattern and mix of orders to secure a stable production plan and facilitate the achievement of maximum production output and optimum unit production costs.

Balancing the needs requires a careful segmentation of customers based on their strategic importance.

Company Q produced processed raw materials for the food industry. The product range had recently been updated, sales volumes had increased steadily and the plant was now working on a six-day three-shift system, Sunday being a maintenance day.

The demand for the improved products was forecast to be greater than plant capacity, particularly since a major competitor had plant problems and was missing delivery dates. The product manager saw this as an opportunity to weed out the bad customers from the good and secure a firm base of good customers who would be afforded a five-star service. The choice in a manner not unlike the example shown in Table 7.6.

**Table 7.6** Identification of five-star customers

|  | Customer | | | | |
| --- | --- | --- | --- | --- | --- |
|  | A | B | C | D | E |
| Volume customer | 5 | 4 | 2 | 3 | 1 |
| Customer for standard product | 5 | 5 | 5 | 0 | 5 |
| Existing customer | 5 | 5 | 0 | 0 | 5 |
| First-time customer from competitor | 0 | 0 | 5 | 5 | 0 |
| Prompt payer | 4 | 3 | 2 | 5 | 2 |
| Demand for specials | (−1) | 0 | 0 | (−5) | 0 |
| Customer score | 18 | 17 | 14 | 8 | 13 |
| Five-star status | Yes | Yes | No | No | No |

The system was introduced as follows.

Five-star customers were divided among a number of customer service staff members. These handled all the orders, queries, and communications with their allocated customers. Sales executives visited five-star customers and explained the system and offered improved standards of service in return for a quarterly forecast of needs and firm fortnightly delivery at call. These customers provided the base production load and were given a guaranteed service.

The difficult customers — those requesting non-standard products and late payers — were offered longer but firm dates but, more importantly, were quoted a premium price for the special formulations, making it worth while to run a special batch once in a while but not weekly.

Other customers were considered on a week-by-week basis and offered realistic delivery dates determined by the capacity available after five-star cutomers had been satisfied.

The five-star customers became more loyal, and other customers recognized the benefits of securing this status. Win–win situations were achieved, with gains in sales, repeat orders, referrals, increased market share, ability to drop sales visits to and the servicing of bad customers, and a significant improvement in financial results. Most importantly, both customers and the sales force began to believe that

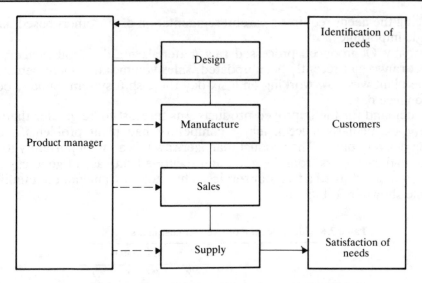

**Figure 7.5** Driving for customer satisfaction

the manufacturing team cared. Similar case histories abound in banks, airlines, hotels and manufacturing industry.

Product managers often play a key role in leading or supporting a chief executive in initiating, securing and sustaining such programmes. Product managers are after all in a key position (see Fig. 7.5).

## Chapter 7 — Key point summary
*Product managers and the manufacturing function*

1. Establish close working relationships
2. Clarify manufacturing strategy
3. Preplan prototypes and new products
4. Integrate the design, make or buy processes
5. Drive productivity and quality towards competitiveness and value for money to the customer
6. Instil enthusiasm for the product down to the shop floor
7. Respect customers by giving them a five-star service
8. Establish the marketing concept in manufacturing

# 8. Product managers and finance

**Product managers' key task**

To establish, with support from the management accountant and systems development manager, effective product-related systems and procedures for financial planning, budgeting, monitoring, control and investigatory analysis

### Product financial objectives

In Chapter 1 the fundamental objective of introducing product management was stated as the achievement of a level of product profitability above that which would otherwise be achieved by means of a traditional functional organization structure. So by introducing a product management structure, corporate management will expect the trend in profits to demonstrate an incremental improvement. Improved levels of profit will be achieved through a variety of decisions and actions, some influenced directly by the product manager, and some indirectly.

The product manager needs to establish a framework of financial plans, budgets and controls which enable the impact of his or her own decisions to be evaluated, monitored and controlled; and the impact of decisions and actions by other persons, involved in development, manufacture, marketing, sales and servicing, to be monitored and investigated, where significant positive or negative variances occur.

Fig. 8.1 provides a framework for establishing product financial objectives and controls, and illustrates the relationships between the various objectives. It hardly needs to be said that profit, the accounting difference between sales and total expenses, is a major objective. Corporate management and product managers involved in decisions on the location of factories, warehouses and service centres will be interested in profit after tax, as well as in profit before tax and gross profit levels. Profit after tax will be affected by the tax rates, depreciation allowances and regional development grant structure of the various regions and countries in which the fixed assets associated with a product group are located.

All product managers should monitor and consider how to improve profit before tax, since decisions on prices and expenses affect cash flow and, therefore,

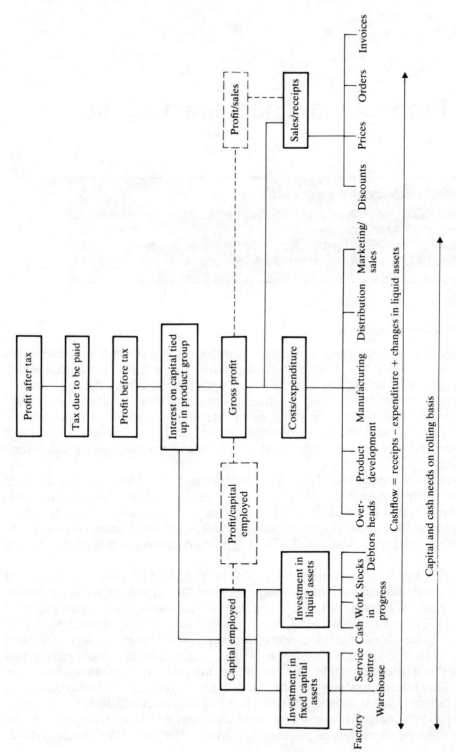

**Figure 8.1**  Financial framework for product objectives and controls

working capital, interest payments and gross profits, the rolling difference between recorded sales and expenses.

1. *Profit/capital employed* — the ratio between profit generated from a specific capital investment in a product group to the amount invested. The ratio can be calculated as profit/total capital employed or profit/fixed investment
2. *Sales/working capital* — to indicate the utilization and turnover of investment cash
3. *Gross profit/sales* — a quick ratio to indicate the trend in product profitability
4. *Cash flow* — the real-time difference between receipts and expenditure adjusted for any changes in money tied up in work-in-progress and finished stocks. Cash flow is often monitored as cash flow/sales to check on the cash generating power of products

## Objectives and budgets

Financial objectives are an agreed statement of results that can be realistically aimed for and achieved over a period of time, under anticipated market conditions, as illustrated in Fig. 8.2. They need to be specific quantified statements, incorporating a desirable financial improvement and the time-scale for achieving the improvement. The objectives can then be communicated and achievements monitored and evaluated on an ongoing basis. Financial objectives will be established as an integral part of strategic and operational planning and will influence, and be influenced by, the financial budgeting process (see Fig. 8.3).

The financial budget will be a realistic statement of the most likely financial transactions associated with a product group, incorporating all relevant sales and

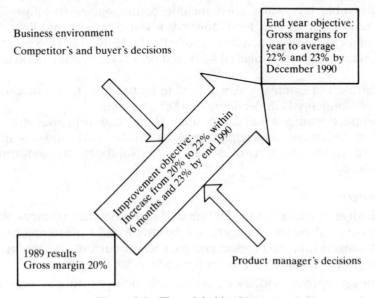

**Figure 8.2**   Financial objectives

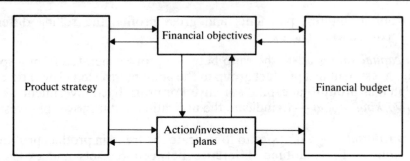

**Figure 8.3** Financial objectives setting process

costs for a period, typically 6, 12 or 24 months, and the cash-generating power of a product or product group

Two important features of the budget are likely to be targets for:

1. *working capital/sales* as an indication of the utilization of the capital tied up in a product or product group
2. *shareholder value* as an assessment of the value of the product group as a business entity to the parent company if retained or sold off as an operating business. This is normally calculated as a multiple of profits, asset value or forecast future cash flows

The relationship between financial objectives and budgets will depend on the company's budgeting philosophy.

Company A has an aggressive approach to budgets. Budgets are challenging and tight, and the objective is to achieve the budgeted figures for profits, sales and costs. In this case budgets tend towards a best-case situation.

Company B has a conservative approach to budgets. Sales levels are set at a safely achievable level, and costs include contingencies to allow for possible adverse trends. The budget tends towards a worst-case or middle position. The financial objectives are set at a level above the budgets, that is to say, the product manager aims to exceed budgeted sales and profits and underspend on budgeted costs.

The approach of Company A will tend to be used in growth market situations and that of Company B in declining market situations.

The product manager needs to understand and influence the company's financial management philosophy, and to ensure that budgets prepared by different functions and territories can be consolidated and interpreted in an agreed manner.

### Product budgets

Product budgets are an essential feature of the product management planning and control process. Product managers will be involved in preparing or collating a variety of budgets for total product groups, specific current and planned products. The basic ground rules for useful budgets are as follows:

1. The budget represents today's most realistic view of future revenues, costs and appropriate interrelationships

2. The budget is prepared on the basis of a profit-centre or cost-centre, dependent on the accountability of the product manager in a specific situation
3. Product group budgets should represent a financial plan for the implementation of the first year of a three- to five-year product strategy, and should anticipate the achievement of specific objectives and the cost implications of specific agreed courses of action
4. Product group budgets can be drawn up by product, by territory, by current and new products, by market segment, by key customers, and so on
5. Special budgets will be required for a specific product development, a product launch, a product strategy session, a training programme or a tour of foreign subsidiaries and affiliates
6. Where possible, budgets should be subject to a sensitivity analysis before being finalized to ensure that they are realistic and reliable under anticipated market conditions

A typical budget and sensitivity analysis is illustrated in Table 8.1. The sensitivity analysis enables a product manager to establish and present a picture of most probable, and possible best- and worst-case financial results. Budgets supported by sensitivity analyses are an essential part of the proposal pack requesting capital expenditure related to a product group, for instance, in proposing new manufacturing facilities, the extension of a product warehouse, point-of-sale merchandizing units, the acquisition of a source of in-fill or related products, etc.

## Monthly financial reports

The product manager requires monthly or four-weekly financial reports indicating actual achievements against budget, and an indication of likely year-end results

**Table 8.1**  Product budget

|  |  | Budget | Best case[1] | Worst case[2] |
|---|---|---|---|---|
| Sales |  | 1000 | 1050 | 950 |
| Costs: | Sales force | 100 | 100 | 105 |
|  | Marketing | 100 | 100 | 100 |
|  | Product support | 50 | 50 | 50 |
|  | Distribution | 50 | 50 | 50 |
|  | Manufacturing | 500 | 475 | 525 |
|  | Product development | 100 | 100 | 110 |
| Total costs |  | 900 | 875 | 940 |
| Gross profit |  | 100 | 175 | 10 |

Notes: [1] Assumes 5 per cent increase in sales and 5 per cent improvement in manufacturing costs possible
[2] Assumes 5 per cent shortfall in sales and 5 per cent reduction in sales productivity, and 5 per cent inflation of manufacturing costs as well as 10 per cent overrun in product development costs

**Table 8.2**   Monthly financial report, product group X period 5, 1990

| | Budget | | Actual | | Variance (%) | | Periods 1–13 | | |
|---|---|---|---|---|---|---|---|---|---|
| | Period | Cumulative | Period | Cumulative | Period | Cumulative | Budget | Best forecast | Variance (%) |
| Sales | 1000 | 4800 | 1100 | 5100 | 10 | 6.3 | 14000 | 15000 | 7.1 |
| Product A | 500 | 2200 | 600 | 2300 | 20 | 4.5 | 7000 | 7500 | 7.1 |
| Product B | 300 | 1600 | 350 | 1900 | 16.7 | 18.8 | 4500 | 5500 | 22.2 |
| Product C | 200 | 1000 | 150 | 900 | (25) | (10) | 2500 | 2000 | (20.0) |
| Territory 1 | 400 | 1800 | 450 | 2000 | 12.5 | 11.1 | 6000 | 6800 | 13.3 |
| Territory 2 | 400 | 2000 | 400 | 2000 | 0 | 0 | 5000 | 5200 | 4.0 |
| Territory 3 | 200 | 1000 | 250 | 1100 | 25.0 | 10.0 | 3000 | 3400 | 13.3 |
| Cost of sales | 900 | 4368 | 985 | 4615 | 9.4 | 5.6 | 12530 | 13380 | 6.8 |
| Gross margin | 100 | 432 | 115 | 485 | 15.0 | 12.3 | 1470 | 1620 | 10.2 |
| Gross margin (%) sales | 10 | 9 | 10.5 | 9.5 | 5 | 5.6 | 10.5 | 10.8 | 2.9 |

compared to the original budget. A typical but simplified report format is illustrated in Table 8.2. In practice, the product manager would also require a breakdown of product sales by territory, and a detailed breakdown of costs in order to monitor the trend of key aspects of both variable and fixed costs.

**Table 8.3** Indication of product cost needs

| | |
|---|---|
| *Investigation needs* | – The need to be able to investigate the extent and cause of positive and negative variances in financial results |
| *Decision-making needs* | – The need to explore a variety of options based on a detailed knowledge of fixed and variable costs, direct and indirect costs |
| *Planning needs* | – The ability to cost and budget for specific action plans and programmes |
| *Control needs* | – The need to identify and monitor the costs that are controllable by the product management team and those controlled by the board or other managers |

**Table 8.4** Illustrative cost analysis, product $X$

| Item | Fixed cost | Variable cost | Total costs |
|---|---|---|---|
| 1. Sales force | | | |
| 1.1 Salaries | | 85 | |
| 1.2 Incentives | | 10 | |
| 1.3 Expenses | | 10 | |
| 1.4 Training | | 5 | 110 |
| 2. *Marketing* | | | |
| 2.1 Advertising | | 20 | |
| 2.2 Brochures | | 20 | |
| 2.3 Exhibitions | | 10 | 50 |
| 3. *Distribution* | | | |
| 3.1 Transport | | 50 | |
| 3.2 Warehouse labour | | 5 | |
| 3.3 Warehouse facilities | 6 | 4 | 65 |
| 4. *Manufacturing* | | | |
| 4.1 Material | | 370 | |
| 4.2 Labour | | 190 | |
| 4.3 Utilities | | 70 | |
| 4.4 Facilities | 84 | 11 | 725 |
| 5. *Product improvement* | 10 | 70 | 80 |
| 6. *Product support* | 5 | 15 | 20 |
| 7. *Allocated overheads* | | | |
| 7.1 Services | 25 | | 50 |
| 7.2 Facilities | 25 | | |
| Total costs | 155 | 945 | 1100 |

## Product costs

An analysis of costs will be important to the product manager for purposes of evaluation, decision-making, planning and control, as outlined in Table 8.3. An illustrative cost analysis indicating the nature of the costs involved, is outlined in Table 8.4.

## Working capital

A key ratio for the product manager will be:

$$\frac{\text{Sales}}{\text{Working capital employed}}$$

This ratio provides a measure of the effectiveness with which all the functions involved in designing, producing, marketing and selling a product or service utilize day-to-day working capital. A ratio of 3:1 indicates that the capital is turned over or utilized three times in a 12-month period; a ratio of 1:2 indicates a disastrous situation with much slow-moving stock or bad debts in which the working money tied up in the product group turns over only once every two years. Naturally, the ratio will vary dramatically between different types of product.

The product manager does not control all the parameters affecting the ratio, and is therefore more concerned with trends. A graphical representation of the trend provides a compact record that will focus the attention of the product team on problem areas for more detailed evaluation. A typical graph is illustrated in Table 8.5.

The information included under each financial heading is as follows:

*Current assets*   Assets that could be realized for cash at reasonably short notice
*Liquid assets*   Cash in hand at the bank, plus investments not held as security against loans or reserves, plus sundry debtors, less bad and doubtful debts
*Current liabilities*   Invoices from customers not yet paid and miscellaneous outstanding payments
*Stocks and work-in-progress*   Working assets as distinct from fixed assets such as buildings and plant
*Debtors*   Invoices to customers not yet paid and miscellaneous monies owed
*Cash*   Cash in hand and balance of bank accounts

## Product cash flows

As discussed in Chapter 5, the generation of cash flow (defined as receipts minus expenditure plus changes in stocks and work-in-progress), is an important objective of companies and product groups. Table 8.6 illustrates the basic calculation required and the impact of a number of product management decisions. This table has the same starting point as Table 8.5, but is affected by the decision to launch a new product.

Product managers need to recognize the impact of their decisions on the working capital needs, cash resources and interest charges incurred by the

**Table 8.5**  Product working capital

| Period | 1 | 2 | 3 | 4 | 5 | 6 | 7 |
|---|---|---|---|---|---|---|---|
| Current assets | 2800 | 2720 | 2650 | 2700 | 2600 | 2000 | 1900 |
| Liquid assets | 2500 | 2410 | 2330 | 2360 | 2240 | 1630 | 1520 |
| Current liabilities | 300 | 310 | 320 | 340 | 360 | 370 | 380 |

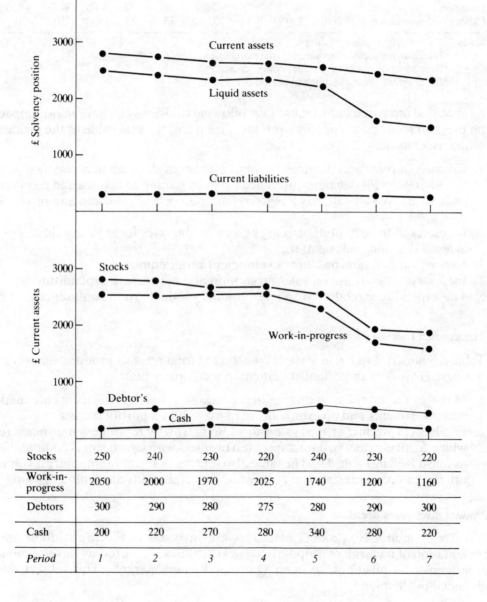

| Stocks | 250 | 240 | 230 | 220 | 240 | 230 | 220 |
|---|---|---|---|---|---|---|---|
| Work-in-progress | 2050 | 2000 | 1970 | 2025 | 1740 | 1200 | 1160 |
| Debtors | 300 | 290 | 280 | 275 | 280 | 290 | 300 |
| Cash | 200 | 220 | 270 | 280 | 340 | 280 | 220 |
| Period | 1 | 2 | 3 | 4 | 5 | 6 | 7 |

**Table 8.6**   Product cash-flow analysis

|  | Period | | | | | | | | |
|---|---|---|---|---|---|---|---|---|---|
|  | 1 | 2 | 3 | 4 | 5 | 6 | 7 | 8 | 9 |
| Opening cash position | 200 | 220 | 230 | 200 | 100 | 75 | 75 | 150 | 250 |
| Receipts from sales | 2000 | 2000[1] | 2100 | 2100 | 2100 | 2100 | 2200 | 2400 | 2600 |
| Expenditure | 1900 | 1950 | 1970 | 2000[2] | 2100 | 2100 | 2100 | 2100 | 2200 |
| Change in work-in-progress | +40 | +20 | +50 | +200 | +100 | −100 | 0 | +100 | +100 |
| Change in stocks of finished product | +40 | +20 | +50 | −70[3] | +100[4] | +100 | +100 | +100 | +100 |
| Cash flow | 20 | 10 | 30 | −30 | −100 | 0 | +100 | +100 | +200 |
| Closing cash position | 200 | 230 | 200 | 100 | 75 | 75 | 150 | 250 | 470 |

Notes: [1] 5% price increase introduced
[2] Increase in purchases to support increased sales
[3] Run-down of stocks of product being replaced
[4] Build-up for product launch in period 5

company on increased bank loans. The following decisions can have major impact on the cash required to support a product group and the real value of the product group as a business entity.

1. Changes in price and the time-lag before changes show up in accounts due to the 30-, 60-, or 90-day time difference between issuing an invoice and receiving cash. The invoice itself may be 90 days after an order was taken and recorded by the sales force
2. Increases in the extent of discounts given by the sales force to sustain sales or arrest a declining sales pattern
3. Expenditure on new product development programmes
4. Increased expenditure on sales promotion and advertising expenditure
5. The expenditure related to an international product group conference

### The product balance sheet

Table 8.8 illustrates a balance sheet constructed for a product group as if it were a business. This is an important statement in a company that:

1. Manages the company as a series of businesses in which investments are made and investments and divestments are managed on a portfolio basis
2. Establishes product groups as business units, run by a business unit manager who effectively runs an unincorporated business with significant accountability as illustrated in Table 8.7. The table also illustrates the accountability levels of other types of organizational units which interface with the product group

### Product investment decisions

Directly or indirectly, product managers are involved in the preparation and presentation of investment proposals for new facilities, new product development programmes, acquisitions, or opening up totally new markets. This subject was discussed in Chapter 5.

**Table 8.7**   Accountabilities of organizational units

| Type of unit | Accountability | Typical title |
|---|---|---|
| Revenue centre | Generation of revenue but with minor impact on expenses to achieve revenue | Sales area |
| Cost centre | Control of total costs and minimization of unit costs but with minor impact, if any, on revenue | Departments or works |
| Profit centre | Excess of revenue over costs, ROI and cash flow; decisions to trade off promotion to increase sales and costs; sales to other parts of the company at equivalent outside prices | Product group or business unit |
| Investment centre | As above, plus total accountability for return on investment and gearing. Can decide on expansion, replacement or disposal of assets | Subsidiary or company |

**Table 8.8**   Illustrative product balance sheet as at 31.12.89

| The finance available for the product group | | Where the finance is invested within the product group | |
|---|---|---|---|
| *Equity* | | *Fixed assets less depreciation* | |
| 1. Share capital if company has acquired companies or products to form the product group | 50 | 1. Manufacturing facilities <br> • plant <br> • buildings <br> • land | 100 |
| 2. Retained profits | 50 | 2. Warehouses | 50 |
| 3. Reserves for future bad debts and abortive investments | 10 | 3. Service centres | 30 |
| | —— | 4. Office premises | 20 |
| | 110 | | —— |
| | | | 200 |
| *Liabilities* | | *Current assets* | |
| 1. Loans raised by company specifically to invest in product group | 255 | 1. Product stock | 50 |
| 2. Outstanding invoices unpaid by company | 110 | 2. Product work-in-progress | 100 |
| 3. Payroll due | 25 | 3. Outstanding invoices unpaid by customers | 100 |
| | —— | 4. Result of positive cash flow held on account | 50 |
| | 390 | | —— |
| | | | 300 |
| Total liabilities | 500 | Total asssets | 500 |

*Note:* Assuming a product group achieved a profit before tax on 10 in the 12 months to 31.12.1989 then the return on total assets or capital employed would be $\frac{10}{500} \times 100 = 2\%$ per annum.

What are the financial calculations and presentations required to make the case? Essentially, the product manager needs to present a financial argument, based on sound assumptions, that demonstrates a financial return at least as attractive as other identified product group opportunities and comparable investment opportunities available to corporate management. The product managers needs to consider corporate management as his bankers.

The product manager may be required to evaluate the likely return on investments proposed on one or more bases dependent on the financial policy and procedures introduced by the finance director. The more common approaches are outlined below.

*The basic average earnings approach*
Using this method, the product manager prepares a forecast of the improvement in profit (before tax, interest and depreciation) over a given number of years from a given investment. The total profit improvement is then divided by the number of years to give an average annual profit improvement over the period, and this is then expressed as a percentage of the original investment to give the average rate of return.

In the example below, £1 million is invested in a new manufacturing facility. The product manager has prepared a five-year profit forecast for this investment:

Year 1      £100 000
Year 2      £200 000
Year 3      £250 000
Year 4      £300 000
Year 5      £350 000

Total       £1 200 000

Average     £240 000

Average rate of return = 24 per cent per annum.

The method is a simple rule of thumb, but does not consider in detail the real value of earnings. It is best used for short-life, high-profit, low-risk investments.

*The payback period*
The payback period is calculated by determining the length of time required in the forecast to generate sufficient cash through profits to repay the original investment. In the above example, it is apparent that the investment is paid back during the fifth year. After four years cumulative profits are £850 000. Year 5 profits are £350 000. Since the original investment was £1 000 000, and £150 000 remains to be paid back after Year 4, the payback period equals 4 + 150 000/ 350 000 years, or about 4 years 5 months.

The payback period approach is simple and useful as a means of ranking a number of investment opportunities. However, the method under- or overvalues profits achieved after the payback period, and takes no account of the real value of money after inflation.

*Discounted cash flow (DCF)*
The DCF approach allows for the decreasing value of money. The advantage of the method to the product manager is that it provides a more accurate assessment of the relative merits of a number of investment opportunities. It has the disadvantage of being more complex mathematically. Two examples of the use of DCF are illustrated opposite.

*DCF yield* This calculation determines the discount interest rate which, if applied to both the cost of the investment and the profit generated, would achieve equal values over the period of the investment. Assuming a five-year life for the investment case outlined under the average earnings approach, the calculation would be as follows:

| | | |
|---|---|---|
| Initial value of investment | | £1 000 000 |
| Income that would be | Year 1 | 120 000 |
| generated at 12% p.a. | Year 2 | 125 000 |
| | Year 3 | 140 000 |
| | Year 4 | 157 000 |
| | Year 5 | 176 000 |
| | TOTAL | 718 000 |
| Value of profit generated | Year 1 | 88 000 |
| discounted at 12% | Year 2 | 154 000 |
| | Year 3 | 170 000 |
| | Year 4 | 179 000 |
| | Year 5 | 185 000 |
| | TOTAL | 776 000 |

The internal rate of return or yield approximates to 12 per cent.

In practice the calculation is a trial-and-error iterative process commencing at 10 per cent and moving in 1 per cent increments.

*DCF net present value* This method determines whether the future value of profits generated by an investment exceeds the present value of the investment required when both future profits and current investment are discounted at a common interest rate, normally the anticipated cost of capital to the company.

The following calculation applies a 10 per cent discount rate to the previous example.

| Year | 1 | 2 | 3 | 4 | 5 |
|---|---|---|---|---|---|
| Value of investment £1 000 000 | 900 000 | 810 000 | 730 000 | 657 000 | 591 000 |
| Present value of future income | 90 | 162 | 183 | 197 | 204 |
| Net present value over 5 years | 836 | > | £590 000 value of investment after 5 years | | |

An excess indicates that the investment is worth considering as it will generate in excess of the cost of capital.

### The presentation of financial results

Product managers need to present financial results in a variety of reports and at a variety of meetings and conferences. For impact, the presentation of information needs to be simple, visually pleasing, easy to read, easy to cross-reference and backed up by more detailed analysis should this be necessary.

Fig. 8.4 outlines four ways of illustrating similar information, each with its own benefits and problems in specific situations. The product manager needs to decide:

- What financial results should be plotted for his or her own reporting and presentation purposes
- How frequently the information should be updated and reissued
- What presentation format to use

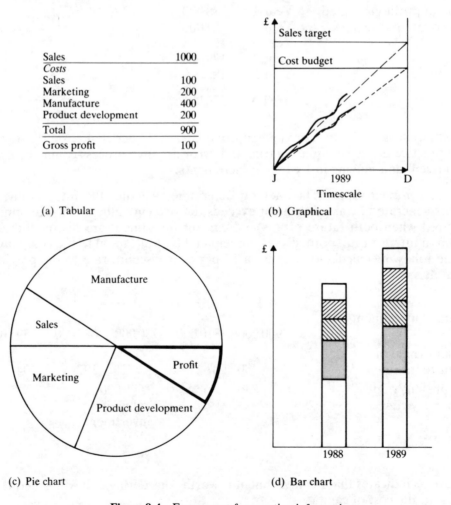

Figure 8.4   Four ways of presenting information

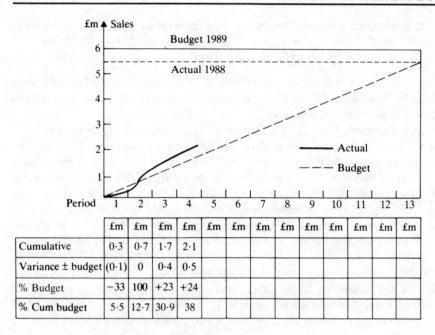

| | £m | £m | £m | £m | £m | £m | £m | £m | £m | £m | £m | £m | £m |
|---|---|---|---|---|---|---|---|---|---|---|---|---|---|
| Cumulative | 0·3 | 0·7 | 1·7 | 2·1 | | | | | | | | | |
| Variance ± budget | (0·1) | 0 | 0·4 | 0·5 | | | | | | | | | |
| % Budget | −33 | 100 | +23 | +24 | | | | | | | | | |
| % Cum budget | 5·5 | 12·7 | 30·9 | 38 | | | | | | | | | |

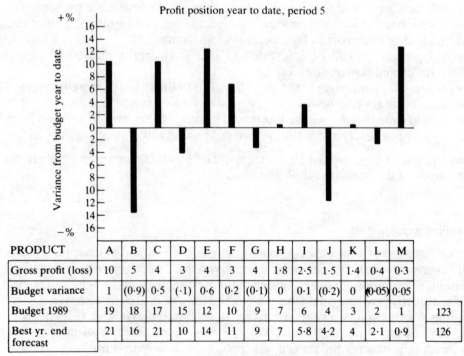

| PRODUCT | A | B | C | D | E | F | G | H | I | J | K | L | M | | |
|---|---|---|---|---|---|---|---|---|---|---|---|---|---|---|---|
| Gross profit (loss) | 10 | 5 | 4 | 3 | 4 | 3 | 4 | 1·8 | 2·5 | 1·5 | 1·4 | 0·4 | 0·3 | | |
| Budget variance | 1 | (0·9) | 0·5 | (·1) | 0·6 | 0·2 | (0·1) | 0 | 0·1 | (0·2) | 0 | (0·05) | 0·05 | | |
| Budget 1989 | 19 | 18 | 17 | 15 | 12 | 10 | 9 | 7 | 6 | 4 | 3 | 2 | 1 | 123 | Σ |
| Best yr. end forecast | 21 | 16 | 21 | 10 | 14 | 11 | 9 | 7 | 5·8 | 4·2 | 4 | 2·1 | 0·9 | 126 | Year 1989 |

**Figure 8.5**  Examples of product control charts

- Whether the presentation should be maintained manually and displayed visibly or maintained and kept on a personal computer database, printing out transparencies or prints for specific presentations

The product manager will need to experiment before finalizing a series of charts and presentations that highlight the most important trends in results and potential opportunity and risk areas for analysis.

The trend charts outlined in Fig. 8.5 represent a useful starting point for they combine financial and statistical information. Other charts to be considered on the basis of product, territory or product and territory include the following: sales, market share, gross margins, net profit, costs, prices/discounts, sales/working capital, cash flow, return on investment, expenditure on product development programmes, achievement of product development milestones, manufacturing productivity, stock levels, orders in hand and deliveries achieved. The charts selected will depend on the scope of the product manager's job, as discussed earlier.

In preparing presentations of financial results and trends, the product manager needs to identify the audience in advance and assess their expectations, motivations and approach to reading and analysing financial reports. In practice, four types of manager will be met in a variety of combinations in any given audience.

1. *The analytic ferret* will be determined to analyse the information presented in a wide variety of ways, seek supporting evidence and additional information, and be looking for errors in figures and calculations
2. *The risk perceiver* will be interested in marginal profits and costs, input/output ratios and downside risks
3. *The laissez-faire* manager is the disbeliever in figures, and is more interested in what actions are planned
4. *The objective supporter* will be interested in clear objectives, clear trend lines and evidence of corrective action where potential problems are identified

All four exist in most groups of 10 managers. The product champion needs to be able to satisfy and work with all of them.

### The planning gap

An important aspect of the strategic planning process outlined in Chapter 2 is the establishment of realistic financial objectives for sales, profit, return on investment, working capital/sales, added value/unit salaries and wages and so on. Financial objectives will normally be established for a period of three to five years. The figures for the first two years are likely to be based on reliable statistics and trends. Figures for subsequent years will be based on an extrapolation of recent results, with adjustments for known new products, anticipated product obsolescence, and the growth pattern of priority market segments and assumptions about the best- and worst-case business conditions that can be anticipated with information currently available.

Fig. 8.6 plotted for sales and profits, is a useful technique for identifying and

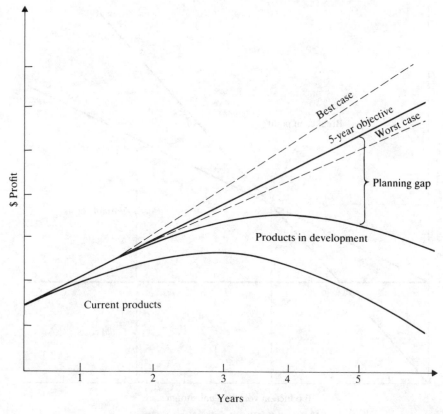

**Figure 8.6**   The planning gap

illustrating the profit gap that will need to be filled by the planning and addition of new products, market segments or territories.

## Breakeven charts

Breakeven charts are a means of calculating the current or potential volume or cost points at which a product group starts to make a profit or alternatively, starts to make a loss. The breakeven chart for each product in the product group will assist the product manager to analyse options such as:

– What is the sensitivity of product profits to incremental increases or decreases in sales prices and costs?
– What would be the impact of installing a new production unit with 15 per cent increased fixed costs but 25 per cent reduction in variable costs?

The analysis is particularly useful in the launch, maturity and decline phases of the product life cycle.

   In practice, the straight lines illustrated in the breakeven chart in Fig. 8.7 are likely to be curves and to feature a number of step changes. Inflation of sales prices

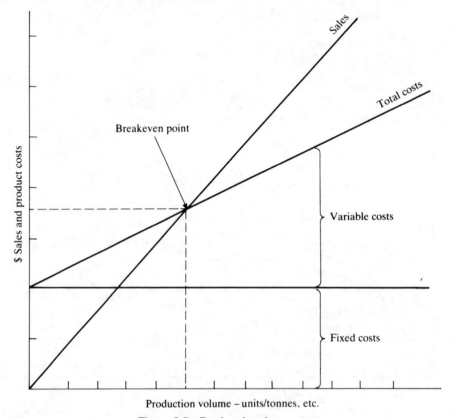

**Figure 8.7**   Product breakeven curve

and costs needs also to be allowed for. However, used with common sense, breakeven charts provide a useful support for a number of strategic and operational decisions, including a speedy assessment of the impact of changes in raw materials costs, currency exchange rates and labour contracts.

### The 80/20 rule

The 80/20 or Pareto rule describes a natural phenomenon observed in many businesses in both industrial and consumer markets and is illustrated in Fig. 8.8.

Personal experience has demonstrated that in an uncanny number of situations the rule applies within ±10 per cent variations to such ratios as:

● 20 per cent items in stock represent the fastest moving line
● 20 per cent products in market generate 80 per cent market share
● 80 per cent overdue accounts are with 20 per cent customers
● 80 per cent profits come from 20 per cent of customers, products, countries or applications
● 20 per cent of customers account for 80 per cent sales of new product introductions in year one

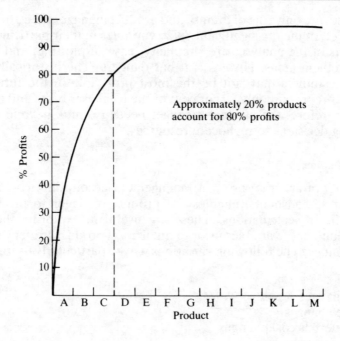

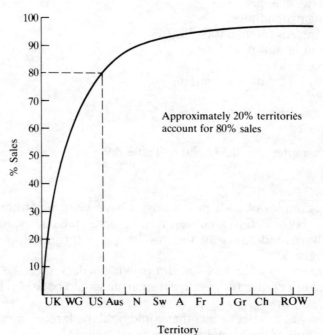

**Figure 8.8** Pareto charts

These examples are only rule of thumb, and product managers need to plot a series of graphs to determine the significant 80/20 variables in their particular situation.

The benefits of the analyses are simplicity, ease of plotting, and visual highlighting of problem areas. However, it has dangers. The historically profitable products or customers may not be the most profitable in the future; current customers may represent only 20 per cent of the total user base, and not the most profitable. Therefore, the product manager needs to think beyond the analysis before making decisions to reallocate resources.

### 'What if' calculations

The availability of accurate product management accounting, cost information and computer spreadsheets, enables the product manager to produce a wide variety of 'what if' calculations. These are useful in exploring the impact of changes in a number of variables prior to finalizing a product strategy and product marketing strategy. The following variations will be particularly useful to product managers.

1. ± price changes
2. ± volume changes
3. ± raw materials cost changes
4. ± productivity changes
5. ± marketing expenditure
6. ± product improvement expenditure
7. ± investment in new plant
8. ± sales discounts
9. ± savings by international sourcing
10. ± stock levels
11. ± work-in-progress
12. ± debtor policy

A number of examples are illustrated in Table 8.9.

### Product statistics

A number of examples of statistical analysis have been illustrated in previous chapters: ratios, 80/20 Pareto analyses, trend graphs, pie charts, and so on. The choice of analysis, and the way the results are interpreted, are critical, as illustrated in Fig. 8.9.

If the decision was to select box sizes for packing orders, then the calculation of the median, and upper quartile and lower quartile would be useful in deciding on four standard box sizes.

If the decision was to select a box that could hold the largest number of orders, then the calculation of the modal point or mode point would be useful.

If the need was to extrapolate future cumulative order values, then the weighted average would be a useful figure, but the use of this statistic would assume significant change in the size mix of orders during the period of the forecast being prepared.

**Table 8.9**   Assessment of impact of product management decisions

| Factor | Base | | Price adjustments | | | | 10% Productivity improvement | | International sourcing | |
|---|---|---|---|---|---|---|---|---|---|---|
| | Products A | B | Product A | | B | | Product A | B | Product A | B |
| Price | 10 | 15 | 9 | 11 | 14 | 16 | 10 | 15 | 10 | 15 |
| Unit volume | 100 | 60 | 105 | 95 | 65 | 55 | 100 | 60 | 100 | 60 |
| Total revenue | 1000 | 900 | 945 | 1045 | 910 | 880 | 1000 | 900 | 1000 | 900 |
| Marketing | 40 | 70 | 40 | 70 | 40 | 70 | 40 | 70 | 40 | 70 |
| Product development | 10 | 30 | 10 | 30 | 10 | 30 | 10 | 30 | 10 | 30 |
| Manufacturing materials | 400 | 450 | 420 | 380 | 487 | 412 | 400 | 450 | 680[1] | 680[1] |
| Labour | 300 | 100 | 315 | 300 | 108 | 100 | 270 | 90 | | |
| Utilities | 50 | 50 | 50 | 50 | 50 | 50 | 50 | 50 | | |
| Depreciation | 80 | 100 | 80 | 80 | 80 | 80 | 80 | 100 | 20 | 20 |
| Total costs | 880 | 800 | 915 | 910 | 775 | 742 | 850 | 790 | 750 | 800 |
| Profit before tax | 120 | 100 | 30 | 135 | 135 | 138 | 150 | 110 | 250 | 100 |
| Fixed assets | 400 | 500 | 400 | 500 | 400 | 500 | 400 | 500 | 100 | 100 |
| Stocks | 300 | 200 | 300 | 200 | 300 | 200 | 300 | 200 | 400 | 300 |
| Debtors | 150 | 150 | 150 | 150 | 150 | 150 | 150 | 150 | 150 | 150 |
| Creditors | 100 | 100 | 100 | 100 | 100 | 100 | 100 | 100 | 150 | 150 |
| Net assets | 950 | 950 | 950 | 950 | 950 | 950 | 950 | 950 | 800 | 700 |
| Return on investment Net assets % | 12.0 | 10.5 | 4.2 | 14.2 | 14.2 | 14.5 | 15.8 | 11.5 | 31.2 | 14.2 |

Note: [1]Imported price of products

| Order size | Frequency |
| --- | --- |
| 100 | 1 |
| 90 | 3 |
| 80 | 5 |
| 70 | 10 |
| 60 | 15 |
| 50 | 20 |
| 40 | 25 |
| 30 | 35 |
| 20 | 40 |
| 10 | 10 |
| Total no | 164 |

1. The simple average of levels of order size =55
   (but no one order in this size!)
2. The weighted average =38.5
3. The modal value =20
4. The median =30
   i.e. 50% equal or greater, 50% equal or smaller
5. The upper guartile =60
   i.e. 25% orders 50 or above
6. The lower quartile =20
   i.e. 25% orders 20 or below

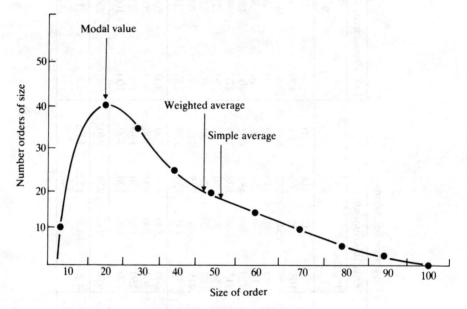

**Figure 8.9**   Statistical variations

In all cases the product manager needs to isolate the decision he or she wants to make; to ascertain what information would help him or her make that decision; and to work out the most useful way of presenting the information to help him or her making the decision. Having decided on the information, and used it in reaching a tentative decision, the manager needs to be satisfied that the accuracy and reliability of the information is appropriate to the seriousness of the decision being taken. This applies to all forms of information, be it financial, market, competitive or environmental trends assembled and reviewed by product managers.

**Chapter 8 – Key point summary**

*Product managers and finance*

1. Be clear about the current position
2. Plan for specific improvement objectives
3. Prepare and monitor detailed budgets
4. Evaluate variances in detail
5. Manage profits, volumes, costs, capital and cash
6. Present results and analyses for ease of understanding
7. Be careful in use of statistics

# 9. Introducing product management

**Key task of sponsor of product managers**
To ensure that an appropriate approach to product management is introduced to the company in a timely and productive manner, through the creation of an effective structure and a team of high performance product managers

### Why? Clarification of objectives

The agreement of clear, concise objectives for the introduction of a product management structure is fundamental to the success of both its initial introduction and its ongoing operation. An obvious statement perhaps, but discussions with product managers in recent years, in a wide range of industries and companies and in many countries, highlight five common and interrelated reasons for the failure of product management:

1. Lack of clear rationale and poor timing of introduction
2. Lack of understanding of structure and system
3. Poor-quality product managers
4. Poor image of job as a career step
5. Lack of top management support

The primary objectives expressed by the senior management of a number of companies committed to the introduction of product management are summarized below.

*Company A   A national specialist food products company*
- To accelerate the search for, development and launch of new products
- To improve the profitability and market penetration of the full product range, in both the consumer and bulk industrial products market
- To commence an active export of ingredients within Europe in preparation for the European single market in 1992

*Company B   A multinational high technology engineering company*
- To coordinate the company's international trade in products important to the future corporate profitability and growth
- To establish closer and productive working relationships between head-

quarters, marketing, product development and customer support functions; and national sales and international territorial marketing and sales functions
- To keep under review the product group's manufacturing policy in terms of where to produce, and whether to produce in-house or by domestic or international sourcing from subcontractors

*Company C   A European sports goods company*
- To improve the profitability and market share of sports goods products in all EEC markets
- To improve the design and quality of goods by exploring the use of the best European and Far East design houses
- To establish a network of South-East Asian suppliers to achieve competitive costs, quality and delivery

*Company D   A Japanese motor car company*
- To improve understanding and penetration of the European market

*Company E   A university department attempting a more market-led approach by appointing product managers*
- To refocus academic work on the needs of the 1990s and promote and deliver academic courses, continuous education, and contract research in a professional and cost-effective manner

*Company F   A mechanical engineering company*
- To establish the marketing concept across the company so as to achieve a greater customer focus and accelerated launch of value added products that match customer needs correctly first time, not after extensive field modifications within the warranty period

Each set of objectives is different in emphasis and derived from the specific needs of the company at the time.


### The importance of timing

Two aspects of timing are important: the best time to introduce product management into an organization; and the best time to appoint product managers within the product life cycle.

*The corporate decision*
The benefits of product management are greater discipline in the direction and coordination of profit improvement programmes for individual products and product groups. The introduction of product management, whether through brand managers, product group managers or business unit managers, should therefore be matched with a corporate need for integration, coordination, delegation of authority and strategic thinking below board level.
    Such needs occur at times of:

- Significant international expansion
- A major redesign and relaunch of a product range
- The design and launch of a totally new range of products

- Preparing the company for the eventual establishment of profit-accountable business units
- Mergers of companies with similar competing or compatible product ranges
- The introduction of a new generation of high technology products
- A dramatic drop in product profitability
- A step change in the speed of new product introduction and reductions in product life cycles
- Major growth following a long period of retrenchment and functional insularity
- Significant changes in market conditions requiring a tight harnessing and refocusing of corporate effort, such as will occur in companies based within both the EEC and EFTA in preparation for the single market conditions planned for 1992

If such conditions exist, or are anticipated, chief executives need to consider whether a group of well-trained, motivated, disciplined middle managers would support them in stimulating, directing, coordinating and controlling a company-wide profit improvement programme, and whether marketing and product development are the best starting point for the focus of the programme.

Marketing directors need to ask whether product managers would assist them in achieving a profit orientation to marketing and sales and an accelerated introduction of the marketing concept into the total organization structure.

*The product manager decision*
The timing of the appointment of individual product managers to manage specific product groups will naturally be affected by the overall corporate decision. However, the timing of appointments against the product life cycles of the company's products needs to be carefully considered. The factors outlined in Table 9.1 apply equally to the appointment of a second and third generation of product managers in companies that have operated product management successfully for a number of years.

In terms of background, product managers with technological education and experience at some stage in their career are likely to be most effective when appointed at the design and development and maturity phases, product managers with a marketing background at the concept, growth and maturity phases, and

**Table 9.1** Factors affecting the success of product managers

| *Phase of product life when product manager is first appointed* | *Likely impact* | *Likely resistance from:* | | *Likely motivation of product manager* |
|---|---|---|---|---|
| | | *Functions* | *Territories* | |
| Concept, design and development | High | Low | Low | High-provided not for 10 years |
| Launch | High | Low | Low | High |
| Growth | High | High | High | Medium |
| Maturity | High | Medium | Medium | High |
| Decline | Low/medium | High | High | Low |

**Option A**

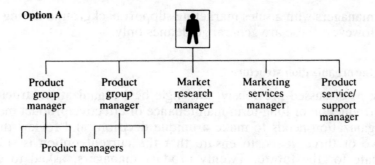

| Product group manager | Product group manager | Market research manager | Marketing services manager | Product service/ support manager |

Product managers

**Option B**

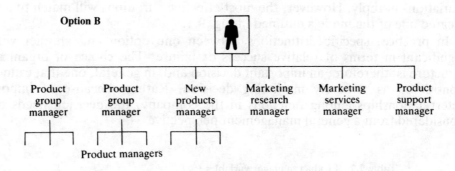

| Product group manager | Product group manager | New products manager | Marketing research manager | Marketing services manager | Product support manager |

Product managers

**Option C**

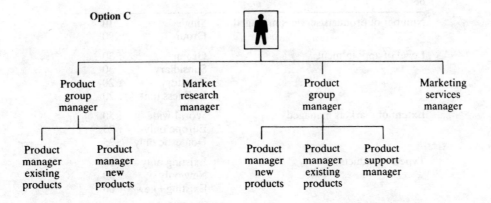

| Product group manager | Market research manager | Product group manager | Marketing services manager |

| Product manager existing products | Product manager new products | | Product manager new products | Product manager existing products | Product support manager |

*Code:*

Typically marketing director, divisional general manager or marketing manager in a large organization

**Figure 9.1**   Product management organization

product managers with a sales/marketing support background during the growth phase. However, these are general guidelines only.

### Deciding the organization structure

There is, as discussed previously, no single best organization structure for the initial introduction or long-term maintenance of effective product management. Each organization needs to make a unique decision, and review that decision every two or three years, to ensure that the current option is still the most appropriate for the future. Twenty product managers, asked to explain the organization structure within which they operate, are likely to offer 8–16 variations in reply. However, the most effective variations will match to a large degree one of the models outlined in Fig. 9.1.

In practice, specific distinctions between one option and another will be significant in terms of relative success or failure. The choice of organization structure is, therefore, an important decision and, in general, one that cannot be considered as a purely marketing decision. Rather, because of important interrelationships among functions in the company, the decision needs to be considered from a general management perspective.

**Table 9.2**   Product manager variables (%).
*Source:* The result of a survey of 200 European product managers 1987–88

| | | |
|---|---|---|
| Number of products/services managed | Single | : 10 |
| | Group | : 90 |
| Level of appointment | Group | : 30 |
| | Subsidiary | : 30 |
| | Territory | : 20 |
| | Business unit | : 20 |
| Extent of markets managed | World-wide | : 50 |
| | Europe only | : 25 |
| | Domestic only | : 25 |
| Type of products | Existing only | : 10 |
| | New only | : 30 |
| | Existing+new | : 60 |
| Time dedication | Full-time | : 90 |
| | Part-time | : 10 |
| Functional background | Marketing | : High |
| | Sales | : High |
| | Technical | : High |
| | Production | : Medium |
| | Finance | : Low |
| Timing of appointment | First job | : 15 |
| | Second job | : 40 |
| | Mid-career | : 40 |
| | Late in career | : 5 |

A recent analysis of 200 product managers from a cross-section of industries undertaken in 1987–88 is summarized in Table 9.2. Each of the dimensions needs to be considered in developing and evaluating detailed organizational options.

Practical means of processing the decision include the following:

1. The marketing director analyses the options and makes a functional decision. The conclusions are then presented to the directors responsible for the other functions affected by product management — research and development, sales, personnel, manufacturing, finance — as a *fait accompli*.
2. The marketing, sales, research, design and development, and personnel directors consider and make the decision as a corporate task force, and present the conclusions to the board as a cooperative decision.
3. A multidisciplined, perhaps multilevel, group of middle managers from the functions involved in the various facets of total product management consider (as a special task force or part of a product management audit (see Chapter 10)) the options and present the conclusions to directors for consideration.

As with all major decisions, both potential benefits and potential risks need to be taken into account in the final analysis. Risks such as non-availability of good staff, the impact of changes in organization and status, the cultural changes implied in a change from unifunctional authority and accountability to matrix authority and accountability, require careful consideration.

Product management is a successful form of organization structure but it requires dedication, commitment and a deep understanding of multinational executive aspirations, motivations and relationships to achieve full success.

### Preparing to implement the structure

Once the decision to introduce a new or modified organization structure has been taken, the outline structure needs to be developed to provide a framework for day-to-day operation.

Job descriptions describing the main purpose, reporting and working relationships, key tasks and accountabilities, and the extent of authority for each job need to be prepared. Job descriptions need to be compared across functions to ensure that conflicting and political overlaps in specific key tasks and related limits of authority are avoided. Personnel specifications need to be prepared to define the type of person required for those jobs which need to be filled by internal promotion or lateral career moves, or by external recruitment.

The planning processes need to be reviewed to clarify the accountability for preparing, communicating and controlling product and market plans. Particular attention is required to the agreement of separate and joint sales and product management accountability for market planning and results, product design and development, product planning and results.

### Selection of product managers

The appointment of a product manager is a high-risk decision. A wrong appointment can have a negative effect on product profitability, the market image

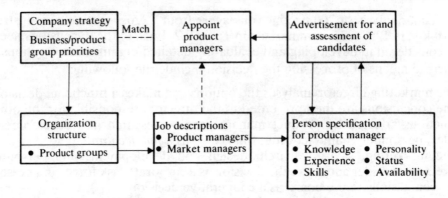

**Figure 9.2** Outline recruitment process

of the company, the corporate support for product management in general, and be a disastrous career step for the product manager involved.

Product managers need a fair chance of early personal credibility, built on a combination of factors:

1. A corporate history of successful product managers
2. A strategic need for a product manager
3. A selection process that matches appointments to strategic needs, as illustrated in Fig. 9.2.

The following selection criteria provide an objective starting point for the preparation of personal specifications for specific recruitment situations.

*Position: product group manager*
1. *Previous experience*
   1.1 A product development or project management role
   1.2 A marketing services, territorial marketing manager, or product management role
   1.3 A senior sales support role or area sales management role
   1.4 Experience in two or more functions

2. *Knowledge*
   2.1 Depth of related product and technological knowledge and/or market knowledge
   2.2 Good understanding of application of marketing concepts to type of products or services to be managed
   2.3 An engineering graduate with a postgraduate marketing specialism

3. *Previous accountability*
   3.1 Leadership of a small functional or project team
   3.2 Personal or shared accountability for profits, margins, programmes and productivity
   3.3 Implementation of a change programme

4. *Personal skills*
   4.1  Ability to communicate
   4.2  Ability to provide leadership and direction
   4.3  Commercial judgement in decision-making
   4.4  Ability to make things happen and control budgets and deadlines
   4.5  Ability to listen, digest and analyse a situation objectively
   4.6  Ability to establish a wide variety of interpersonal relationships
   4.7  Ability to achieve support by leadership and persuasion rather than from rank and status
   4.8  Ability to identify and translate customer needs
   4.9  Ability to learn by experience
   4.10 Ability to respect, use and support role of senior managers and peer groups
   4.11 Financial numeracy

5. *Personality*
   5.1  Outward-going
   5.2  A self-starter
   5.3  Empathy with others within and without the company, including customers
   5.4  Disciplined
   5.5  A challenging mind

6. *Availability*
   6.1  Probably difficult to free from present job as seen as a promising manager in present situation
   6.2  Family situation would permit regular travel to regions and international territories
   6.3  Available for appointment and training within three to six months

The above time-scale is realistic as product management appointments should be planned ahead and not as a crisis event.

### Success characteristics

The views of some 200 European product managers on the personal characteristics most frequently demonstrated by the behaviour of successful product managers during the 1980s are summarized in Table 9.3. The table provides a useful checklist in preparing personal specifications of, searching for and interviewing candidates and in designing a management development programme for both potential and appointed product managers. It also provides a starting point for the design of assessment centres to identify candidates with preferred personal attributes.

### Advertisements

Vacancies for product managers are normally advertised internally and externally through appropriate trade, national and international media. They need to make

**Table 9.3** What personal characteristics do successful product managers demonstrate in practice? (*Source:* Result of personal survey of views of 200 European product managers)

- Leadership skills, both as team leader and team member
- Good communication and presentation of ideas
- Ability to get on with people at all levels
- Excellent organization abilities, good use of resources in achieving product productivity — ability to get things done
- Ability to set priorities well, to concentrate on what is significant
- Capacity to challenge situations with objectivity and empathy
- Diplomacy, concentration on doing own job well, and respect for roles and accountability of related jobs, particularly in marketing and sales
- Open-mindedness: willingness to look and listen
- Depth of product knowledge and appreciation of product related technology
- Ability to identify and relate to customers' strategic needs
- Determination to gain corporate knowledge of marketing, sales, manufacturing, research and development, and finance
- Ability to translate and progress ideas into successfully marketed products
- Intuitive knowledge of where to search for information
- Ability to motivate persuasively, generate ideas, ask the right questions in order to extract the information needed, make decisions objectively, and use lateral thinking skills
- Conviction, both visionary and pragmatic
- Willingness to stick neck out, and be a product champion
- Above all, basic common sense on a day-to-day basis

clear the objectives of the proposed appointment, the nature of the challenge and the type of person most likely to be successful. Extracts from typical advertisements are listed in Table 9.4. The full advertisements would reflect the company strategy, the personal specification and identified likely sources of product managers.

### Sources of product managers

The source of product managers varies widely from company to company or product range to product range as a result of differences in customer and market demands, the pace of change of product technology and the previous experience of the company. Typical examples are given in Table 9.5.

In practice, obvious and innovative sources need to be explored both within the company and in related industries. The age range will extend from the 22–26-year-old MBA graduate, taking up a junior product management or brand management appointment, to the 28–45-year-old commercially minded research and development manager moving into product management in mid-career.

Typical personal benefits recognized by product managers include:

1. Early general management experience and responsibility
2. A chance of a second commercial career after many years in a technical position
3. A chance to add a technical dimension to a marketing background
4. Multifunctional, international exposure
5. Accelerated development of business knowledge and skills

**Table 9.4**  Extracts from typical product management advertisements

*Junior product manager*
Young product manager required, superb experience for rising professional with at least one year's marketing or product support experience in manufacturing or retail. Personality and enthusiasm to steer products crucial to achieving deadlines on many fronts, as is the courage to innovate

*International product manager*
To sustain record of continuing growth, based on market-leading products, exceptional marketeer required to be responsible for marketing major range of products in important international markets, including roll out of impressive range of new products. Business graduate or science graduate with strong sales background and understanding of marketing essentials required

*Product manager*
The world leading manufacture of product X requires a product manager to develop and promote an existing major product range. Experience in marketing industrial products and ideally a chemical engineering or process industry background

*Product development manager*
Market leader intends to strengthen position and secure further growth through increasingly effective utilization of engineering expertise. Product development manager required to manage process of introducing new products through a number of multidisciplinary development teams. Demonstrated man-management and project management skills and ability to liaise at senior level internally and externally

*Business development manager*
Rapid expansion requires business development manager with responsibility for identification and creation of new products and services and their early introduction to the marketplace. Commercial flair, technical awareness and excellent interpersonal and negotiating skills required

6.  A chance to innovate
7.  An interface with senior management

**The induction of new product managers**

The effective induction of new product managers is critical to their early and long-term success. An early misinterpretation of roles, relationships and corporate game rules will be difficult to correct and may create mistrust, even open hostility.

A well-structured induction programme will include individual or group briefing on the following topics:

– The company's future strategy
– The relative importance of specific product groups to that strategy
– The company's organization structure
– The reasons for introducing a product management structure and system
– The current strengths and weaknesses of product management operations and anticipated threats to future success
– The objectives and opportunities for product managers to assist the company to achieve results above the level that would be achieved with a non-product management structure

**Table 9.5**  Typical sources of product managers

| Job | Type of product | Source industry | Typical background | | | | |
|---|---|---|---|---|---|---|---|
| | | | Marketing | Sales | Technical service/production | Research and development | Buying |
| 1. Junior product manager | 1.1 Food products | Food industry | ● | | | | |
| | 1.2 Sports gear | Consumer industries | ● | | | | |
| 2. Brand manager | 2.1 Household products | Consumer industries | ● | | | | |
| | 2.2 Package holidays | Travel/advertising | ● | | | | |
| 3. Product manager | 3.1 Financial services | Banking/computers | ● | ●[1] | | ●[2] | |
| | 3.2 Scientific instruments | Electronics | | ● | ●[2] | ● | |
| | 3.3 Speciality chemicals | Chemicals | ● | ● | ● | ● | |
| | 3.4 High tech electronics | Electronics | ● | ● | ● | ● | |
| | 3.5 School books | Publishing | ● | ● | ● | | |
| | 3.6 Lingerie | Retail, mail order, wholesalers | | | | | ● |
| 4. New product manager | 4.1 Wine and spirits | Drink/advertising agencies | ● | ● | | | |
| | 4.2 Biotech | Biotech/universities | ● | ● | | ● | |
| | 4.3 Confectionery | Food industry | ● | | | ● | |

Notes: [1] Branch banking   [2] Systems development

- The support senior management is prepared to give product managers to ensure appropriate status and chance of success
- The company's stategic planning, operational planning and budgeting processes and timetables
- The company's product policy and procedures manual
- The company's training and development programme for product managers, product designers and product salesmen
- The current plans, trend in results and competitive position of the product group to be managed
- Personal introductions to the members of the product manager's formal and informal team, as described in Chapter 1

The list is not exhaustive but does provide for the most important elements of an effective series of briefing sessions, and is designed with the following purposes in mind: first, planning and monitoring the induction of new product managers; second, the evaluation of gaps in the knowledge of existing product managers as part of the needs analysis for an ongoing development programme.

### Development of product managers

In companies with clearly defined and communicated strategic guidelines corporate results will depend on a combination of:

- Short-term improvements in product performance and productivity
- The timely and profit-effective achievement of agreed strategic milestones
- The achievement of changes required to secure innovations in products, marketing and customer relations
- The development of the commercial, technical and management capabilities of the total management team, including product managers

The competitive and fast-moving international business environment requires that product managers are not only well selected but well trained and developed. The development of product managers will be an ongoing process of learning by experience, supported by a formal management development programme. The formal development programme for product managers needs to achieve a practical balance between management theory and practice. An effective programme will concentrate on ideas, processes and experience that can assist the product manager to improve both personal and team performance. The product manager has a three-legged role, as a creator, as a co-ordinator and as a change agent. The design of a development programme needs to reflect and balance the demands and needs of each of these three dimensions and the business environment in which the product manager will operate. A practical framework for the development of product managers is illustrated in Fig. 9.3. Its essential features are:

1. An in-company core programme
2. The core programme organized for a single company, or for an in-house club of subsidiaries, or an external club of non-competing companies

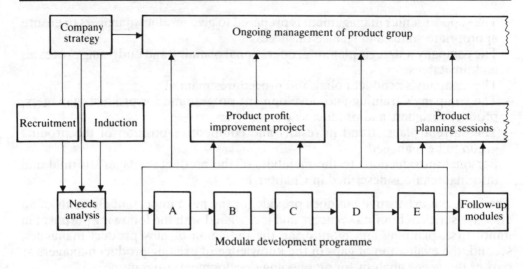

**Figure 9.3**   Practical framework for developing product managers

3. A modular design, including appropriate basic training modules, practical planning sessions (see Chapters 2, 3, 6 and 7 for examples), follow-on modules to reinforce earlier messages and a timely product management audit (see Chapter 10)

4. Basic training modules designed to:

   ● focus on specific aspects of the role of the product manager in turn, e.g. concept and roles; product marketing; product development; product strategies; leadership; interpersonal relations and team building; the international dimension; product financial management
   ● provide sufficient elapsed time between modules to allow participants to reflect on, apply and test out issues discussed in the course room
   ● provide opportunities, at successive modules, for participants to discuss successes and problems and receive help from fellow participants and the programme leaders
   ● achieve a time effective balance between presentations, group case work, practical application, and personal coaching and counselling
   ● ensure that participants understand the markets and organization within which they operate
   ● provide a theoretical base to support the programme project

5. The programme project can be undertaken by individuals or in pairs; the project should focus on using product management theory and practice to improve the profitability and performance of a specific product

6. The modular development programme should be conducted in a manner that enables product managers to relate to the real job of day-to-day product management, so that by the end of the programme what has been learnt or reinforced is being applied on an ongoing basis and in the design and implementation of product planning sessions

7. The product management development programme needs to be reinforced by an objective personal planning and appraisal system as outlined in Chapter 2
8. Cumulatively the modules need to include sessions on the following topics:

   - the product management concept, processes and practices
   - product management organization structures and culture
   - product marketing, planning and control
   - product development and control
   - appointment and management of agencies
   - the buying process through which business is conducted in the industries within which the product manager operates
   - the entrepreneurial process of taking a product concept into the market-place via design, development, manufacture, distribution, marketing, selling and servicing
   - strategic planning and competitor analysis
   - decision-making
   - team leading and memberships
   - interpersonal motivation and communication skills
   - product knowledge
   - selling skills, to be able to sell ideas and understand problems faced by the sales force
   - basic financial planning and control

The approach outlined links the management development process directly to the corporate strategy of the company and the day-to-day job of the product manager. The approach is designed to be profit-effective and ensure an ongoing improvement in the quality of results, products, product managers and their teams, and can be readily adapted to match the needs of specific national and multinational companies.

### The importance of senior management support

The introduction of product management is a corporate decision and, therefore, requires the support of senior management during the introduction phase and beyond. The six essential needs are as follows:

1. A clear company-wide communication of the purpose of product management and the reason for introduction
2. A clear directive to territorial and functional management that senior management has stimulated the introduction of product management, and that company-wide support is expected
3. The agreement that managers with ability and potential will be appointed to product management positions to ensure that maximum benefit is achieved from the introduction of product management
4. Communication, by policy and practice, that experience as a product manager is an important career step for future general managers and heads of functions
5. An insistence that effective development programmes for product managers are budgeted and implemented

6. That the performance and career aspirations of product managers are assessed, evaluated and acted on in a professional manner to ensure that high-performance, competitively knowledgeable persons are not lost unnecessarily to other companies, especially competitors

---

**Chapter 9 – Key point summary**

*Introducing product management*

1. Know why? Base decision to introduce on an objective product management audit (Chapter 10)
2. Select the appropriate organization structure
3. Communicate the purpose, structure and benefits widely
4. Recruit high-quality product managers
5. Establish an effective induction and ongoing development programme
6. Assess and evaluate objectively
7. Ensure initial and continuing senior management support

# 10. Keeping product management alive

**Product managers' and Corporate managers' key task**

To monitor and audit product management needs, benefits and practices, and introduce timely action plans for improving the performance of the product management systems, with the support and commitment of corporate, functional and territorial managers

### The demands on product managers

Product management is a demanding task, ever visible and under time pressure. Product managers are rarely without a backlog of ideas they would like to explore, initiatives they would like to implement, relationships they would like to improve and a host of management challenges.

The introduction of a product management organization structure implies that change is required to ensure that specific product groups are competitively reviewed at the right time, are marketed in a profit-effective manner, and yield regular added stockholder value. But change, with its implication of criticism of previous attempts to manage markets competitively, is not always welcome. It is therefore important that the pressures on product managers, as illustrated in Fig. 10.1, are recognized and that product managers are provided with relevant training, development experiences, functional support and, most importantly, senior management support. There are many common pressures:

- Pressure from senior managers for results, reports and responses to special requests
- Pressure from functions for support, information and proof that product managers are more than an overhead
- Pressure from subordinates for advice, authority, access to information and challenging careers
- Pressure from peer groups to be in many places at once, tying in product plans with the corporate strategy cycle, sales planning and budgeting cycles, and for

215

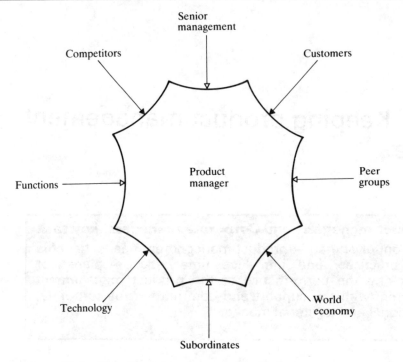

**Figure 10.1** Typical pressures on a product manager

progressing the multitude of initiatives that overzealous product managers attempt to coordinate
- Pressure from the marketplace for new responses to customers, competitive moves, changes in the rules and conditions of international competition and step changes in key technologies

Unless such pressures are managed professionally product management benefits will be suboptimal. For success, action is required by both the product manager and senior management.

**Actions by the product manager**

1. An insistence on being briefed and updated on the strategic role of the product group within the total corporate strategy
2. Dedication to an ongoing audit and improvement of the effectiveness of product management processes, practices and structure through timely formal and informal product management audits
3. Regular updates and communication of product strategy, objectives and plans
4. Regular development sessions for self, product team and functional associates
5. Personal time planning to ensure that the product manager is in control of 60 per cent or more of personal time

Experience indicates that ineffective product managers tend to allow corporate

**Table 10.1**   Product manager's annual time utilization (days)

| | | Product manager A | Product manager B |
|---|---|---|---|
| Corporate controlled time | Functional Management Meetings | 50 | 20 |
| | Special 'urgent tasks' | 50 | 30 |
| | Annual personal appraisals | 5 | 5 |
| | Budgeting | 15 | 10 |
| | | 120 | 65 |
| Corporate/ personally controlled time | Annual/national holidays | 30 | 30 |
| Personally controlled time | Product strategy/planning sessions | 0 | 15 |
| | Market planning/coordination | 20 | 30 |
| | Territorial visits/reviews | 10 | 20 |
| | Strategic customer visits | 5 | 15 |
| | Product development reviews | 5 | 20 |
| | Monthly management report | 10 | 5 |
| | Personal/team development | 0 | 10 |
| | Personal thinking time | 10 | 25 |
| | Crisis problem solving | 50 | 25 |
| | | 110 | 165 |
| | Total days/annum | 260 | 260 |

pressures and practices to overtake their time schedule, with the result that essential product group tasks are poorly progressed or not achieved at all.

The effective product manager is likely to recognize the time squeeze and aims to put system and structure to the company's timetable as illustrated in Table 10.1.

**Actions by senior management**

1. Prepare, issue, communicate and reinforce from time to time a corporate statement defining:

   – the purpose of product management
   – the role in the strategic direction and management of the company
   – the type of product management appropriate to each division or product group
   – the relative roles and accountabilities of marketing, product management and sales management within the company

2. Require and review annual business and strategy review documents from each product group manager as part of the corporate planning process and prior to finalizing next year's corporate budget

3. Ensure that the personnel policy related to product management is creative, resulting in the appointment and development of a cadre of future marketing and territorial general managers
4. Support the product group managers and product managers, whether seasoned professionals or post-MBA learner drivers, in their efforts to audit and improve the management of their allocated product groups
5. Initiate a company-wide product management audit from time to time as an initiative within the corporate development programme

### The need to audit and plan product management activity

Managing the product management process is a major management task, one that becomes more demanding and challenging as the company grows and the longer product management exists in the organization. It is a management task requiring dedication and painstaking care in the design, launch, implementation and ongoing maintenance phases. The initial introduction needs to be well planned and implemented, enthusiasm, change and profit improvement ensuring that product management is believed in and achieves early success. However, complacency and the protection of functional and territorial boundaries and accountabilities can result in a less than satisfactory result and early concept maturity and decline.

The importance of communication in preventing this happening has been emphasized a number of times. However, communications can only set the scene and provide an arena within which product managers can operate. But what happens in the arena in practice over a period of time?

Fig. 10.2 illustrates the general pattern of the impact of management concepts, systems and techniques in many organizations.

A recent survey of a wide cross section of companies in Europe highlighted five common and basic reasons for this failure pattern:

1. Individual management concepts, systems and techniques had been launched one after the other without a common framework of objectives, or with objectives that were in conflict

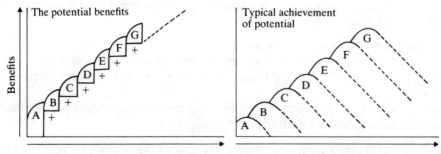

Time and number of management concepts, systems and techniques introduced

**Figure 10.2** Impact of management initiatives

2. Even where the efficiency of individual management techniques was high, their combined integrated effectiveness was often low, caused by poor interpretation of the application by line departments and support departments and project groups. Sometimes technical and functional objectives were being pursued rather than objectives expressed in terms of user and company benefits

3. Many managers do not carry out a formal self-appraisal of how well they and their team use available concepts, systems and techniques, particularly when interacting with other departments

4. Too few managers implement their full responsibility for coaching and counselling their team on an ongoing basis in the use of management concepts, systems and techniques through face-to-face review meetings, departmental meetings, task forces or project groups

5. A failure to match concepts, systems and techniques with the culture of the company and existing good practices

The future of product management may be no different unless managed professionally with the following important questions asked from time to time:

- Is product management right for the company in the future?
- Are the product management processes and practices focused on the needs of the 1990s?
- Have the subsystems and techniques been introduced in a planned, integrative sensitive manner?
- What are managers' current attitudes to product management? Is it seen as drowning the organization in paper, controls and techniques and a process starved of real management focus and professionalism?
- Is the adopted approach to product management coping with the stress and interplay of national, international and interfunctional competitive pressures?
- What changes or adjustments to the product management practice should be considered, planned and implemented?
- What product management organization structure is most appropriate to the future?
- Who should have accountability for what?
- What profile of product managers is required at headquarters and the territories?

Such questions need continually to be asked and answered to ensure that the benefits of product management, as defined by two recurring themes in this book, are achieved and sustained.

1. Product management was defined in the opening chapter as the dedicated management of specific products and services to improve the profit contribution from current and potential markets, in both the short and longer term, above that which would be achieved by traditional approaches to territorial sales, marketing and product management

2. Product management has been presented in many sections of the book as essentially an innovative, integrating and improving force across the

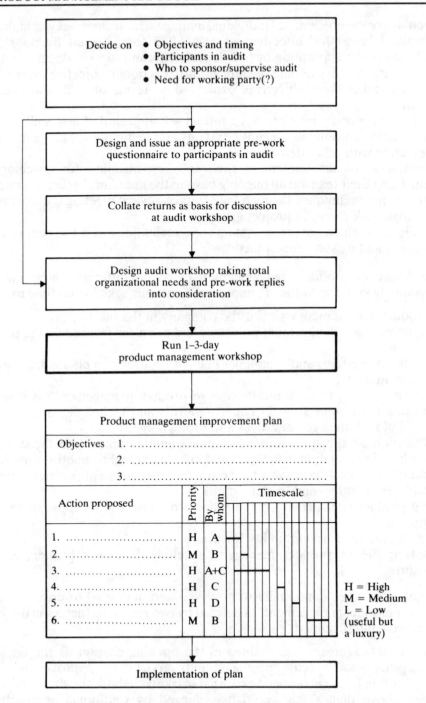

**Figure 10.3** The product management audit process

organization from the initial product/market visionary concept to the end customer application

Increasingly, companies are finding it of benefit to build a review of product management into the company's planning cycle through formal product management audits, on a one-off, annual or biennial basis.

## The product management audit

The process for a typical product management audit is outlined in Fig. 10.3. It is designed to be:

1. A process that is practical, objective and time-effective
2. A process that could be implemented:

   ● for the total organization
   ● for a representative section of managers across the organization
   ● for a specific product division or marketing department
   ● for the product management team only

3. A process that would involve those managers in a position to have a significant impact on the product management process
4. A process that meets the needs of a wide range of company situations
5. A process that audits the effectiveness of existing product management practices against:

   ● the current and future needs of the company
   ● the international best practices

   A typical product management questionnaire is outlined in Table 10.2. This table is designed for personal use or for incorporation in a product management audit session. Consider each statement in turn by asking yourself: 'To what extent is the statement an accurate description of the state of product management in your company, division or business unit?'

6. A process that meets the need of a wide range of company situations

### Typical company applications of the product management audit

Company A had formally practised product management for a number of years.
   Product management was considered a success but the company wished to review, update and sharpen existing practices on an ongoing basis to combat anticipated market conditions and organizational stresses. The product management audit was introduced as a two-day module in the corporate planning/development process, and would take place biennially. In this way product management was given renewed impetus and kept alive.
   Company B had been less successful for a number of reasons. The audit was used in two ways to achieve improvement:

1. As a two-day audit within the product management department to achieve an objective self-analysis

**Table 10.2**   Basic product management audit questionnaire

The table is designed for personal use or for incorporation in a product management audit session. Consider each statement in turn by asking yourself 'to what extent the statement is an accurate description of the state of product management in your company, division or business unit'.

| A. *Positive statements*<br>Is the statement true of your organization? | *Score*<br>True  4<br>Partly true  2<br>False  0 |
|---|---|
| 1. Product management is given total and visible support by senior management | |
| 2. Product managers are established and accepted as product champions able to make an impact on profits | |
| 3. The key tasks and accountabilities of product managers are clearly communicated across the organization and accepted by the functions involved | |
| 4. Product managers have the ability to work in harmony with other functions and achieve this in practice | |
| 5. The company's planning process is participative and aims to integrate product plans and territorial plans | |

| B. *Negative statements*<br>Is the statement true of your organization? | *Score*<br>True  1<br>Partly true  ½<br>False  0 |
|---|---|
| 1.1 Product management seen as a latest fad | |
| 1.2 Product management has lukewarm support | |
| 1.3 Product management doesn't match today's needs | |
| 1.4 No communication of purpose of product management | |
| 2.1 Product managers seen as an overhead | |
| 2.2 Product managers seen as trainee jobs | |
| 2.3 Product managers given little authority | |
| 2.4 Product managers seen only as coordinators | |
| 3.1 No involvement in product development | |
| 3.2 No involvement in product promotion | |
| 3.3 No involvement with sales | |
| 3.4 No involvement with market research | |
| 4.1 Regular conflicts occur with sales | |
| 4.2 Regular conflicts occur with product development | |
| 4.3 Regular conflicts occur with marketing services | |
| 4.4 Regular conflicts occur with manufacturing | |
| 5.1 Territories ignore product manager's plans | |
| 5.2 No real link with manufacturing plans | |
| 5.3 Product launches are often a problem | |
| 5.4 Emphasis on paper and not participative decisions | |

| Column A | | Column B | |
|---|---|---|---|
| 6. The development of marketing strategies analyses and focuses on the total 'competitive mix' and 'marketing mix' | | 6.1 Sales use discounts for volume growth | |
| | | 6.2 No time for comprehensive analysis | |
| | | 6.3 Concepts are regarded as academic | |
| | | 6.4 Only a short-term planning focus | |
| 7. Up-to-date intelligence about the activities of current and potential competitors is readily available | | 7.1 No regular feedback from sales | |
| | | 7.2 Mainly historic trends | |
| | | 7.3 Inadequate focus on tomorrow | |
| | | 7.4 Poor analysis of competitors' strategies | |
| 8. Product managers regularly travel to meet with the sales force and strategically important customers | | 8.1 There is no travel budget for product managers | |
| | | 8.2 Field visits are poorly organized | |
| | | 8.3 Only current and not potential customers are visited | |
| | | 8.4 Only salesmen contact customers | |
| 9. Product management is recognized as an interesting and important career opportunity | | 9.1 No mid-career appointments | |
| | | 9.2 Product managers not easily promoted | |
| | | 9.3 Inadequate training is provided | |
| | | 9.4 Few applicants for positions | |
| 10. The performance of product managers is evaluated six-monthly or annually in an objective manner | | 10.1 No regular appraisals | |
| | | 10.2 Confused performance criteria are used | |
| | | 10.3 Qualitative criteria only are used | |
| | | 10.4 Fight with territories over contribution to results | |
| Total Score Column A | | Total Score Column B | |

Score A minus Score B

*Indicators:*

20–40 Product management working well
0–20 Product management could achieve more; an audit could help
–20– 0 Product management needs an urgent audit and overhaul
–40–20 Product management is probably not right for the company

2. As an integral part of a four-day corporate workshop in which all functions were present and which featured a product management audit, an inside product management case study, an outward bound 30-hour session including a number of exercises which mirrored many of the design, communication, leadership and marketing skills essential to product management, and a multifunctional improvement planning exercise. The benefits were high

Company C had not introduced a formal approach to product management. However, it was interested in examining what assistance a more formal approach might bring to the implementation of an ambitious strategic plan. An audit was incorporated in the company's annual corporate weekend. The audit was adapted to examine the weaknesses of current practices and whether a more formal approach to product management would help in overcoming the weaknesses — and if it would, how current practices might be improved and new practices introduced in a complementary manner.

Company D was a medium-sized company with an informal approach to product management. Functions worked well together. No special coordinating product managers were appointed, but project teams were used to steer and coordinate the development and launch of new products. The company had an active training and development programme with a number of one- and two-week programmes for all levels of management, generally with a multifunctional participant group. The product management audit was introduced as a one-day module in many programmes. Tentative improvement plans were produced for discussion with a director on the last but one day of the programme. On the last day of the programme, groups of between two and four participants worked agreed initiatives into concrete action plans and committed themselves to ensuring that the action plans were implemented and followed up.

Company E was a small individually owned business with a simple but growing product group. The company used a modified audit to examine how the existing formal management practices might be made more professional but without losing or diminishing the sense of individual accountability, entrepreneurship and team spirit fostered by the owner.

*Typical participants*
A full product management audit process would involve the following mix of persons, and a partial audit an appropriate cross-section.

- The product management team(s) of a specific product group or related groups, i.e. product group managers and product managers with responsibility for new products, existing products and specific markets
- The executive management supervising product management operations: varying from company to company this will typically be the marketing director or manager, a divisional general manager, or the manager of a business unit
- The appropriate product design and development team(s)
- The national and international sales managers accountable for selling the product groups involved, plus the international service manager
- The marketing services manager and independent market research manager, if existing in the organization

- If a close marketing relationship exists, the account executive of the marketing and advertising agency supporting the product groups
- The accountant supporting the product group with market and product based management information

The exact choice should be made on the basis of the following questions:

- On whom does product group success depend?
- Who is or should be intimately involved in, and supportive of, the product management process?
- Who are objective and open-minded contributors?
- Who is prepared to champion the concept of product management?

### Planning the next phase

The outcome of the product management audit proces will be the product management improvement plan, as illustrated in Fig. 10.3. The audit will have initiated a searching analysis of concepts, commitments, communications, planning processes, organizational and personal relationships, team development needs and barriers to successful product management. The audit will also have involved those persons accountable for initiating or suggesting changes to senior management.

Therefore, the action plan should clearly spell out:

- Improvement objectives in terms of significant changes to be aimed for
- Specific action to achieve these objectives with clear milestones and time-scales
- Specific and clear accountability for making things happen

As with all action plans, the plan needs timely and diligent follow-up to ensure that agreed actions are initiated, milestones and objectives achieved, and barriers to progress overcome. Progress can best be monitored by a product group manager, the chief executive or a multidisciplined steering group.

### The benefits

Typical benefits from formal product management audits include the following:

1. For the company senior management
   - A more in-depth understanding of the nature and benefits of product management
   - The evaluation of a management approach that is a better match with the needs of today and anticipated needs of tomorrow
   - Improved cooperation between the functions, territories and levels of management involved in product management
   - A renewed determination of product managers and territorial sales teams to work in cooperation

2. For product managers
   - A greater understanding of roles and relationships

- Improved working relationships and practices with design and development, marketing services, sales and manufacturing and the advertising agency, if involved in the audit process
- Requests for personal assistance
- A better feedback of information from product development project leaders on the progress of new product initiatives; the sales force in respect of market initiatives by customers and competitors; and the finance department in terms of improved product financial reports
- Agreed access to key customers
- Improved territorial product and key account planning, control and sales forecasting

3. For territorial sales managers

- A more personal contact with and response to the need of the market on the part of the product management team
- Improved timing, briefing and involvement in product launches
- A greater awareness of corporate efforts to support customer needs
- New ideas for improving the productivity of the sales force
- Improved and more timely product training support

4. For the marketing executive

- A product management team with a more rounded corporate perspective
- A step forward establishing the marketing concept as a multifunctional reality
- Clarification of and balance between the roles of product development managers, product managers at headquarters and in subsidiaries or associate companies; marketing managers at headquarters and in subsidiary and associate companies, the product support manager, sales managers and sales training managers; all of whom exist in the structure of many multinational companies

5. For the personnel executive

- An objective basis for a development and training needs analysis for the product management team
- Insight into the quality of interdepartmental and interpersonal relationships
- A practical team-building exercise
- A refinement of the job and personal specification for the product manager for tomorrow
- A purposeful process that requires no new management knowledge or skills, but rather utilizes and reinforces the generic management skills and processes common to all managers in all functions

6. For the owner-manager of a small company

- A valuable team-building exercise
- The appreciation of the benefit of a professional management approach to managing the company

- The starting point for developing improved business plans
- The identification and resolution of critical issues that would constrain the development of the company

7. For the customer

- A more responsive developed organization
- A next generation of available products that, through improved styling and enhanced productivity features, help the customer's management team achieve its strategic objectives
- The beginnings of a close relationship with the managers in the supplier organization who decide on the product specification and method of distribution of future products
- A speedier processing of technical enquiries, request for off-location support and product complaints

Total success requires early successes that can be built on progressively. Easily accepted ideas should be introduced first, to gain the confidence that change will be of benefit, and followed by the more controversial and difficult changes once a foothold, foundation or stepping stone has been achieved.

Product managers are unlikely to achieve all essential changes alone, but will need to present a commercial case and seek support from more senior managers with a broader power base.

If time can be found to analyse the concepts and practices of product management, many diarized opportunities exist to monitor and follow up agreed improvement actions on a regular basis: strategy reviews, progress reviews, budget meetings, management conferences, day-to-day dialogue, coaching and counselling sessions with subordinates and product managers in territories, and annual appraisal meetings.

From experience, product champions will have no difficulty in striving for improved and sustained results via a more professional personal and corporate approach to product management. In practice, where there's a will a way ahead will be found.

**Making it happen**

This book was conceived and developed to provide a framework of practical guidelines for the day-to-day practice of product management; it is not a rewrite of management theory.

The framework will have provided the reader with a number of challenges, new ideas, reminders of the elements of good management, a basis for improving the way in which the product and service portfolio of the company is conceived, developed and managed.

For some readers one or two of the ideas will be of importance, for others many ideas may be identified as important. In each case, the reader faces the problem of introducing change; change aimed at improving working practices; change that challenges existing practices, the organization structure and corporate culture.

The reader therefore needs to plan ahead objectively and thoroughly and should ask:

– What changes are essential and what changes are desirable?
– Who needs to be involved in authorizing and providing support for the change?
– Who needs to be involved in and committed to the change?
– Who is most likely to resist change?
– Who is likely to be the greatest cynic on day 1, but the greatest supporter by day 100?
– How can the change be most effectively communicated?
– Where and when should the change first be introduced for the greatest impact and benefit?
– How fast should the change be introduced? Should the strategy be stealth, evolution or revolution?
– What risks can be anticipated? And how can they be prevented or overcome?

As discussed in Chapter 1 a thorough analysis is required to achieve optimum benefit from the concept of production management.

---

**Chapter 10 – Key point summary**

*Keeping product management alive*

1. Recognize the demands of product management
2. Plan actions by product managers and senior managers
3. Audit practices objectively on an ongoing basis
4. Establish improvement plans
5. Achieve commitment
6. Make change happen
7. Establish product management as

**The dedicated management of specific product(s)/ service(s) to *increase the profit contribution* from current and potential markets, in both the short and longer term, *above that which would otherwise be achieved* via traditional approaches to territorial sales, marketing and product development**

# Postscript

*The Product Management Handbook* was conceived as a sharing experience. Hopefully, readers have discovered new ideas and a stimulus and motivation to introduce and improve the international practice of product management.

The author is interested in learning about new product management successes, innovations, problems and applications of the product management audit to sustain the international learning and sharing processes.

Richard S. Handscombe
Windsor, UK

# Index